PEN

ANGLO-INDIAN

Patricia Brown was born in Bombay, India, and grew up in various cities since her father, an army officer, was transferred every two years. She attended La Martiniere Girls' High School, Lucknow, and passed out from the Convent of Jesus and Mary, Pune. She showed a keen interest in the written word from a very young age, and dreamed of becoming a writer. At school, every year, she walked away with the first prize for English literature.

Upon immigrating to Canada in 1969 with her husband and three sons, Patricia did various jobs before settling down to become a writer. She has had several short stories, poems, and feature and culinary articles published in Canada, the United States, India and Malaysia. Her recent article on the immigrant experience will be featured in a book titled *Of Maples & Mounties*, to be published by Prentice Hall in Toronto.

Anglo-Indian Food and Customs

Patricia Brown

Illustrations by Lena Weyer

PENGUIN BOOKS

Penguin Books India (P) Ltd, 11 Community Centre, Panchsheel Park, New Delhi-110017, India
Penguin Books Ltd., 27 Wrights Lane, London W8 5TZ, UK
Penguin Putnam Inc., 375 Hudson Street, New York, NY 10014, USA
Penguin Books Australia Ltd., Ringwood, Victoria, Australia
Penguin Books Canada Ltd., 10 Alcorn Avenue, Suite 300, Toronto, Ontario M4V 3B2, Canada
Penguin Books (NZ) Ltd., 182-190 Wairau Road, Auckland 10, New Zealand

First published by Penguin Books India (P) Ltd. 1998

10 9 8 7 6 5 4 3 2

Typeset in *Garamond* by SÜRYA, New Delhi

For

Gordon, Bruce and Mike
In loving Memory of Andrew (1963-1995)

Contents

Acknowledgements ix
Preface xi

Introduction 1
Festivals 12
Rites of Passage 38
Birthday Celebrations 58
Summer Holidays 63
A Few Notes and Helpful Hints 77
A Note on Weights and Measures 91
Soups 95
Side Dishes 115
The Pigman 161
Rice 173
Curries and Masala Fries 203
Vegetables, Lentils and Eggs 271
Cakes, Cookies and Custard 299
Pickles, Chutneys, Sauces and Salads 345
Snacks and Appetizers 373
Tea, Coffee and Refreshments 393

Glossary 406
Index 411

Acknowledgements

To the Peters, the Thompsons, the Pages and Burbys,
The Moores, the Majors, da Cunhas and Kirbys—
To friends and relations, kith and kin
Whose recipes I have included within.
I offer my thanks and implore your critique,
Remembering no formula is ever unique.
Since my efforts are begged, borrowed and 'nicked',
If you see yourself in here, by gosh, you were picked!

Preface

The Anglo-Indians—how they came into being

The following is an excerpt taken from W.T. Roy's book, *Hostages to Fortune*. Mr Roy's definition best describes the 'Anglo-Indian' in India, as the term came to mean after Indian Independence: '. . . a member of a group possessing a distinctive subculture whose characteristics are that all its members are Christians of one denomination or another, speak English, wear European clothes on almost all occasions, have substantially European dietary habits though addicted to the fairly lavish use of Indian spices, are occupationally engaged in a restricted number of trades and professions, and are by and large endogamous.'

The first Europeans arrived in India nearly five hundred years ago. Vasco da Gama, a Portuguese explorer, landed at Calicut on the Malabar coast in 1498. He was sent by King Emmanuel of Portugal who was curious to find out more about the legendary treasures in silks and spices that India was rumoured to have in vast quantities. Upon his arrival he encountered hostility from Muslim merchants, and was unable to institute a trading station in Calicut. However, another Portuguese explorer, Pedro Alvares Cabral, who arrived soon after was successful in establishing a post.

As the Portuguese awareness of the country grew, they were amazed at the opulent lifestyle enjoyed by the wealthy princes and merchants. The natives proved to be warm and hospitable, and the Europeans were invited to stay by the local rajas and enjoy India's traditional hospitality. Looking around they saw a country immensely rich and fertile, where it was possible to reap a harvest of boundless treasure in gold and spices. The idea of colonization that was but a seed at first took root, and soon became the main objective. The Portuguese were the first in a succession of European visitors. Soon Dutch, French and, later, English merchant ships weighed anchor along the shores of the great subcontinent; they came principally as traders. The Portuguese, however, stayed, acquiring land and establishing colonies along the coast at first. Growing bolder with time they slowly crept inland, but always favoured land hugging the shore. The Europeans traded with the Indians, carrying away to their homeland cargo ships laden with spices, silks and gems.

Seeking to root themselves even deeper in Indian soil, Alfonso d'Albuquerque, one of the more famous Portuguese governors of the territories, whose principal aim was colonization and missionary work, used the prevailing policy of assimilation to encourage marriages between his men and Indian women of noble birth, after the latter converted to Catholicism of course. The children of these unions came to be known as Luso Indians, and were in fact the first Eurasians. They, together with the offspring born from the union of numerous other European men and Indian women were the first Anglo-Indians.

In 1510, Goa, a district on the Malabar coast of India, was conquered by the Portuguese. The town of Daman was sacked in 1531, becoming a permanent colony by 1558. Daman subsequently became an important port, as trade with the eastern coast of Africa was established. The island of Diu, which is about thirteen km long and about three km wide, lies off the southern tip of the Kathiawar Peninsula in the Arabian Sea. In 1535 the Portuguese made a treaty with the native princes and erected a fort on the island.

The Dutch did not have any colonial aspirations. They came principally as traders and established trading posts on the Malabar and Coromandel coasts, and also in the state of Bengal. However, there must have been a certain amount of intermarriage between them and the local Indians, evident from the number of people bearing Dutch surnames that can be found in the towns of Negapatam, Chinsurah and Pulicat. Other European sailors and explorers took Indian wives, which served to increase the Eurasian population of the subcontinent.

Shortly after 1664, the French colonies were founded. The French in India were engaged in a constant struggle with the British to gain dominance in trade and in the acquisition of land. Pondicherry, a seaport on the Coromandel coast, changed hands many times. The town was acquired by the French in 1674, captured by the Dutch in 1693, but was restored to France in 1697. The British captured the town on three occasions during the eighteenth century. The French freely intermarried with the local Indians, and there was a sizeable Eurasian population in the French settlement towns of Pondicherry and Chandernagore.

The term 'Anglo-Indian' originally referred to British colonials residing in India. Their prolonged stay in the country resulted in the emergence of a race of people born to British fathers and Indian mothers, who also called themselves Anglo-Indians. In the course of time Eurasians of every description came to be known as Anglo-Indians, and since they intermarried freely with one another, they were soon indistinguishable, with entire families bearing British, French, Portuguese and Dutch surnames. The common denominator was the fact that they all had one Indian parent; it was the European half that contributed a different facet to the cultural melting-pot. Despite the variance in customs and cuisine, and the fact that they came from different parts of the subcontinent, the new 'Anglo-Indians' shared many of the characteristics that set them apart from their Indian and European parents. They did not fit comfortably into either Indian or European society, and from the very onset experienced some difficulty in developing a self-image. What helped them overcome this hurdle was perhaps the fact that they never took themselves very seriously. This, coupled with a puckish sense of humour and a penchant for good living, helped them to emerge culturally as a distinct people.

Both my parents were products of this mixed race, and growing up I was exposed to all the idiosyncrasies of this unique community, which has moulded my character and coloured my life. Anglo-Indians are a gregarious lot; they can party until sunrise—eating and drinking, or dancing the night away at the local gymkhana. A generous and hospitable people, they feel no compunction about setting an extra place at the table if an unexpected guest should happen to arrive before a meal. Friends can drop in for a visit uninvited, without feeling they are encroaching on their host's hospitality, or privacy; and one is always invited to stay the night. Impromptu gatherings need no reason: pot luck lunches, dinners, and picnics often evolve from a mere suggestion. Pooling their resources they have a party!

Today, the Anglo-Indian is a dying breed. Only about one hundred and fifty thousand of them remain in India, with the rest of the community scattered all over the world. They have intermarried with Hindus, Muslims, Europeans, Americans and Australians. When India won her independence in 1947, many of them used their British passports to gain entry into England. Large numbers emigrated to Australia, many went to Canada, and a few went to Europe and to America. But wherever they have travelled, and however much they distance themselves from the subcontinent, India remains an enigma. The country they left behind has never left them; it continues to haunt and beckon, with the time spent in India often viewed in retrospect through rose-tinted glasses. At any Anglo-Indian gathering, no matter where in the world, sooner or later the topic of conversation always veers around to 'the good old days'. With great animation, oft told tales of dances, picnics, shikar and high jinks on the estates and plantations are recounted with many embellishments. One hears of all the golden opportunities—some taken, and some lost.

Each year, from points far and near, scores of Anglo-Indians make a journey, nay, a pilgrimage back to India. Everyone agrees the country has changed, but then a hint of nostalgia creeps into their voices, and they are quick to point out that with enough money, in India one can still live 'the life of Riley'.

Among those Anglo-Indians' who remained behind, there are many who have carved out very successful careers, distinguishing themselves in the Army, Navy and Air Force. A fair number are still employed by the railways, customs and Port Trust. For the most part they are urban dwellers who enjoy the hustle and bustle of India's teeming cities, but a handful can still be found on the plantations, and in the more obscure backwaters of the subcontinent.

The Anglo-Indians' rambunctious way of life, generosity, and love for the underdog has endeared them to their fellow Indians. Wherever the community gained prominence, there was a subtle shift in the lifestyle of the local population. Being for the most part a people totally oblivious of caste and creed, they accept and are accepted at every level of society.

Though they have adopted the religion,

mannerisms and clothing of their European forefathers, the Anglo-Indians since Independence have successfully integrated into the mainstream of Indian society. Their dietary habits are definitely Indian. Notwithstanding the fact that they prepare roasts, stews and pies that bear English names, the lavish use of spices renders them Indian to the palate. Over the decades a unique cuisine has evolved, a delicious blend of east and west, rich through the liberal use of coconut, yogurt and almonds, flavoured with an assortment of spices.

Anglo-Indians celebrate all the feasts in the Christian calendar, and bring in the New Year with 'Auld Lang Syne'. Indians, after two hundred and fifty years of British rule, are also well acquainted with these festivals and enthusiastically join in. Of course, from the Anglo-Indian point of view, 'the more the merrier'.

In the following chapters I have tried to capture the life and spirit of the Anglo-Indians at the time of Independence, and as they are today. The culture and customs, food and festivals. Particularly their carefree lifestyle and devil-may-care attitude that has allowed them to flout convention, and for the most part live happily beyond their means.

List of References

1. Microsoft Encarta '95
2. *The Anglo-Indian Community*, 'Survival in India' by Evelyn Abel
3. W.T. Roy, *Hostages to Fortune*, Plural Societies, Summer 1974

Introduction

The way it was

> Culture is man's medium: there is not one aspect of human life that is not touched and altered by culture. This means personality, how people express themselves (including shows of emotion), the way they think, how they move, how problems are solved, how their cities are planned and laid out, how transportation systems function and are organized, as well as how economic and government systems are put together and function. However . . . it is frequently the most obvious and taken-for-granted and therefore the least studied aspect of culture that influence behaviour in the deepest and most subtle ways.
>
> —Edward T. Hall

On August 15, 1947, India became independent, and with the creation of Pakistan the country was rent asunder and bled profusely as millions of refugees were killed trying to flee across the border from India into Pakistan, and vice versa. Hindus and Muslims alike watched helplessly as an English mapmaker carved out an invisible border dividing their ancient land. The people had chosen, said the decision makers, but who knew for certain. It seemed more the result of crass manoeuvring by egocentric politicians, greedy to serve their own ends. Ultimately it mattered little: India was now two countries.

Amidst this chaos the British were also repatriating, leaving India after more than two hundred years of domination. At this time many Anglo-Indians felt abandoned. For the most part their lives had been spent in unquestioned loyalty to the Raj, and now it seemed they were being cast adrift upon the tide of uncertainty and change. Stunned at first, they watched in dismay as the Englishman retreated, taking with him the safety net that many felt was their only protection against the Hindus and Muslims who were butchering one another. For a group of people which had from the very beginning suffered an identity crisis, the sense of isolation grew and became more acute, as the future in India began to look exceedingly bleak. Most Anglo-Indians held British passports, which allowed them to settle in England, and a great many of them seized the opportunity to leave the country of their birth for what they believed to be greener pastures. In many instances, emigrating to England offered the perfect solution.

My parents decided to remain in India, since my father was a commissioned officer in the Indian Army. He realized the country was in a state of flux, and that with change comes upheaval. In retrospect, I personally do not think that those who left fared better in their adopted country, but that is just one person's point of view. It was ridiculous to imagine that the British who lived in England, bound by prejudices in a rigid class-conscious society, were going to take their 'mistakes' in India under their wing. Rather, they would be only too happy to see the Anglo-Indian quietly disappear into the sub-strata of British society. India by contrast was known as a country that for centuries had welcomed foreigners to her shores, treating them with tolerance and respect.* At any other time in her history, it would have been safe to expect that the Anglo-Indians, though they were Christians and of mixed blood, would not be harmed; they were after all born and bred on her soil. But these were strange, bewildering times, and fear governed many decisions.

I grew up in India, where though the Englishman was gone, he was not forgotten. Vestiges of the British way of life still clung tenuously to the newly independent people who had lived with over two hundred years of the Raj. Besides, the colonial lifestyle suited to a 'T' the new gentry. Living was easy, and one could still afford to hire three or four servants to maintain a household. In many affluent Anglo-Indian homes, the 'memsahib' very seldom troubled herself with domestic chores, preferring to delegate them to her servants. Most households could afford at least an

---

*Today, Anglo-Indians enjoy recognition and political representation in India. Two seats in India's Rajya Sabha (the Upper House of Representatives) are reserved for Anglo-Indians, who are nominated to it.

ayah who cared for the children, and a cook-cum-bearer. The sweeper, gardener and dhobi were often shared by many households. It was the duty of the 'khansamah' to do the daily marketing and prepare the meals. If the memsahib was fortunate enough to avail herself of the services of a khansamah who was also a good cook, and she in turn was graciously full of praise for the excellent meals dished up at her table, while at the same time generously overlooking minor discrepancies in the marketing accounts, things generally worked out very well for the household. But there were too many variables for this type of perfect chemistry to work in every case. Mistresses were often unrestrained in their criticism, while khansamahs had a penchant for cheap country liquor. Besides, many held dubious credentials; and failure upon failure in the kitchen often resulted in an unending stream of cooks.

The only practical solution to this dilemma seemed to be for the lady of the house to master the principles of cookery for herself. A mistress well versed in the rudiments of the culinary art could be relied upon in a difficult situation to turn failure into success. At this time, scores of recipe books were written and published, along with detailed instructions on how to circumvent the many pitfalls that could confront a memsahib. Unfortunately, most of these books were written by retired British colonials with time on their hands, who, during their sojourn in India, had seldom, if ever, ventured into the smoky confines of an Indian kitchen. As a result, some of them laughably chose to present the art of Indian cuisine, and the khansamah himself, as an exact science. Of course, memsahibs rushed to the bookstores in droves as each new publication hit the stands. The outcome of all this feverish purchasing can still sometimes be seen on the bookshelves of many Anglo-Indian households, where they lie in mint condition, their dust covers intact. Testament to the worth of the recipes contained within.

I would like the reader to indulge with me in a bit of nostalgia as I digress in an attempt to recreate the atmosphere that prevailed around our kitchen. The house we lived in was a relic of the British regime. It was a bungalow built of stone and brick, with large airy rooms. The ceiling was high, allowing for hot air to rise and escape from the skylights during the stifling summer months. The house contained six bedrooms with adjoining bathrooms, a large, square living room, dining room, front and rear veranda. From the latter there projected a covered passageway which led to a further block of rooms that comprised a godown, pantry, scullery and kitchen.

The godown housed trunks, suitcases, bedding rolls and other paraphernalia, so essential to the nomadic army life. It had one barred window reinforced with mesh. I hardly ever ventured in because it was infested with mice. Beside the godown lay the pantry, its windows shuttered against the scorching rays of the Indian sun. This was a room I delighted in exploring, but it was kept under lock and key, except for those times when my mother entered its cool confines to dole out the daily 'stores'. The pantry held the month's ration of rice, lentils, flour, sugar and spices. It also held an ample supply of tinned provisions such as English bacon, Danish butter, Australian jams and Kraft cheese in cans. The shelves that lined the walls were filled with an assortment of pickles, chutneys and home-made preserves, while the dark corners sheltered jugs of carrot wine, covered with cobwebs and dust, silently ageing.

Before Advent the pantry was swept out and all its shelves were lined with fresh newspaper. As Christmas approached it took on a magical quality, becoming the centre of attention as rich plum cakes, pudding and sweets—in fact, every type of delicacy, being prepared ahead of time—were stored within. Soon large odd-shaped parcels started arriving, and these found their way too into the pantry's cloistered confines. Whenever I found the door unlocked, I would elude the ever watchful eye of the ayah and lose myself in the enveloping darkness of that room. Intoxicated with the heady, sweet aroma of fermenting wine and Christmas puddings doused with rum, I savoured the smells, sampled forbidden delicacies, and closing my eyes, dreamed of Christmases past and the one yet to come. Unfortunately, I was never allowed to linger long, before being ferreted out by a keen-nosed ayah whose call I had neglected to answer.

Adjoining the pantry lay the scullery, smelling of phenyl and carbolic. It was a white-washed room with a sink and a draining board. On a long shelf above the board rested the detergents and other cleaning agents related to the maintenance of the house. I seldom lingered there as it held no particular enchantment for me.

The same did not hold true of the kitchen, a huge smoke-filled room adjoining the scullery. It was always hot in the kitchen, and the lighting was very poor. A single soot-covered bulb offered all the light besides the filtered rays of the sun. The bulb burned day and night for as long as someone was in the kitchen, and as far as I can remember, it was never empty. A kerosene lantern suspended above the chopping board was lit at dusk, shedding more light on the khansamah's culinary endeavours after sundown. No particular attention had been paid to the kitchen's position with regard to ventilation, and its drainage facilities also left a lot to be desired. There was no chimney either, the only outlet for the smoke being through the skylight. The walls were naturally covered with soot, the smell of which clung to the clothing of persons who stayed too long within, imparting a woody odour that was not altogether unpleasant. The kitchen was white-washed once a year, but this was an exercise in futility, as the lack of a chimney soon restored it to its former blackened state. The floor was swept twice a day and washed with a solution of phenyl and water, which left behind a lingering antiseptic smell.

The focal point of the kitchen was a large stove-cum-oven which had been manufactured in England for use in the colonies. It had two ovens, four hot plates and a fire hole that was perpetually covered with a large pot of water, boiling in readiness for baths, or for the feathering of fowl. Across from the stove stood the chopping table that looked rather like a dresser with a marble slab on top. Here the worthy cook minced his herbs, chopped his onions and cut up his meat. He also used the marble surface to bread cutlets and tenderize chops, achieving the latter by beating the chops repeatedly with a wooden mallet. I heard my mother on numerous occasions admonish him about this barbaric practice, but he would just roll his eyes, apologize and say: 'Understood, memsahib.' He promptly reverted to this method of tenderizing the minute my mother's back was turned.

There were several shelves above the chopping table that held an array of pots and saucepans. The mincing machine had pride of place, being the most prized gadget, serving any number of uses. No Indian kitchen was complete without one. For the rest, there was an assortment of aluminium vessels. These were kept as clean as possible under existing conditions. Once a week they were brought out and scrubbed with a bit of bar soap, coconut husk and coal ash, after which they received a good hosing down.

The most pleasant recollections I have are of birthdays and holidays. The kitchen was a hive of activity as extra hands were employed to help clean rice, peel garlic and ginger, and chop onions. Only the khansamah had charge of dressing the meat, fish and fowl. His wife unceasingly fed the oven with wood on one side, and with cakes, pastries and savouries on the other. These were baked to perfection without benefit of a thermometer, or regulated heat.

When my parents entertained, we children were served dinner early and sent to bed a little after sundown. Motor cars rolled up the driveway as guests arrived and were seated on the lawn. The evening air was filled with laughter and the tinkling sound of ice in crystal. As the evening progressed, the party moved indoors. At around 9.00 p.m. dinner was served. Vicariously, I lived the excitement, and sleep being out of the question, I would creep out of bed and find my ayah's lap as she sat gossiping on the steps of the back veranda. Gazing at the company within—catching the aroma of mouth-watering food as it passed from the cook to the butler, who placed it on the sideboard, ready to be served. Eventually my eyes would grow heavy, and I would fall asleep amidst snatches of servant gossip, with the acrid smell of wood smoke in my nostrils.

The meals prepared in that kitchen, primitive as it was, proved to me that knowledge and a true love of cookery were all the ingredients necessary for becoming a really good cook. Over the years my interest in the culinary art grew to become a passion. I was taken hunting with my parents, and we spent a lot of time in dak bungalows deep in the jungles of Madhya Pradesh. Sitting silently, crouched on a milking stool in a corner of the kitchen, I helped clean ginger and garlic for the cook, just for the privilege of being allowed to remain and be part of the pageant. Undetected I chopped onions and undertook a million menial tasks, all the while watching with fascination as venison and wild boar were dressed and made ready for the table. My mother, I am sure, despaired of ever making a lady of me. Those dark, cavernous, smoke-filled kitchens, brightened only by the dancing flames of the woodfire, touched a primeval spot within my being. I luxuriated in their enveloping warmth, injected with the pungent aroma of blended spices.

Khansamahs were, and are even today, for the most part unlettered men who often dish up the most delicious fare, with all the ingredients blended to perfection. Using the time-honoured measure of 'andaz', for which there is no literal translation, except perhaps, 'a pinch of this' and 'a dash of that', they work their magic. I tried to duplicate their successes, using recognized measures, and after a lot of experimenting have finally achieved the same delicious results. It is this collection of recipes, together with others tried and true, that I would like to share with enthusiastic lovers of cookery.

However, it is not enough merely to know about the cuisine of a people; one must have some knowledge of the people themselves in order to fully appreciate their food. It is necessary to delve into their psyche and explore their culture and customs. The ensuing pages, while offering a wide range of recipes, also strive to illuminate the Anglo-Indian way of life by documenting their festivals and celebrations. I have recorded numerous anecdotes drawn from memory which, I hope, will serve as illustrations as I attempt to capture the spirit of my people.

Today we watch the rapid demise of the Anglo-

Indians as we know them to be. Future generations will be assimilated into other cultures, and during the next century they will no doubt be totally absorbed by the global melting pot. Finally, to be swept away, without a trace, by the tide of time.

Writing this book has been a labour of love, and it is my hope that it will become for the reader as much a book for reading as for reference.

Festivals

Celebrations with a difference

All Christian feasts revolve around the birth, ministry and death of its pivotal figure, Jesus Christ, who was born between BC eight and four, in the town of Bethlehem of Judah, which today lies in Israel. Jesus is regarded by all Christians to be the Son of God, divinely conceived by the Virgin Mary, who was the wife of a carpenter called Joseph. The family lived in the small town of Nazareth. The title 'Christ' is derived from the Greek translation of the word *Christos*, meaning the 'anointed one'. The life and times of Jesus Christ are set down in the gospels written by his four apostles: Matthew, Mark, Luke and John. Jesus preached a gospel of love, which is an integral part of Christianity.

For most Christians December 25 is the day when the Nativity of Jesus Christ is celebrated. Many of the rituals surrounding Christmas, such as the use of mistletoe and holly, the Yule log and even the wassail-bowl, trace their origins to ancient Germanic and Celtic pagan customs. The evergreen Christmas tree symbolizes the paradise tree from the Garden of Eden. When Albert Emmanuel of Saxe-Coburg-Gotha married Queen Victoria of England in 1840, he brought over with him to Britain the delightful custom of celebrating Christmas with an evergreen tree. British colonists introduced this custom to the colonies, and immigrants took it with them to the New World. In much the same way Dutch settlers brought the celebration of St Nicholas's Day on December 6 to America. Traditionally, on the eve of St Nicholas's feast, children were given gifts. On Christmas Eve, traditionally, the British also gave their children gifts. The name Santa Claus, given to the jolly old man in a red suit, is derived from the Dutch Sinterklaas, which is a modification of St Nicholas. With the passage of time, the feast of St Nicholas (Santa Claus) moved forward in the calendar to coincide with the date of Christ's birth. And so it is that all over the world Christmas is celebrated on December 25 and gifts are exchanged.

The first missionaries to India gave their converts the tradition of Christmas. Children born to European fathers and Indian women were baptized Christians, and adopted all the traditional feasts and celebrations associated with Christianity.

Christmas

Bring me flesh, and bring me wine,
Bring me pine logs hither;
Thou and I will see him dine,
When we bear them thither.

—'Good King Wenceslas'

Christmas is the most widely celebrated feast within the Anglo-Indian community, and the spirit in which it is observed is best typified by the lyrics of the old Christmas carol, 'Good King Wenceslas', that speaks of generosity, mirth and merriment. The spirit of Christmas generally reaches out and touches all who are even remotely connected with the feverish activities leading up to that special day. It is a state of mind that arrives around Advent, when plans for the celebration of Christ's birth generally begin.

Tradition must be observed, and in our family preparations usually started on a chilly winter morning early in December. My mother would have a large folding table brought out from the godown and set up in a corner of the sitting room. Next, a shallow tin pan that fit the length and breadth of the table was placed on top. A bed of soil covered the base of the pan, and red raggy seeds were scattered evenly over the soil, which was then liberally watered. Each day we children would rush to the table, eager to see if the seeds had sprouted, and in time they did. Soon there was an even carpet of grass that was tended each day by our mali, who would bring his watering can into the sitting room and give the young shoots a thorough soaking. On December 22, a wooden stable was set up on the bed of green, and plaster figures of the Nativity were carefully unwrapped. My mother set each one down in its appointed place. A star was placed atop the stable, and the crib was ready for us to admire. This procedure was repeated ever year for as long as my mother was alive. Nevertheless, the sight of the rough wooden stable with the infant Jesus, and the holy family set on a carpet of grass, never failed to fill

us with wonder. The mali as well was in awe of the crib, and he could often be spotted standing before it in silent admiration.

In order of priority, the next most important task was a visit to the tailor. Fabrics that had been purchased during the course of the year were brought out from the dark recesses of the cupboard where they were stored, and once more saw the light of day. Pattern books gained a new significance and were in great demand. Tailor shops were suddenly crowded with clientele poring over illustrations of the very latest fashions. Arguments erupted and quickly subsided when tailor and customer came to an agreement on the amount of fabric required to sew a certain style, and the delivery date was established. Harassed tailors seldom delivered as promised, and frantic customers often had to make repeated trips to his shop before they were finally able to retrieve their completed garments. Parents undertook extended shopping trips, arriving home with large odd-shaped packages wrapped in newspaper. These were stored out of sight, in a spot everyone was aware of but dared not pry into.

The Christmases of my youth that I recall so fondly are even today ritualistically observed in many Anglo-Indian homes all over India. The spirit of Christmas touched everyone, from the peons in my father's office to the postman, who would save up all the overseas cards to deliver on Christmas Eve, and claim his baksheesh. The bania, a cheerful old rogue from whom we purchased all our dry goods, raised the prices of essential items such as sugar and flour just before Christmas, in order to make his tidy little profit. My mother felt she outwitted him every year because she would start buying items for her cakes and confections early, but somehow, I felt, he always had the last laugh. Even the dhobi, who was notorious for his tardy delivery of clothing that had priority, arrived punctually with linen and curtains, washed and pressed, because he knew there was something in it for him.

The kitchen was a hive of activity as cakes and biscuits galore were baked and stored away in an assortment of containers. The pungent odour of spices being ground in vinegar filled the air as preparations commenced for making pickled pork, which, when cooked, was allowed to soak in stone 'burnees', awaiting the week of festivities. Beef hump and tongues were salted in a bath of brine to which limes and pickling spices had been added. The ritual actually commenced on that Sunday before Christmas when every family member was recruited and had to devote the whole day to making kul kuls. The tiny balls of sweet dough were rolled on the tines of a fork, which gave them a unique shape. They were then laboriously deep fried in oil, after which they were sugared and allowed to cool before being filled into containers that found their way into the pantry. While passing the kitchen a wide variety of aromas reached the nostrils, but nothing was more tantalizing than the delicious redolence of chocolate fudge being stirred over a slow fire to a perfect 'soft ball'.

In the last two weeks of December, family and friends who were invited to stay converged upon the house for the holidays. A general air of merriment prevailed, and Yuletide carols were played on the gramophone. December days were crisp and cool.

The early morning sun streamed through doors and windows, radiating warmth. One rose and hastily donned a cardigan and a pair of socks, because the stone floors felt uncomfortably cold against unshod feet. After breakfast, a clear cloudless sky usually beckoned the family outdoors, and we often sat around on the veranda until lunchtime, playing draughts, or chatting—basking in the winter sunshine. After lunch, a siesta always looked inviting, and even though there were innumerable tasks to be attended to, everything came to a halt as even my mother slid between the covers for a nap. The evenings were short, with night descending abruptly.

As the waning year rapidly drew in the days that moved forward at a feverish speed, one was caught up in the momentum of the fast-approaching holiday season. December 22 soon arrived, and every home was magically transformed as streamers of crêpe paper and tinsel adorned sitting and dining rooms. Large intricate decorations cut from metallic sheets of myriad-coloured paper were suspended from the fan, and bunches of balloons adorned the corners of each room. A bunch of preserved mistletoe was carefully unwrapped and hung from a strategic entrance. The mistress of every household ensured that linen was freshly laundered, and the cobwebs had been swept out from the nooks and crannies all around the home. Lace antimacassars graced the backs of sofas and chairs. Fresh runners and doilies were placed on sideboards and dumbwaiters, while impeccably laundered drapes were hung over doorways. A zinc tub filled with soil was brought in and placed in a corner by the window, and in it was firmly buried a great branch cut down from one of the trees outside.

We then commenced decorating the Christmas tree, which sported innumerable little branches. A string of miniature lights was deftly woven through them, followed by garlands of crêpe paper and strings of beads. Glass baubles were suspended at strategic points upon delicate boughs, together with tiny painted wooden ornaments, some of which were very old. Finally, a star of breathtaking beauty was set upon the highest branch. I can remember gazing at it hypnotically for hours on end. The decorations complete, my parents would switch off the lights so that we could all admire the beautiful tree. The glass baubles swayed gently among the branches and mirrored the twinkling tree lights, while the star of Bethlehem cast a radiant glow in the darkened room.

Christmas Eve was always memorable—our dresses arrived from the tailor's shop; boxes of new shoes were scattered about the bedrooms while trinkets and hair bows lay untidily upon the dressing table. Everyone was busy getting ready for Midnight Mass. The sitting room, cloaked in velvet darkness except for the winking tree lights and the star of Bethlehem glowing on high, was the scene of much furtive activity, and if one peeked out long enough, one was sure to spot the figures of my parents as they furtively arranged gifts around the tree. At 11.00 p.m., we trooped out into the crisp night air on our way to church, which was within walking distance from the house. Warm shawls and coats hid all the finery, and as the men walked briskly ahead, fidgeting uncomfortably with their new shirt collars, we children skipped alongside our mother, oblivious of the cold. Our family always arrived early and took a pew halfway down the centre of the church. My mother considered it a disgrace if one was late for Midnight Mass and had to stand outside 'holding up the pillars of the church'.

Midnight service was filled with prayers and hymns—the overpowering fragrance of incense hung heavy in the air. The lines for Holy Communion seemed endless, and those of us who were too young to receive it soon grew restless. After Mass we all joined another line, taking turns visiting the crib and the scene of the Nativity, after which the congregation spilled out of church, and everywhere one could hear the joyful exchange of Christmas greetings. When one grows up within a small community, neighbours become almost as close as family. Being young and always impatient, we walked ahead in anticipation of the gifts and treats awaiting us at home.

Great gasps of delight filled the room as the lights were turned on, and we saw the bejewelled tree with the gifts arranged beneath it. This was truly a child's moment of magic and suspense. Our Uncle Alfie always played Santa Claus and distributed the gifts. We ripped away the flimsy wrappings of tissue paper, anxious to find the treasures within. It was difficult to judge which was more exciting, enjoying one's own gift, or examining another's. After all the presents had been handed out, what remained under the tree were a few parcels for friends, and several envelopes and packages for our faithful retainers who would receive their gifts the following morning. Even though we were allowed to stay up as long as we pleased, our eyelids soon grew heavy with sleep, and one by one everyone trooped off to bed.

Everyone slept late on Christmas morning except for my mother and the cook. On entering the kitchen sleepy eyed around 10.00 a.m., one would find them both hard at work—they had already been up for hours. All the gift wrapping from the previous night was cleared away, and the sitting room was spic and span once more, in readiness to receive friends and relatives who would soon start arriving. On Christmas day there was always company for lunch. Old friends whose children lived far away, or had left the country joined us, as also house guests, and occasionally the parish priest who had said Mass the night before. The main course generally consisted of chicken korma, peas pulao, raita and papadums. A platter of fresh pomfret coated with spices, crumbed and fried to a delicate brown colour, arrived garnished with wedges of masala fried potato. A garden salad, cauliflower and cabbage foogath rounded off the meal. For dessert, Christmas cake and an assortment of other treats were served. Fresh fruit was always offered at the end of the meal. Everyone ate with gusto, and the conversation was lively. However, as the fruit was passed around, one noticed a definite lull between the periods of chatter, and these silences grew longer as the afternoon progressed. The meal ended, and after a decent interval our guests began to take their leave. House guests retreated to the sanctuary of their bedrooms, and soon everyone departed, dictated by the need for an afternoon snooze. The servants cleared away the dishes.

Christmas dinner was a much grander affair. Our well-rested guests generally arrived around 7.00 p.m. Everyone milled around excitedly, exchanging season's greetings. Laughter and light conversation filled the house. A large bowl of rum punch graced the centre of the table, surrounded with trays of hors d' oeuvres. We children darted unrestrained between the guests and helped ourselves to the savoury delights spread out on the dining table. It was an evening of great excitement. Dinner was served around 9.00 p.m., and everyone trooped into the dining room where a wonderful array of dishes were arranged on the sideboard. We children were always seated at a separate table set up specially for us. A light, clear broth was generally served, and after it was cleared away, diners helped themselves to the many dishes set out on the sideboard, before taking their places at the table to enjoy the meal.

Entrées usually consisted of succulent duck roasted in orange sauce, served with stuffing on the side, ham with pineapple glaze, roasted potatoes and carrots, stuffed tomatoes, a beetroot salad and a fresh garden salad. Crusty rolls and butter were passed around. A little way into the meal, the pièce de résistance arrived—it was my mother's famous biryani that she served on a large oval platter. Streaked with kesar, adorned with plump raisins and cashewnuts fried a golden brown, it was carried in by our cook. The fragrance of this delicately spiced dish of rice in which nestled morsels of rich mutton, permeated every corner of the room. What followed was curious and indicative of our Indian heritage—everyone made a beeline for the rice. The platter was repeatedly emptied and replenished. It took pride of place at the dinner table.

Plum pudding swathed in a dancing blue flame was set upon the table. Two kinds of sauces accompanied it—a brandy hard sauce and a rich custard sauce. My favourite was the latter. While my father served guests and members of the family with portions of pudding, my mother once more recounted the tale of how she had acquired the recipe. It seems a cousin had 'nicked' it from a world-famous chef who worked at the Dorchester Hotel in London, while he was busy making amorous advances in her direction. Upon receiving our portion, each of us children promptly proceeded to sift through the pudding in search of the coins that always lay buried within its depths. Shouts of glee accompanied each find. The meal ended, our elders sat around the table until the early hours of the morning, drinking and reminiscing on Christmases past. We children were dispatched to bed as the excitement of the day caught up with us, and we could no longer stay awake.

December 26 or Boxing Day was spent in relaxation. Our parents awoke later than usual, and some of the servants had the day off. We children did as we pleased, entertaining ourselves with our gifts, or reading curled up in a chair on the veranda. Our parents were generally invited out for dinner that night, and we retired early to bed after a light repast.

Bringing in the New Year

'Tis noise and nonsense are their dear delight
And stupid pleasures crown the drunken night.

—Anonymous

New Year's Day is celebrated on January 1. It is the first day of the year in the Gregorian calendar, which was introduced in 1582 and adopted by England in 1752. Prior to this the Julian calendar was observed, and New Year's Day fell on March 25, which was the feast of the Annunciation. It was on this day that an angel first appeared to the Virgin Mary and informed her that she would give birth to Jesus Christ. New Year's Day has traditionally been observed as a religious feast, but it is December 31, New Year's Eve, that is the occasion of much spirited celebration and revelry as people gather in a festive atmosphere and count down the hours to midnight—'to ring out the old and ring in the new.'

In Anglo-Indian homes everywhere, a typical New Year's Eve celebration would start on the evening of December 31. Dinner was generally a light repast, often missed by the excited younger members of the household. Several dances were always held within the community, but we girls were only allowed to attend the one approved by our mother. Of course, the young men had greater freedom, and some would in the course of the night, visit two or three dance halls, finally ending up at the place where they met the most friends, or the most interesting girls.

We were four sisters, and on this evening there was always a great scramble to use the bathroom, the iron and the dressing-table mirror. The topic of conversation revolved around clothing, shoes, accessories, and invariably—boys. The atmosphere was one of feverish excitement. Friends arrived, who would accompany us to the dance, and everyone proceeded to giggle and talk all at once, appraising and comparing new clothes and shoes. One of us sisters was always skipping out of the room, leaving the chatter behind to run to the back veranda and shout for the dhobi who happened to live in an outhouse in the next compound, a decision, I am sure, the poor chap bitterly regretted. The harassed little man would come running over with an article of clothing on his arm, and this he kept up for most of the evening. Finally the impossible was achieved, and we all trooped out of the house with clothing and accessories matched. The endless fussing with hair and eye make-up had paid dividends; we were impeccably coiffed!

Arriving early at the dance hall, one generally encountered friends milling around. Young men with

loud, self-conscious voices congregated in groups while the girls giggled in corners—chattering about clothes, or discussing the young men. The dance hall was brightly lit and draped from end to end with crêpe paper streamers that were caught up in the centre of the room with a large bunch of balloons in a variety of colours, boldly proclaiming the new year. Tables were set up around the hall, while the centre was bare except for a liberal sprinkling of French chalk. Upon each table were hats and noisemakers with trailing metallic tendrils, all the necessary accoutrements for heralding the new year. The live band on the stage would be rehearsing while the crooner, gorgeous in a sequined evening gown, sat practising her notes. As people began to arrive in increasing numbers, the hall began to fill. Greetings were loudly exchanged over the din of conversation as groups arranged themselves around the tables. The tension mounted.

The meat patty and chicken salad stall in one corner of the room did brisk business, and beside it, the bar was equally crowded. In the great hall the lights were dimmed as the band struck up the opening number that always filled me with excitement . Having attended numerous functions during my teenage years, I found it uncanny, and could never quite get over the fact that nearly every dance started with the number 'Cherry Pink and Apple Blossom White'; it was definitely the favourite of the Fifties! Men led their partners onto the dance floor. Twirling our frosted glasses of lemonade, we cooled our perspiring palms while steadfastly avoiding the appraising glances from members of the opposite sex. When one of them broke away from the group and made his way to our table, an air of expectation hung in the air until he led one of the party onto the dance floor. Each one of us desperately wanted to be asked to dance, but there were few glances of encouragement. The evening was still young and this type of bravado would have to wait until we were well into the night, and feeling more sure of ourselves. It was a pretty game, prettily played out.

The crooner wailed out a medley of slow romantic numbers, then soothed her husky voice with a glass of amber-coloured liquid. Spot dances were followed by the Paul Jones, and an assortment of games were played. Amorous partners, glued to each other, swayed gently to the music. Dramatically, there would be a change of tempo, and dancers twirled or jived around the floor with great enthusiasm. The air was heavy with cigarette smoke, combined with the underlying odour of alcohol.

At around ten o'clock the hall was flooded with light once more as the music ceased, and a buffet dinner, the price of which was included in the ticket, was served. Many of us had satisfied our pangs of hunger with sandwiches or beef patties; nevertheless, the queue stretched through the room. The dinner table held a wide array of food, diverse and delicious. There were roasted chickens surrounded by tiny baked potatoes, mutton curry and rice, pea and potato sabzi, and large platters of Hakka chow. Fresh rolls, butter and two types of salad generally rounded off the meal. Coffee and assorted cakes were served for dessert. During the meal music played softly in the background, and the conversation was generally subdued as the company concentrated on the food.

After dinner, amidst much clapping and cheering, the organizers proceeded to call out the lucky numbers of tickets that had won prizes. Members of the band, their spirits refreshed with food and drink, would start up the music by playing a lively tune. Spirited dancers took to the floor, and many of them, in spite of the food and alcohol they had just consumed, kept perfect time with the music. The ice was broken and everybody now seemed relaxed, having captured the spirit of the event. Couples floated around the room with the greatest of ease—many had paired for the night, or at least for the duration of the dance, finding romance or friendship in the magic of the moment.

As the hands of the clock moved closer to the witching hour, the countdown began, starting at 11.50 p.m. At the stroke of midnight the revellers cried out in unison: 'Happy New Year!' The band would strike up, and the strains of 'Auld Lang Syne' echoed through the hall. Everyone joined in. Ladies donned their masks, and men wore their ridiculous hats of varied colours. The hall was filled with merry laughter, and greetings were exchanged between friends and strangers alike. All this amidst the shrill cries of the noisemakers, and the loud bursting of balloons. The hall was a cacophony of sound as the old year slipped into history.

The dancing resumed and sometimes continued into the early morning hours, but the celebration had lost momentum. People began to leave. We girls would hurry out into the bracing night air, pile into the car and drive silently home, each one filled with her own thoughts. Hastily shedding our finery, we tumbled into bed, oblivious of our bedrooms, now in a state of complete disarray, with clothing carelessly draped over chairs, shoes strewn about, and the dressing table cluttered with hair ornaments and costume jewellery. Sleep came instantly as we slid between the covers. The new year arrives, notwithstanding.

New Year's Day

> The New Year is when some people drop in for a call
> And others call in for a drop.

Traditionally, on New Year's Day, Christians are required to attend church service. Several services are held at different times during the day, and very often there is also an evening service, but many people, worn out from the previous night's festivities, often find it impossible to be present at any one of them. Those that do make the effort, generally attend the 12.00 p.m. service, and evidence of its popularity can be seen by simply passing the church at this time and witnessing the faithful who spill out of the church into the front compound, and beyond. This service is very often also the shortest, as the attending priest invariably has a luncheon date to keep.

People generally wake up later than usual on New Year's Day, and even the bright winter sunshine often proves to be no enticement as they avoid the glare and stay indoors. In our home it was customary to entertain intimate friends in the evening. They would arrive at around 6.00 p.m. to exchange 'compliments of the season', and stay for a light dinner that would be served around eight o'clock at night. Dinner usually consisted of chicken velvet soup, followed by crumb chops, slices of salted beef tongue, a cauliflower boiled and served whole with a dusting of fresh ground pepper, country-fried potatoes and a fresh garden salad. For dessert my mother served an assortment of Christmas treats, fruit cake and coffee to the elders.

On New Year's Day a sense of anticlimax often prevails after the mirth and merriment of the previous week. It has always been a day in limbo; people generally spend the time recovering from the excesses of the festive season, and contemplating the year ahead. All the calendars proclaim the fact that we are in a new year, but for many people it is often difficult to relinquish the year just past. This is especially true if it proved to be a year marked by an event of great sorrow; it almost seems as if one is leaving a loved one behind. Nevertheless, the year must be surrendered so that it can flow from our beings into the past where it belongs. For there is the future to be reckoned with, a continuance of life's journey that requires all our attention.

Lent and Easter

For Christians, Lent is traditionally the forty-day period that starts with Ash Wednesday and ends on Holy Saturday, the day before Easter Sunday. It is a time for fasting and penance, and one is required to eat sparingly during the entire period, except for Sundays. In 1966, however, Pope Paul VI relaxed these rules, after which fasting and abstinence were only obligatory on Ash Wednesday and Good Friday. The observance of fasting and self-denial during Lent differs in the Protestant and Anglican churches, whose emphasis is primarily on penitence.

Shrove Tuesday or 'Fat Tuesday' is the day before Ash Wednesday, and in many Latin American countries around the world it is a festival day (Mardi Gras), during which there is a great deal of indulgence in food and drink. Shrove Tuesday traces its origins to pre-Christian, spring fertility rites. In India, Shrove Tuesday was commonly known as 'Pancake Tuesday', because on that day in every Anglo-Indian home pancakes were prepared. These thin delicate crêpes were made from a batter of cake flour, coconut milk, sugar, eggs and vanilla. Filled with a delicious combination of freshly grated coconut, sugar, a dash of vanilla and plump dark raisins we called 'plums'. The pancakes were rolled into cylindrical shapes, sprinkled over with a dash of fresh lime juice, and served with hot cups of sweet, milky tea.

Ash Wednesday marks the first day of Lent. The day gets its name from the traditional ceremony of placing ash on the forehead as a sign of penitence. Roman Catholics are required to attend Mass, during which the priest places ash on the foreheads of his congregation, officiating priests, and members of the clergy. Over each one he recites the words, 'Remember that you are dust, and unto dust you shall return'. Everyone generally tries to give up something for Lent; in many instances this deprivation consists of an indulgence or craving one is not disciplined enough to otherwise live without. For some it is chocolates, for others alcohol or tobacco. There are no hard and fast rules governing this sacrifice and in many cases, try as one might, it becomes impossible to still the craving and endure deprivation for the entire Lenten period.

Palm Sunday marks the triumphal entry of Jesus Christ into Jerusalem, after which commences Holy Week. On the Monday of that week Christ drove the money changers from the temple. On Tuesday, he spoke to his disciples of the second coming, and on

Wednesday, the New Testament tells us that Jesus was anointed in Bethany to prepare him for burial. He shared the Passover supper, traditionally known as the Last Supper, with his disciples on Thursday. During the meal he informed them of his imminent death; and in blessing the bread and wine, he called the bread his body, and the wine his blood, which was going to be shed for the forgiveness of sins. He broke the bread, and his disciples shared both bread and wine with him. He entreated them to 'do this in remembrance of me' (Luke 22:17-20). This ceremony, first performed by Jesus Christ, lies at the very core of Christianity, and today is the most sacred ritual known as the Eucharist, celebrated by Christians of every denomination.

After the meal Jesus and his disciples went up to the Mount of Olives, and knowing that his time of betrayal was near, Jesus entered the Garden of Gethsemane to pray. He was then betrayed by one of his apostles known as Judas Iscariot, tried and sentenced to die on the cross.

Good Friday is a day of fasting, and Christians are required to attend church. Traditionally, hot cross buns are eaten on this day. In the Roman Catholic Church, the 'three hours agony' that Jesus Christ suffered on the cross before he died is observed. After his death, Christ was taken down from the cross and laid in the tomb of Joseph of Arimathea. On Holy Saturday at midnight, the Lenten period of penitence comes to an end.

Easter Sunday marks the glorious resurrection of

Jesus Christ, and is the principal festival of the Christian religion. On this day, the Gospels tell us, he rose from the dead. Early that morning, 'Mary Magdalene and Mary, the mother of James' (Mark 16:1) arrived at the tomb , and were dismayed to find it empty. Within they saw 'a young man' (Mark 16:5) who informed them that Jesus was risen. The festival of Easter is celebrated at different times during the months of March and April each year, and is known as one of the moveable feasts. Even though Easter is a Christian festival, it involves many pre-Christian traditions. The word '*Eastre*' is the Anglo-Saxon name for the goddess of spring and fertility. To her was dedicated the month of April. The Easter bunny is also a sign of fertility, as are Easter eggs. The celebration itself most probably embodies quite a number of traditions, since it also coincides with the Jewish festival of Passover. Remembering that the first Christians were all brought up as Jews, it is easy to see how they interpreted Easter as a feast that celebrated the coming of the Messiah, as was foretold by the prophets in the Old Testament of the Bible.

Even though Easter is the principal feast in the liturgical calendar, with great significance, because of the death and resurrection of Jesus Christ and the first celebration of the Eucharist, it is a sedate feast. Coming so soon after the crucifixion and death of Christ, it lacks the *joie de vivre* of Christmas. On Easter Sunday most Christians experience a quiet inner joy and peace. They attend church services in the morning, and upon returning home, the younger members of the family receive Easter eggs. Depending on how deep one's pockets are, the type of Easter egg can vary from a simple hard-boiled egg with its shell painted in brilliant hues, to the most exquisite confection wrought in the shape of an egg. The more luxurious types of eggs sport an outer shell made from marzipan or chocolate, and upon breaking them open one is often delighted to find a delectable assortment of toffees and bon-bons. It is a common sight on Easter Sunday to see children gnawing at the outer shell of a marzipan or chocolate Easter egg.

In our home we always celebrated Easter with an afternoon luncheon. Friends began to drop in any time after 11.30 a.m. The atmosphere was casual, and everyone sat around chatting and drinking beer from large tankards. The months of March and April can be very hot in Central India, with the afternoon sun blazing down from a clear blue sky. My mother and her friends enjoyed their shandy in the cool, dark interior of the house. On this day we teenagers were also allowed to imbibe some of the frothy stuff, liberally watered down with lemonade.

In the kitchen the cook slaved over a hot fire, preparing the lunch. My mother would leave her company from time to time to ensure the meal was progressing satisfactorily and would be on time, which, of course, it never was. Eventually, at around two o'clock, we all assembled in the dining room and lunch was served. A large oval platter piled high with coconut rice was placed upon the table, and everyone caught a whiff of the delicious aroma of blended spices coupled with the scent of coconut, liberally garnished with crisp fried onions. Accompanying the rice was a large tureen filled with koftas swimming in a rich dark gravy (ball curry). A platter of fish cutlets followed, set on a bed of fresh lettuce, garnished with sliced tomatoes and radish roses. Country fried potatoes, French bean foogath, devil chutney and a bowl of raita rounded off the meal. It was a veritable feast for the senses. Dessert was a large fruit salad, accompanied by a custard sauce. Many of the guests having eaten and drunk to capacity would be invited by my father to take their afternoon nap in one of the spare bedrooms, and return to their homes after sundown. The offer was generally accepted with alacrity. Those who were intent on leaving departed soon after the meal, while everyone else retired for an afternoon siesta.

A full stomach was the opiate that allowed one to fall into a deep sleep. Overhead, the fans whirred around ineffectually, only serving to redistribute the hot air within the room. Awaking from a drugged slumber at around 5.30, a quick wash-up in a basin of cool water revived one. Tea, with an assortment of petit fours, was served. We could also have slices of toasted bread with butter and jam, or treacle. The men folk generally limited themselves to a cup of strong, hot tea.

As the brilliant sun set in the western sky, a cool breeze would sometimes start up and stir the leaves and branches of the trees, bringing a little respite from the stifling heat. Our guests, once more refreshed, continued to celebrate late into the evening. Many held tall glasses filled with the 'hair of the dog that bit them'. Snacking on bhujias, sandwiches and cheese straws, they sat around engaging in conversation that was generally light and full of banter. Night descended rapidly, and slowly everyone started to take their leave. Dinner often consisted of no more than a light broth, and leftovers for anyone who could stomach food—after which we retired early to bed.

Rites of Passage

Anglo-Indians observe all the sacraments of the Christian church. The word 'sacrament' is derived from the Latin word '*sacramentum*', which during the pre-Christian era denoted something given in pledge, like the water of baptism, or the bread and wine shared in the Eucharist. The function of the sacrament, therefore, is to sanctify, and this is achieved by bestowing grace.

It would not be far wrong to suggest that many of Christianity's sacraments are closely affiliated with ceremonies that follow a human being's rites of passage, marking the different phases that carry a person from one period in his life to the next. When a child is born, the sacrament of baptism grants him/her admission into the Christian faith. Through the sacrament of marriage a man and woman are united before God, establishing a new status for them within the community. Their children are legitimized by the rite of parenthood within the sanctity of marriage. The final rite of passage is of course death, which marks the termination of life in much the same way that birth marks the entry. The funeral and mourning process allows the dead person to leave this world in the prescribed Christian manner, while at the same time furnishing the deceased's family and friends with a sense of finality.

In the Roman Catholic church there are seven sacraments: baptism, penance, holy Eucharist, confirmation, holy orders, matrimony and the anointing of the sick. Baptism and penance are known as the sacraments of the dead, mainly because the grace they bestow gives new life to those who are spiritually dead, either through the blemish of original sin, with which they are born (inherited from Adam and Eve when they fell from grace), or through mortal sin committed knowingly and with a free will. The other sacraments are called sacraments of the living because, in order to receive them, the recipient must be in a state of grace. The sacraments of baptism, confirmation and holy orders may only be received once in a Christian's life, because it is believed they imprint an ineffaceable seal on the soul, and thereby fulfil their purpose completely when first received.

Baptism

Baptism is the universal rite of initiation among Christians. Infants born to Roman Catholic parents are generally baptized within months of their birth, primarily because the parents fear the infant may fall sick and die while not in a state of grace. It is believed the souls of persons who die before baptism are consigned to 'limbo', a place which is neither heaven nor hell. During the ceremony of baptism, the officiating priest asks God to cast out the devil. Both he and the sponsor recite the Apostles' Creed and the Lord's Prayer; the priest anoints the head of the infant with oil, and when a desire for baptism is expressed, he pours the baptismal water on the head, saying: 'I baptize you in the name of the Father, and of the Son, and of the Holy Spirit.'

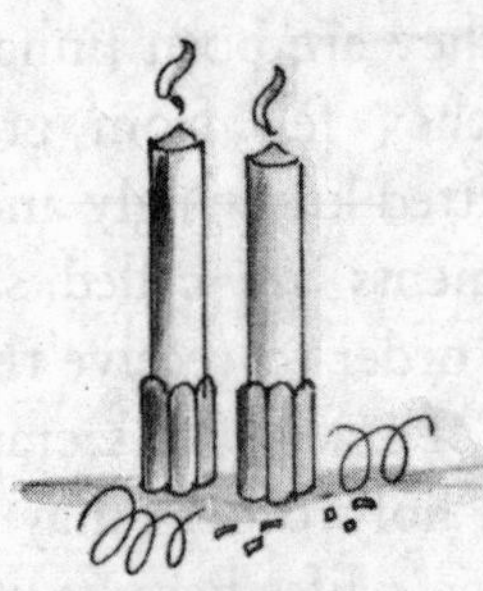

The ceremony of baptism is carried out in that area of the church known as the baptistery, and the baptismal font may in some instances be dedicated to John the Baptist. Holy water blessed by a bishop or a priest is sprinkled over the head of the infant in a ritual cleansing that traces its origin to the ancient rites of Judaism. The baptized infant through the sponsor agrees to undertake the obligations of Christianity.

In the Baptist and Anabaptist faith they insist on adult baptism as they believe that only adults can be called upon to account for their misdeeds. These faiths also require total immersion in water, which is a symbol of purification in many religions.

In the days before the technique of 'ultrasound' indicated the gender of the unborn child, women indulged in a lot of speculation and superstition regarding its sex. Even today not every mother is willing to submit to modern science, preferring to discover the sex of her child at the time of birth. Within the Anglo-Indian community, garments for the unborn child are often sewn or knitted in three colours: blue for a boy, pink for a girl, and yellow—well, yellow can be worn by either gender. Once the child is born, of course, it matters little. As the infant grows, he or she goes through the complete layette in a matter of months, and if it happens to be a second child, promptly dons its elder siblings' hand-me-downs.

As soon as the baby is brought home from the hospital, setting the date for the baptism of the child is the next important concern. A name has to be chosen, and there are plenty of suggestions and advice. 'Don't be choosing some strange name from a gravestone,' my grandfather would admonish, and thereafter proceed to give me a selection of names which he thought were suitable. Of course, they were all quite acceptable, for a child born during the turn of the century, but for the 1960s? Generally, a mother knows in her heart what she is going to call her child, and, in fact, will call it by that name when they are together. Naming one's child is a private matter that only requires the agreement of the parents in question.

Choosing godparents for the child is another hurdle that must be overcome before baptism. Often this is a difficult task, as the most unsuitable friends and relatives offer themselves as candidates. They must be dissuaded tactfully, and the pair considered most appropriate discreetly asked to accept the responsibility. In the event it is the first-born, a christening robe, cap, booties and shawl are necessary for the baptism. Doting grandparents on both sides have been known to provide these items. In some cases the fortunate baby is presented with two sets of everything, while the unfortunate mother has the task of determining which set will actually be worn.

Most christenings take place on Saturdays, in the early afternoon, after which the parents of the newly christened child generally invite family and friends over to their home for a small celebration. Countless photographs are taken of the baby with its proud parents, grandparents, godparents, and other family members. It is traditional to bring a gift, and during the celebration guests generally take turns holding little Caroline or Andrew, cuddling and cooing as the fretful infant squirms in their arms.

Today the custom is to give practical gifts that the infant can use or wear. In the past, however, it was fashionable to give electroplated nickel silver mugs, teaspoons and hairbrushes. I can remember finding an assortment of such articles tarnished with age, carefully wrapped in tissue paper, packed away in my mother's cupboard. She had five children, and that meant five christenings, which all added up to a fair bit of silver.

After all the fuss has died down, the christening cake is cut and slices passed around to the guests along with an assortment of finger food such as sandwiches, meat patties, lemon tarts, cocktail sausages and prawn puffs. Tea and coffee is also served. Beer and sherry is generally available, with soft drinks for the children. Most christening parties conclude at sunset, but I have known a few where toasts to the new-born continued well into the night!

Penance—Confession

In the Christian faith there are two types of confession: private confession that the penitent is required to make to the priest in the privacy of the confessional; and public confession that is made before the congregation. Private confession is an essential part of the sacrament of penance in the Roman Catholic faith, and Catholics are expected to go to confession at least once a year. In the Roman Catholic and Orthodox churches, the sacrament of penance is dispensed by a priest, whereby he forgives sins that are confessed to him. The confessor must be sorrowful, penitent and determined to make amends. The priest then grants him/ her absolution. He is bound by the seal of the confessional never to repeat what he has heard. In the Roman Catholic church, when a penitent person kneels before the priest in the confessional, he/she begins by saying: 'Bless me, Father, for I have sinned; my last confession was—'. He/she proceeds to name all the serious sins committed since that time. If the priest judges the person is truly penitent, he will impose a penance, and after asking for God's mercy, he will pronounce absolution by saying: 'May Our Lord Jesus Christ absolve you from every bond of excommunication and interdict, to the extent of my power and your need. Finally, I absolve you from your sins, in the name of the Father, and of the Son, and of the Holy Spirit. Amen.'

The confessing of sins and gaining absolution is taken from the Gospel according to St John (20:22-23), when Jesus appeared to his disciples after his death. He breathed upon them and said: 'Receive the Holy Spirit: whose sins you shall forgive they are forgiven them; and whose sins you shall retain, they are retained.' Confession is also an accepted sacrament in the Orthodox, Coptic and other Eastern churches. The Church of England and many other Anglican denominations also have confession, though many prefer general confession and absolution before the communion service to private confession.

In the Roman Catholic faith, before a child receives its First Holy Communion, he/she is required to make a first confession. Special classes are held to prepare children for their first confession, and for Holy Communion. Here they are taught about sin, penance, and the need to confess with true penitence. When the necessary instructions are completed, the child makes its first confession, receives a penance and absolution, after which it is believed the soul is ready to receive the Eucharist.

Holy Eucharist— First Holy Communion

The Holy Eucharist is a Christian sacrament commemorating the Last Supper, during which the apostles received the body and blood of Jesus Christ, which brings grace to the soul. The bread and wine are consecrated by an ordained priest and thereafter consumed by him and the congregation, in obedience to Jesus's command at the Last Supper: 'Do this in remembrance of me.' It symbolizes a Christian's union with Christ. The Eucharist lies at the core of Christianity, and ranks first among all seven sacraments. The celebration of the Eucharist is called the Mass by the Roman Catholic church, and by some Anglican churches as well. In most Protestant churches it is called the Eucharist or the Lord's Supper, while the Eastern churches call it the Eucharist or the Divine Liturgy.

During the sacrament of Communion, the priest holds up a consecrated host and speaks these words: 'Behold the Lamb of God, behold Him who takes away the sins of the world.' The priest and the congregation then say together three times—'Lord, I am not worthy that you should come under my roof. Speak the word and my soul shall be healed.' When the priest places the host on the person's tongue, or in the palm of his/her hand, he says: 'Body of Christ.' Before receiving the host the communicant says: 'Amen.'

The act of receiving the host for the first time is traditionally known in the Roman Catholic church as one's First Holy Communion. Adults baptized into the Catholic faith must receive their First Holy Communion as well. Children born into the church between the ages of seven and nine are prepared to receive this sacrament at catechism classes, and the day on which they receive their First Holy Communion is one of celebration and joy. Girls and boys wear white to signify their purity, and they may also carry a white candle. First Holy Communion is generally received at Mass, on a Sunday morning. The communicants—boys in their shining white suits and girls in white dresses of silk and taffeta, with flowered wreaths and veils of lace—walk sedately to the very first pews at the front of the church, and take their places. The service begins, and consists of two parts. The first is the 'service of the word', consisting of scripture readings, a sermon and prayers. The second consists of the offering of bread and wine, the central Eucharistic prayer (of consecration), and the distribution of the host and wine. At this time the first communicants go up and kneel before the altar to receive the sacrament. The rest of the congregation follows behind. After the distribution of Communion, the priest gives the final blessing, followed by the dismissal. After Mass, photographs are generally taken of the first communicants, and they return home with their families.

A celebration breakfast generally follows, to which friends and members of the family are invited. The communicant receives gifts of a religious nature, such as prayer books, rosaries, stories on the lives of saints, etc. It is a joyous occasion at which both adults and children mix happily together. Breakfast is served, and may consist of a mixed grill with fried eggs, sausages, mutton chops, bacon and fried calves liver, served with thick slices of tomato and fried potatoes. A fresh garden salad and rolls with butter are served alongside. An assortment of pastries, or one large golden sponge cake with lemon or chocolate icing, which the children enjoy, is usually served for dessert. Refreshments generally consist of tea, coffee and cool drinks.

Confirmation

Confirmation is a rite within the Christian church, whereby a baptized person receives the Holy Spirit, and is strengthened in grace to become a soldier of Christ. This rite is usually administered when the person has reached adolescence. In the Anglican church only bishops are allowed to administer the sacrament. In the Roman Catholic church, if confirmation is conferred during Mass, a bishop generally celebrates the service. He will confer confirmation while wearing the Mass vestments. In the Lutheran and Orthodox churches, the rite is generally performed by pastors and priests. The Orthodox church omits the laying on of hands.

In the Catholic church confirmation is effected by laying on of hands, and by anointing with consecrated oils. Before the ceremony, each person who is to be confirmed must have a sponsor or godparent, and also choose a name to be confirmed with. The ceremony begins with the bishop asking the Holy Spirit to come upon those who are to be confirmed. He then prays with hands extended, asking that those about to be confirmed may receive the seven gifts of the Holy Spirit. As each person who is to be confirmed comes forward, he or she is presented to the bishop by a sponsor, and is anointed with a chrism on the forehead. The bishop says: '(confirmation name), I sign you with the sign of the cross, and I confirm you with the chrism of salvation. In the name of the Father, and of the Son, and of the Holy Spirit.' The confirmed person answers, 'Amen.' The Bishop then administers a light tap on the cheek of the newly confirmed, saying: 'Peace be with you.' This concludes the ceremony.

Holy Orders

Holy Orders is the sacrament that confers on a priest the right to conduct services, and discharge other duties of the church. It establishes upon the person receiving the sacrament the rank of spiritual leader. In the Roman Catholic church, a priest is ordained during Mass; he receives this sacrament from a Bishop who recites: '. . . Bestow, then, we beseech Thee, Almighty Father, the dignity of the priesthood upon Thy servant; renew in him the spirit of holiness, that he may receive from Thee, O God, this office, and that his life may be an example to others, an incentive to virtue . . .' There is a laying on of hands by the bishop at a priest's ordination.

Women who seek to enter a convent and devote their entire lives in the service of the order in the name of Jesus Christ, must first be accepted into a noviciate. Here they spend a stipulated period of time living and working in accordance with the dictates of the order they have attached themselves to. There are teaching orders, nursing orders, and orders in which prayer and silence are required. After their time as novices has been successfully completed, they are then accepted into the order by way of a church ceremony.

The Betrothal

The betrothal or engagement is a custom that traces its origins to ancient biblical times, when it was accepted practice for parents to arrange a suitable marriage partner for their children. Formal betrothals were also enacted by the royalty, which often pledged sons and daughters in marriage to neighbouring kingdoms in the interest of establishing diplomatic alliances or increasing their fortunes. Although in

Anglo-Indian society men and women generally choose their own spouses, the old custom of getting engaged with a ring that signifies a promise to wed still exists.

Depending on one's inclination and circumstances, an engagement can be a private affair during which the man proposes to the woman he loves, asking her to be his wife. If she agrees, he slips a ring on the third finger of her left hand, and the agreement is sealed with a kiss. They are then considered formally betrothed. Alternatively, there can be an engagement party with no expense spared, where the local parish priest is invited to dispense the appropriate blessing on the couple in the presence of family and friends. This ceremony is generally followed by an elaborate dinner at which repeated toasts are raised to the prospective bride and groom. Here, a date is generally set for the wedding.

The Wedding

The sacrament of matrimony is a contract between a man and a woman, by which they consent to live together for the purpose of begetting children, and cherishing each other in mutual affection for all the days of their life. Christian marriages traditionally take place in church. Roman Catholic marriage ceremonies are often held during a Mass, after the gospel and homily. The bride and bridegroom with two witnesses stand before the altar, and the priest puts the following questions to the bridegroom: '. . ., do you take (bride) as your lawful wife, according to the rite of our Holy Mother the church?' He asks the same of the bride, and when they both answer, 'I do,' each says in turn: 'I (name), take you, for my lawful wedded wife (husband), to have and to hold from this day forward, for better or for worse, for richer, for poorer, in sickness and in health, until death do us part.' The priest then blesses and confirms the marriage bond, after which he sprinkles the pair with holy water. After the blessing of the rings, the priest asks God to remain with the newly married couple for the duration of their married life.

Within the Anglo-Indian community, a wedding is an event not to be taken lightly, and family and friends all get involved to make it a gala occasion. Since we were four sisters with countless relatives and friends, there was a time in our lives when it seemed all we did was plan weddings within the family, or give unsolicited advice to friends regarding their nuptials. In retrospect, it was actually the last fling of our youth before we settled down to domesticity and motherhood. At the time many of us were still unmarried, or newly married, with the 'gilt not yet off the gingerbread', so to speak. Unencumbered, we attended numerous engagement parties and weddings, dancing the night away. It was a magical place in time, and I am sure the practice continues to this day among the young and carefree.

Preliminary preparations for a wedding always involve that first awkward meeting between the bride and groom, and their respective parents. At this meeting the talk is all about money, who pays for what, and how much. The preliminary guest list is compiled, though names will be added and deleted innumerable times before the invitations are finally sent out. However, at this juncture it seems necessary to have at least an approximate number. Today there are scores of books dealing with almost every eventuality and detail involving wedding etiquette, but few give any advice on how to come away from this first meeting without ruffling feathers, especially those of a future mother-in-law!

Once the budget is established, notwithstanding the fact that most weddings end up grossly over-budget, the bride can turn her attention to other details. The next order of business is generally sewing the wedding gown, selecting the bridesmaid's dresses, and suitable outfits for the mothers of the bride and groom. Attending to these details is often the cause of much hysteria, and a great deal of anxiety on the part of the bride and the entire wedding party. After months spent poring over 'bridal' magazines, within whose glossy pages every type of elaborate gown is described down to the minutest detail, the fabric and pattern is purchased and taken to the tailor, who often proves to be both difficult and vague. Patterns are amended, and the bride is forced to deal with reality—the wedding party marches on to the next crisis. At this point it seems as though neither seamstresses nor caterers have any understanding or compassion. As for the father of the bride, he would do better to just relinquish his cheque book if he can afford to and remain discreetly in the background. He will, of course, be required on the wedding day to walk his daughter down the aisle, a considerably poorer man. The larger the wedding, the more hectic the preparations.

The bridegroom, vicariously caught up in all the hysteria, often wonders if indeed it would not have been cheaper and far less trouble all around if they had decided to elope. However, the bride must have her day, and as she walks down the aisle, a picture of serenity and radiance, all the turmoil of the past months fades into oblivion. Once the ceremony is over, she gracefully tosses her bouquet. Traditionally, the spinster who catches it will be the next to wed.

After the ceremony there is generally a photography session where pictures are taken of the newly married couple, both sets of in-laws, and members of the wedding party. The entire group including invited guests, then repair to the hall where the wedding reception is to be held. Here, the newly married pair accept the good wishes of friends and relatives who deposit their gifts on a table set aside for the purpose. Gifts of money are often deposited into a 'wishing well', which is discreetly emptied by a designated member of the family, who delivers the envelopes to the newly-weds. Toasts are raised and speeches made. The wedding cake is cut and the meal commences; wine and spirits are served.

After the meal the centre of the hall is cleared as the music starts up, with a disc jockey generally presiding. The bride and groom have the first dance, after which other couples take the floor and the evening's celebrations commence. Around midnight, the newly married couple leave to change into casual clothing in preparation for their departure. They may spend their wedding night at a hotel, or leave directly for their honeymoon location.

Anointing the Sick

The sacrament of anointing the sick is performed by a priest when a Christian is very ill, in many cases at death's door. The sick person is anointed with Oil of the Sick, and through prayer the priest asks God for health of body and soul. Before conferring this sacrament, the priest says three prayers asking God to bless the house in which the sick person lies, and all who reside in it. Those present around the sick bed say the Confiteor (I confess, or I believe). The priest extends his right hand over the sick person's head and requests the help of the heavenly court. He anoints the eyes, ears, nostrils, mouth and palms of the patient, saying: 'May the Lord forgive you by this holy anointing—and in his most loving mercy, whatever sins you have committed by the use of your sight, hearing, etc. Amen.' The feet are not anointed. Finally, the priest says prayers for the sick person's soul, and for his physical recovery, if this be God's will.

Death

Within the Anglo-Indian community, the Christian funeral rites and customs are observed. These are distinctive, as they are in every religion. Observing rites pertaining to death have important psychological and symbolic implications for the survivors. In fact, much of what transpires at a funeral is dictated by custom—for instance, mourners wear black, the church bells toll, and the deceased is laid to rest after a church service in which a priest delivers a eulogy.

The body is generally buried in a cemetery plot, and married couples often buy plots beside one another so that they may lie side by side in death as they did in life. Today, however, cremation has become very popular, and an ever-increasing number of people request it. It used to be that if a person died, the corpse was required to be interred by sundown of the same day; now, the deceased may be carried to a funeral home, embalmed, dressed in his best clothing and laid to rest in an open or closed casket. Here, grieving relatives and friends pay their last respects and condole with the immediate family. On the day of the funeral the body is carried in a hearse, accompanied by a procession of mourners that form a cortège to the church. During a Mass in the Roman Catholic tradition, or a funeral ceremony in the Anglican church, the deceased is commended to God, after which the cortège proceeds to the cemetery if there is to be a burial. In the event that cremation has been requested, the hearse bearing the casket continues on to the crematorium without the mourners.

After the funeral, in many instances the mourners accompany the family home, where food and drink is served at a wake, which is traditionally an Irish ritual.

If one would like to know more about how the dead are remembered in the Christian tradition, one has only to visit a cemetery. The older ones are far more interesting, and visiting them can be both an inspirational and sobering experience, bringing us face to face with our own mortality. There is after all nothing to fear from the dead; it is the living we should be wary of. Many old cemeteries lie in the heart of cities and cantonments spread across the length and breadth of India. In these melancholic surroundings, set amidst overgrown vegetation and high grass, one often stumbles upon crumbling monuments of marble and stone, relics of another age. Inscriptions, poems and laments, etched upon tablets of stone, serve as windows, giving us glimpses into the lives of those who lie buried beneath our feet. Here among the ruins, one finds the graves of soldiers who died bravely in the Mutiny; young women who lost their lives in childbirth; and children who succumbed at a tender age to one of a multitude of tropical diseases. Unfortunately, many of these old cemeteries are not well-maintained by a country struggling with weightier problems, and so they lie forgotten, crumbling into dust, much like their occupants.

Newer cemeteries sport no imposing busts or mausoleums, as a lack of space and monetary constraints have served to streamline both cemetery plots and gravestones. Of course, one does come across the occasional cross or headstone, but generally moderation prevails. Walking between the rows does not spark as much interest, for the gravestones lack the imagination and character of the old crumbling edifices. Nevertheless, they serve to remind us of the swift passage of time, that sooner or later brings each one of us face to face with death.

Birthday Celebrations

Mothers, brothers, sisters, friends, and members of one's extended family all celebrate a birthday during the course of the year. After Christmas and New Year, birthdays rank next in order of importance, and are always occasions for a celebration and get-together. Be it a child's first birthday, or Granny's eightieth, it's all the same: a birthday is never overlooked within the Anglo-Indian community. If there are sufficient funds in the coffer, a 'bundobust' is made, and everyone gets together for a 'bash'. In the event times are tough, a pot-luck dinner is easy enough to arrange, with friends and relatives arriving with food and drink.

Anglo-Indians are an intrinsically gregarious people who have carried the spirit of hospitality with them to every corner of the globe where they have settled. Magically they find their own, and immediately have a party! Today in Toronto, where I reside, there is a sizeable group of Anglo-Indians, in whom this spirit is alive and well. They journey undaunted by the cruel weather, plunging temperatures, screeching winds, and intimidating snow drifts, to congregate in each other's homes for a party—eating, drinking, and having a bit of fun, into the wee hours of the morning.

As a teenager, I well remember sixteenth and twenty-first birthday parties being milestones in our lives. Of course, every birthday was enthusiastically celebrated, with friends and classmates invited. There was plenty of cake, chips, sandwiches and lemonade, and we made little pigs of ourselves, often spoiling the prettiest dresses with spilled lemonade. As we grew older and entered our teens, birthday parties had to

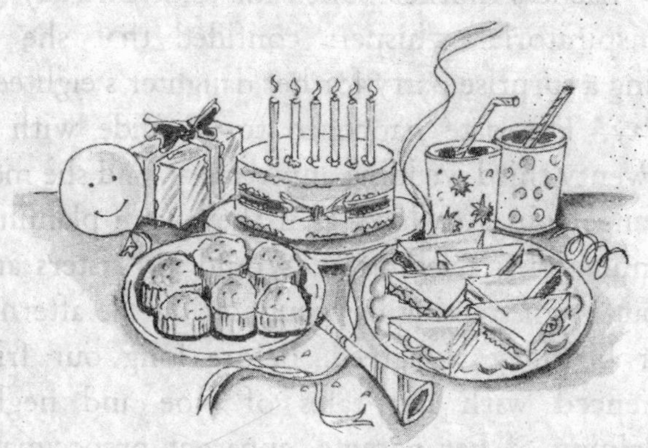

be staged a little differently, if indeed there was to be one. 'I don't want any kids running about at my party,' I once heard a friend cry irrationally, while her harried mother, who had just been through the crisis of choosing a birthday dress, looked incredulously at her. 'Why ever not? What's wrong with children? You were a child once, a very long time ago,' she replied tiredly as her daughter stomped out of the room. The situation was of course resolved by the time her birthday arrived, as the excitement, or a change in temperament, found her greeting each one of her guests, including children bearing gifts, with, 'I am glad you could come.'

Eighteenth and twenty-first birthday parties were often a 'surprise', which sometimes proved very tiresome for the person whose birthday it happened to be. The events that led up to a close friend's birthday party stands out in my memory because it perfectly illustrates the emotional see-saw experienced before a 'surprise' party.

My friend's mother pulled me aside one day, and in conspiratorial whispers confided that she was planning a surprise party for her daughter's eighteenth birthday. The date happened to coincide with her own twenty-third wedding anniversary, and she meant to arrange things to look as if they were planning a gala anniversary celebration. Would my sisters and I help out by distracting her daughter on the afternoon of her birthday? I agreed. Before long our friend commenced with her tales of woe and neglect, complaining of her parents' apparent preoccupation with their anniversary party. 'It's not even twenty-five years,' she pouted. 'I wonder why they are having such a big party.' We tried cheering her up to but no avail; she continued to sulk.

On her birthday she received no gift, and spent the entire day brooding in her bedroom, only emerging to join us that afternoon for a film. At seven o'clock we walked over to her house; there were plenty of cars parked all around. Stepping into the front veranda, we were greeted by a chorus of voices crying out, 'Happy Birthday!' Tears of surprise and guilt sprang to my friend's eyes. Her mother came forward and gently wiped them away. Her father wished her, and a little sister handed over the gift. Many hugs and good wishes were exchanged, and all was forgotten in that joyous moment. A radiogram started up in the sitting room, and everyone took their seats as the party commenced. Her many friends were present, along with family friends and relatives. Alcoholic drinks were poured, but we were only allowed 'soft' drinks and non-alcoholic party punch that, during the course of the evening, would be spiked by one of the daring young men present. Tiny meat patties, vegetable samosas, sandwiches of cheese, roast beef and chicken, were passed around along with alu bondas and chips.

Within the Anglo-Indian community, age discrimination is non-existent, and one can often find three generations from a single family at the same celebration. When a family is invited out, unless specified, every member living under one roof is included. The old ladies get together and huddle in corners nattering about this and that, while the old gentlemen pontificate, airing their views on politics, and recounting tales of shikar in the 'good old days'. Their sons and daughters sit around, and while discussing the cost of living with each other, worry about the future. The young are carefree; these are their salad years, when their only burden may be an uncompleted homework assignment. Children are very seldom sent to bed at any given time on nights like these, and run about freely until they finally drop with fatigue into their mothers' laps. An atmosphere of love and tolerance for old and young alike prevails.

Dinner is served at around 9.00 p.m., or later. Entrées may include platters of carved roast chicken and potatoes, pork indad, salted beef hump or tongue, a green masala pulao with chick peas, a foogath of okra, cabbage or green beans. A fresh garden salad, raita, pickles, chutneys and fresh rolls with butter enhance the meal. After dinner the cake is brought in and everyone sings 'Happy Birthday', a wish is made, and the candles are blown out, after which the cake is sliced and passed around for dessert. Everyone has a piece, and the children run around with butter icing smeared all over their faces.

Birthday gifts are opened amidst squeals of delight. Each gift is carefully examined and commented upon before being stored away. The girls re-emerge to join the young men sitting around on the veranda. Some smoke, furtively cupping the cigarettes with their hands. They eye the girls and flirt carelessly with the ones they fancy. Couples hold hands self-consciously in the shadows, quickly separating when they see an elder approach. The night air is filled with soft laughter and shy giggles. It is a wonderful enchanting time.

Suddenly, of course, it is all over as parents decide to leave, and we trail behind. It isn't until we are much older that we will be allowed to stay out later without being chaperoned.

Summer Holidays

An Ode to Grandpa

I often recall the days of yore and the tales that Grandpa told,
Of dashing Indian princes and their coffers filled with gold.
He wove stories around old crumbling walls, and dusty courtyards came to life.
My childish mind absorbed, enthralled, those ancient tales of loot and strife.
A veritable Pied Piper, he led me into the distant past—
Dacoits lurked within the mango grove, as the brilliant moon dark shadows cast.
Unafraid I followed him, through old decrepit burial grounds,
Clutching tight to his strong hand, careful not to make a sound.
But time does not stand still for man, and Grandpa passed away.
And I have wandered far afield since those distant bygone days.
I sometimes dream of going back in the hope that I may find,
That same enchantment lingering there, suspended by the hands of time.

Summer holidays are a part of Anglo-Indian tradition. For a people who love the carefree, easy life, the two-month summer break their children have from school proves to be an excellent opportunity to escape the stifling heat and daily grind in the city. Nearly every family has relatives or friends who live 'up country', where they are always welcome. Hospitality being reciprocal, at Christmas time it is quite common to be inundated with these same 'up country' folk, who all descend en masse to spend the Christmas holidays with their 'city' kith and kin. Everyone arrives with a bountiful supply of cakes, kul kuls, rosa cookies and biscuits, all prepared especially for the occasion.

In the past—and I am sure the same holds true of the present as well—for those who worked on the railways, purchasing a ticket was not a monetary drain; they simply hopped onto the train with their wives and children in tow, and travelled with their passes to their holiday destination. Opening their tiffin baskets, filled with potato cutlets, crumb chops, hard-boiled eggs, sliced bread and butter, or parathas, bananas and sweet limes, they made themselves

comfortable, creating a picnic atmosphere within the carriage. Their children ran all over the compartment while the parents snoozed comfortably throughout most of the journey, lulled by the motion of the train.

One never actually needs a great deal of money, nor a special invitation to have a holiday—'Come on up and stay with us' is an oft-repeated request, genuinely meant. Simply 'landing' up on an old friend's doorstep with a couple of 'chips' in your pocket is quite acceptable. You are given a 'cot' to sleep on, and an extra place is set for you at the table. In many cases, lifelong friendships have created these special bonds, but it is not uncommon to receive an invitation to 'stay' from a person one has just met, if you 'hit it off'. This is a facet of the Anglo-Indian personality, inherited from his traditionally hospitable Indian ancestors.

There are occasions when the family is unable to spend the entire two months together, because one parent or the other has to return to work. It is not unusual in these instances to leave the children in the care of family and friends who will look after them, and see them safely home by summer's end. This was often the case in our family; sometimes we spent our entire holiday in Burhanpur in the care of our grandparents. Grandpa allowed us every type of liberty, if the request was not too 'outrageous', as he put it. I recall dancing in the front compound with my sister Tina, drenched to the skin as the first warm rain of the monsoon came pelting down. We shouted to one another with cries of joy as we splashed and slid upon the oozing earth. Grandpa, sitting in his old camp chair on the veranda, joined with us in the exuberance of the moment, much to our grandmother's annoyance. Trifling incidents such as these have remained with me over the years, like nuggets of gold embedded in my brain; a panacea when the harsh realities of life refuse to relinquish their tenuous hold.

Today I see Burhanpur through rose-coloured lenses. The memories are sharp, and possibly tinged with illusion—it seems like a long, long time since I was a child.

The ancient city of Burhanpur, surrounded by fields, nestles in the foothills of the Satpura range. I once heard that Rudyard Kipling roamed these hills, and wandered in the forests beyond. I fancied he concocted his jungle stories there while stalking the tiger and the leopard, and listening to the endless chatter of the langur monkeys in the trees above.

Burhanpur remains embedded in my memory for I believe I was conceived there. My parents were married on the front veranda of the house, and spent their honeymoon in the jungle on the banks of the Jheerie, one of the many tributaries of the Tapti river. Burhanpur and my grandfather were synonymous. He filled the place with his presence and gave it meaning. After Grandpa died, I left the country and did not visit for many years, afraid to return to a place where I had known so many happy times—afraid of facing change. Then, suddenly on a whim, I decided to pay a visit to my grandmother, who now lived on the old farm alone, and take my youngest son Michael along with me. I had filled the boy's head with so many stories about the place: Grandpa, the hunting expeditions, picnics in the jungle, the food and the faithful retainers. Excited and anxious for him to see everything and experience the atmosphere that I had so loved, we arrived at the farm to find that not much had changed. It was all there, covered in the dust of ages—the city, the farm, and even some of the faithful retainers. But the ambience that I had known as a child eluded me. I felt the boy searching as well, in vain; all he saw was cattle, dust, and deforestation. I myself could only fleetingly recapture the atmosphere of those bygone days which, I soon began to realize, were associated with a presence, the presence of Grandpa. The farm itself was haunted by memories, but the spirit of the old man had flown.

Despondent, we did not linger long, catching the mail train out of the city the following Sunday. As it sped into the night, I looked out of the carriage window and recalled a chilling experience I once had with Grandpa, on a dark night such as this one.

We were hurrying towards the farm after an evening walk through the jungle, and I turned, looking in the direction of the railway tracks to see a train streaking through the night, with the brightly lit carriages dancing on the rails. 'Oh! Look at the lights,' I exclaimed, excited. Grandpa chuckled, and in a momentary flight of fancy, replied, 'Those are not lights, silly, but devils dancing in the dark upon the tracks.' Afraid, I shivered and clutched his hand ever more tightly as we hastened home. Back in boarding school after the summer holidays, I recounted this tale on numerous occasions to friends who were not quite sure of whether to believe me or not.

As the train gathered speed, leaving the city and its outskirts behind, I looked out at the landscape, now blanketed by nightfall. In the distance, the faint silhouette of a clump of trees came into view. I knew it to be the farm, and silently said goodbye, knowing I would never return. At the same time I resolved to describe this place one day in the written word, and thus keep its memory intact.

Ancient crenellated walls surrounded the city that was once the proud capital of the Deccan, and the holiday resort of the Mogul emperors. Vestiges of its past splendour still remained, and could be seen in the crumbling marble baths and trellis work, intricately carved with birds, fruit and flowers. The city had for the most part fallen into decay, but still teemed with a lively populace.

A few miles outside the immediate perimeter of the city lay the farm of my grandfather Jim Peters. An avenue of tall cork trees formed a stately entrance to his modest home. Spread around the circumference were mango groves, trees of guava, custard apple, papaya, tamarind and neem. They provided a cool refuge for man and beast from the scorching summer sun.

Grandpa's presence dominated the property. He tended his meagre crops and took care of the few chickens he had in the back. Keeping snakes and other predators out of the coops kept him busy, for he was eternally mending the henhouse with chicken wire and a pair of pliers. The chickens were not good layers, and I sometimes wondered whether they warranted all the attention they received. He also kept a few buffaloes. With a few trusty old retainers, both Granny and he managed to survive on the small pension he received from the Indian Telegraph Service.

In retrospect I marvel even more at the man. He was a dreamer, an armchair politician and a man of letters. To me he was always the beloved teller of tall tales. He never allowed the vagaries of life to upset him too much; he had chosen a lifestyle and was content with his choice. I relished his humour; forever youthful, I remember him posing for us in imitation of the famous actors of his day. He called himself 'Natty Jim', and, indeed, I cannot ever recall him leaving the house, even on the hottest summer day, without a coat and tie.

As far back as I can remember, our family always spent the summer holidays on the farm. I looked forward to these visits with great excitement, but to reach our destination, a long, tiring train journey had to be first endured. We arrived late in the evening, hot and covered with coal dust. It always took a good night's rest to release all my pent-up energy.

Day broke early in summer, and the intense dry heat caused one to awake in a bath of perspiration. The sun high in the eastern sky would within the day fulfil all of its fiery promise. Water that had been drawn from the well the night before lay in zinc tubs in the bathrooms. Chilled and tempting, it awaited our sweat-soaked limbs. I bathed before breakfast, splashing mugs of fresh, cold water over me, shivering. Morning baths in Burhanpur were a pure delight. Dressed in frocks of cool cotton or muslin, we sisters sat down with the family to enjoy a breakfast of omelette with parathas, and a glass of creamy buffalo milk.

After breakfast, Granny, armed with her umbrella and a few jute bags, would set out on the long walk to Burhanpur City. I always accompanied her, with a servant girl trailing behind. I would get very tired by noon, but as it was still early in the day, I tripped along beside her through the fields, over the railway tracks, and into the city.

Burhanpur City was dusty, a noisy conglomerate of human beings, cattle and crows. Its streets were narrow, winding and squalid. The central market place was housed within the crumbling walls of what was once the proud palace courtyard of the Mogul emperors. Here one could find grain and spice merchants cheek by jowl with vegetable sellers and tinsmiths. A constant din prevailed as they loudly advertized their wares. Pariah dogs, goats and scrawny country fowl foraged underfoot. This was where the local populace congregated each morning to haggle over prices and purchase whatever provisions their money could buy. Granny made a trip to the market once every month to ensure that she was being charged correct prices by the servants who were sent there once a week to purchase grain, fruit and vegetables for the farm.

Mission accomplished, our next stop was usually a visit to the veterinary hospital, a focal point of the area. It was here that all the farmers brought their sick and ailing cattle. The compound, shaded by an ancient banyan tree, was the scene of pure bedlam, with stamping cattle, tinkling cow bells and the restless braying of nervous donkeys. Several goats and buffaloes fed on bales of hay, stacked lopsidedly in a corner.

The hospital itself was housed in what appeared to be an anteroom of the palace alongside the bath or 'hamam'. The large, sunken bathing pool of a bygone era now served as an ample watering trough for cattle, and the smell of dust mingled with dung stung the nostrils. In the centre sat the farmers and field hands, their handloom dhotis tucked beneath them. Oblivious to the cacophony around them, they smoked their endless beedis and loudly debated among themselves on various issues of mutual concern—the arrival of the monsoon, crop failure, and the policies of the local and central governments. They raised their palms in namaste as we entered. Granny was well known to them as a shrewd and wily woman who was not to be trifled with.

As a child tagging along behind my grandmother, I hardly ever paid attention to them, but as I grew older I began to observe with greater interest their weather-beaten faces and gnarled limbs. I sensed their resignation. Sons of the soil, most of them had grown old trying to scratch a living from it. I knew them to be the backbone of India, tired, ageless and karmic. Believing their lot to be preordained, they accepted the struggle, the poverty, and their endless broods of children with equal resignation.

Dr Majid the vet had his office behind an intricately carved marble trellis at the far end of the anteroom. Granny visited him, recounting to him the various afflictions suffered by her cattle and chickens, for which medication was prescribed. The compounder deftly made up the packets of powders. The visit concluded, we crossed the road to pay a further visit to the family doctor who was also an old friend. He shared offices with a dentist, and adjoining their chambers was the showroom of the marriage band rental business. This was a most propitious arrangement, according to Grandpa, who would chuckle as he recounted how the cries of over-lusty dental patients were soon drowned by the band, which on cue would start up a resounding march advertizing their talents.

Our chores completed, tired and dusty, we made our way back to the farm. Granny still walking briskly ahead, while I tagged along behind with the weary servant girl laden with bags of provisions. Once more we passed the fields and followed the orderly lines of sooringhees or deep wells that lined the path that led to Grandpa's house. These sooringhees were another vestige of the past, a further tribute to Mogul architecture and civic planning. They had been dug deep where continuous natural springs supplied fresh water, even when the land around lay baked hard and dry in the scorching summer sun. Upon entering the house we were always greeted by a servant carrying two tall glasses of sweet lassi—a welcome refreshment after the trip.

Lunch was always a hot and heavy meal. A platter of cooked white rice was served along with a curry of beef or venison. Side dishes of dal and sautéed vegetable completed the meal. For dessert there was always fresh fruit—mangoes, bananas, custard apples, or Grandpa's luscious ripe papayas. Conversation at the table centred around the next shoot. Plans were made to go camping or on picnics beside one of the many streams that flowed through the jungle. I joined in eagerly, always keen to be out roaming the forests that I loved.

After lunch everyone dispersed into the bedrooms for an afternoon nap. A bed was always made up for me in the front veranda, and I retired there, taking with me the book I happened to be reading. The heat was oppressive outside, not a leaf stirred. It was breathlessly still. All around the house, over every window and along the front and rear verandas, the khus khus tats were lowered; they were bone dry even though a servant boy had tossed endless cool buckets of well water over them. They did, however, darken the house, making it cooler. One lay down to rest drenched in perspiration, often sinking into a heavy dreamless sleep until about four o'clock in the afternoon.

After bathing our faces in the chilled water lying in the zinc tubs, we sat down for tea, which was a small meal in itself. Milky, sweet tea was poured. A plate of banana fritters or onion bhajias was passed around. Granny always served her delicious guava jelly, the like of which I have never tasted since, and with it came a large bowl of heavy cream and a stack of freshly made parathas.

Dusk in Burhanpur was perhaps the best time of the day. The distant tinkle of cow bells and the steady stream of woodcutters filing past the farm on their way home all proclaimed the end of the day. Dust hung heavy in the air, and crows cawed as they restlessly flitted from branch to branch, seeking a perch for the night. One could smell the wood and dung fires as they were kindled for the preparation of the evening meal.

In the evening it was customary to take a stroll through the fields at the back of the house and make our way into the jungle. After walking awhile we sometimes stopped to cool our hot tired feet in one of the shallow streams that flowed through the forest. On those evenings we stayed at home, camp chairs were taken from the veranda and placed out in the front compound. Grandpa's cronies (mostly Bhils) drifted in. Lighting their beedis they would sit hunched in the lengthening shadows. The evening air was cooler, bringing with it the sweet scent of 'raat ki rani' (queen of the night). A faint breeze rustled the leaves while the men smoked silently.

'What news?' Grandpa always asked, starting up a conversation. 'Have you heard anything new out of the hills?' There followed the inevitable clearing of throats as they roughly spat in the dust around them. The men drew closer, often speaking of man-eating tigers which had mauled a grasscutter, or of leopards which had stolen cattle. They would inform Grandpa in conspiratorial tones of how the villagers were afraid and had sent word that he should come to their aid and shoot the animal in question. Grandpa demurred, pleading his age went against him. He was reassured time and again that he alone was the best shikari they had ever known. The conversation would shift as titbits of local gossip were recounted. Conversation died, and I could hear the cattle restlessly stamp their feet in the barn at the back. One of the old retainers would light the lanterns, bringing one out to the front veranda; it flickered and danced in the night air. Conversation resumed, the topic was politics. They argued back and forth with each other. Unlettered they were, but not uninformed. Listening gravely, they nodded as Grandpa aired his opinions at length while I gently dozed in my chair.

It was quiet; dogs barked in the distance and disturbed the silence. The men put out their beedis and slowly took their leave. Grandpa would get up and go into the dining room to light the Ditmar while I followed slowly. Dinner was served. A light meal that often consisted of a dish of green pigeon in a thick dark gravy, or chicken, with phulkas. Sometimes we had a dessert of jalebis or gulab jamuns, which were a great favourite of Grandpa's. He would put his share in a large soup plate and cover it with a generous serving of fresh cream. This he proceeded to eat slowly, relishing each mouthful.

The dogs whined as they were tied up in the back veranda for the night. Fireflies flitted into the room from the outside; they rested on the furniture and glowed in the night. We drank our glasses of milk while Granny sipped her cup of coffee and finished her slice of toasted bread and butter.

Dinner ended, we sat outside for a while longer on moonlit nights. Flying fox winged back and forth while jackals howled in the distance. 'To bed, to bed,' Grandpa would say finally, and I needed no urging. Up the steps I tumbled after him, falling asleep as soon as my head hit the pillow.

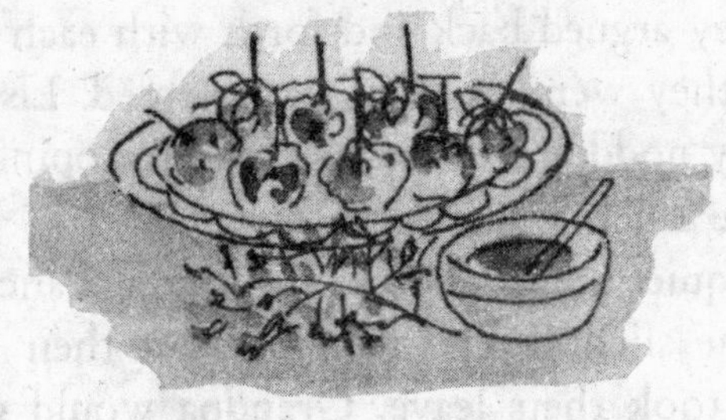

A Few Notes and Helpful Hints

Looks can be deceiving: it's eating that's believing.

—James Thurber, 1894-1961

The early European's arrival in India was most certainly his first real contact with the blend of spices known as 'masala'. Once he smelt and tasted the delicious difference their inclusion made to his otherwise bland meat and vegetables, there was no turning back. Masala, after it is fried in oil, or dry roasted to eliminate its initial raw taste, when added to meat, fish or fowl, enhances the flavour and pungency of food. At the same time it acts as a preservative, and leftovers can safely be eaten the following day. The Portuguese liberally incorporated spices into their food, which today gives us the unique cuisine of Goa. The British, I am sure, with temerity at first, sampled just a soupcon of the blend they called 'curry powder', before becoming addicted to it. Today, 'curry houses' abound in England, and going out for a 'curry' is considered trendy. The first

Anglo-Indians (English men and women in India), having grown attached to the addition of curry powder to their diet, no doubt began to miss this delightful blend of spices when they returned home to England. One can well imagine their dilemma, and the plaintive letters they may have sent to their friends back in India, complaining of the lack of this indispensable mixture, and the effect it was having on their husbands' digestion and temperament. No doubt parcels must have been quickly despatched by sea, containing the precious stuff that arrived months later, sufficiently mellowed by the long journey, rendering it ready for use.

Anglo-Indians, drawing from a mixed bag of Portuguese, British, French and Dutch food, incorporated the many herbs and spices that grew around them, to create a delightful cuisine which, while delivering a distinct sting to the palate, is definitely delicious going down. There are certain spices more commonly used in Anglo-Indian food than others, but for the most part they can generally be found on the shelves of any Indian kitchen.

All the spices required to prepare a delicious curry, pulao or vegetable are readily available, whole or ground. I advocate buying small quantities at a time because ground spices do not have a long shelf life. It is, however, mandatory always to have on hand fresh ginger, garlic, green chillies, green coriander and mint. For grinding the latter into a paste, the blender is indispensable.

Cooking mediums vary from the north of India to

the south. In North India, ghee or clarified butter is used extensively. Ghee is prepared by melting one cup of unsalted butter in a heavy saucepan over a very low flame. When the butter has melted, remove the pan from the heat and allow it to sit for about five minutes or until the milk solids settle at the bottom. Skim the surface of the pan and strain the liquid ghee into a sterilized mason jar through a double thickness of cheesecloth. Store in the bottom shelf of the refrigerator for use as required. One cup of butter will render three quarters of a cup of ghee.

In Central India peanut oil is used in the preparation of most curried dishes, and for frying. The use of ghee, however, is mandatory in the preparation of pulaos. Mustard oil is used for every day cooking in Bengal; its pungent aroma permeates the food, giving it a unique flavour all its own. Mustard oil is also used extensively in the preparation of pickles and for frying fish.

In South India, coconut oil is used as well as sesame (til) oil, not to be confused with Chinese sesame oil. Both oils are from the sesame seed, but in the case of Chinese sesame oil, the seeds are roasted prior to the oil being extracted, which produces a heavier, nutty tasting product. The til oil of South India is light, with a delicate flavour that blends perfectly with spices. In the event that til oil is not available, the same delicious results can be obtained by using the required amount of regular vegetable oil together with a tablespoon of Chinese sesame oil. In the preparation of sweetmeats, both in Central and South India a balance is achieved by using equal quantities of vegetable ghee and pure ghee for added richness. In North India, sweetmeats are prepared exclusively with ghee.

In every recipe that calls for the use of butter or ghee, margarine can be used, though the dish will not be as rich or flavourful. Anglo-Indians generally prefer using vegetable oil for cooking, while butter is used when baking cakes, or making sweet dishes.

Coconut milk is easily made by blending coconut powder in a little warm water to a smooth paste, and then thinning it to the required consistency. There is also available on the shelves of most supermarkets superb coconut milk in cans, which, when added to curries, pulaos and vegetable dishes, imparts an excellent flavour, rich in taste and texture. Of course, nothing can compare with the fresh meat of the coconut which, when ground and incorporated into a recipe, produces a distinctly superior tasting dish.

Here is how one goes about purchasing a fresh coconut: Shake the coconut gently against your ear to ensure that it contains water. If the outer shell is unbroken, this is a further sign of freshness. Do not store your coconut for too long a time even in the refrigerator. It is liable to spoil. Before breaking the coconut, pierce the eyes and drain the coconut water into a glass. The water can later be used to facilitate the grinding. Taste some of the coconut water to ensure that the meat is fresh. Bake the coconut in a preheated oven, 350° F, for about twenty minutes. Split it in half, using a sharp cleaver or a hammer, and remove the meat from the shell by prying it loose with a sharp knife. There is a further brown membrane that should be removed with a vegetable peeler. Dice the coconut meat and grind it in the blender to a paste with a little coconut water. This purée, added to curries, imparts an incomparable flavour. Coconut meat can be covered in plastic wrap and stored in the refrigerator, where it will keep for a couple of days.

Onions, the common red or yellow cooking variety, are essential to Anglo-Indian cookery. Onions are fried in oil or ghee before the spices are added in the preparation of curries, dals or vegetable dishes. Fried onions, topped with slivered almonds and raisins, grace the noble biryani. Onions, sliced fine and fried golden brown, make a delectable garnish for simple dishes of fried meat, vegetable or rice, giving mundane fare a festive look. Onions chopped with tomatoes, green coriander and green chillies, and mixed with beaten curds create a superb raita. Onions by themselves, raw, or roasted over hot coals, eaten with roti or rice and a little pickle on the side, often serve as the Indian farmer's midday meal, and will nourish him as fancier fare may not.

Curry leaf (bot: Murraya Koenigii), the shiny green leaf of a citrus tree native to India, imparts a unique flavour to a dish. Curry leaf trees can be found in most gardens in Central and South India, where use of the leaf is widespread. The stem and leaves are incorporated into curries, dal and vegetable dishes during cooking, with the stems being removed just before the food is served.

Green chillies were carried to India from Central and South America by the first Portuguese and Spanish traders, and soon became intrinsic to Indian cuisine. Green chillies can be hot; therefore, if the chilli is to be used simply to impart flavour, slit it down the centre and discard the seeds. Rinse with cold water, pat dry and use as desired.

Fresh ginger and garlic are essential to Indian and Anglo-Indian food. Fresh ginger/garlic, chopped and puréed, can be stored covered in the refrigerator for two weeks at a time. Once one has developed a taste for this delicious combination, and can truly appreciate the subtle difference its infusion makes to a multitude of dishes, this purée soon becomes an indispensable part of one's culinary needs. Powdered ginger and garlic is also available and can be used as a substitute, but as in many short cuts, the quality of the end result suffers.

Native to India, the tamarind has been known from ancient times for its cooling properties. The fruit of the tamarind is sometimes called the 'Indian date' because, when ripe, it is dark brown in colour. The brown pulp gives food a pleasant tang that cannot be duplicated with the addition of either vinegar or lemon juice. Tamarind pulp sans seeds is now available in jars, and has an almost indefinite shelf life. Tamarind pulp is one of the main ingredients used in the preparation of Worcestershire sauce.

Curd imparts a delicate, creamy/ acidic taste to curries and vegetable dishes, and is used extensively in North Indian cuisine. Since a large proportion of the population of India is vegetarian, curd forms an important part of their diet. Set at home from cow's or buffalo's milk, vegetarians eat curd along with vegetables, dal and rice, and chapatis. In Anglo-Indian homes, curd is used in raita, kormas, and incorporated into marinades for chicken and meat. During the hot summer months, curd is also enjoyed as a refreshing dessert, served with a dash of salt and a little sugar.

Fresh lemon juice is used to impart acidity to a dish. Vinegar plays a dual role, acting both as a preservative and for acidity in many dishes of Goan and Anglo-Indian origin.

Mint (podina) is a herb flavouring from antiquity, that is even today used to flavour mutton dishes and curd-based accompaniments. It is incorporated into cooling drinks served in the summer, and is also used to make a delicious chutney.

It is important not to forget the use of green coriander (cothmir) or 'bastard parsley', as the English in India snobbishly liked to call it. Chopped, fresh coriander adds a distinctive flavour to many meat and vegetable dishes. Lentils such as masoor dal are immeasurably improved in taste with the addition of this delicious herb. Scrambled eggs or 'rumble tumble', as our cook liked to call this dish, is made in a frying pan, with a little oil, two eggs, chopped green coriander, green chilli, onion, tomato, salt and pepper, all briskly stirred together and served up with lightly buttered toast. Served with cups of hot coffee or tea, this is a breakfast fit for a king! Titillating tastes, easily acquired, as the British in India soon discovered.

In conclusion, I would like to set down the common spices used in Anglo-Indian cusine to season curries, fries and vegetable dishes. As mentioned before, there is absolutely no difference between these spices and those found in any other Indian kitchen. Cumin (jeera), turmeric (haldi), mustard seed, powdered and whole (rye), coriander (dhania), red chilli (mirch), fenugreek seed (methi). Whole garam masala consisting of cinnamon (dal cheeni), cloves (lavang), cardamom (elaichi), pepper (kali mirch), bay leaves (tej patta) are used in pulaos, biryanis and some curries. Powdered garam masala in the proportions set down below should always be on hand, but, again, small quantities mixed together and stored in an airtight container ensure a full-bodied flavour when used. In the event some of the recipes found in this book prove to be too hot, one can always temper them by using fewer red chillies, or omit them altogether if preferred. Paprika or Kashmiri chilli powder, the rich red variety, can be substituted with equal success. It is not advisable, however, to tamper with the amounts of other spices specified without a sacrifice to taste.

Given below are a few combinations that allow one to create an impromptu curry or vindaloo with ease:

Garam Masala*

1 level tbsp freshly ground black pepper
1 level tsp powdered cardamom
1 level tbsp powdered cinnamon
2 level tsp powdered cloves
½ tsp powdered mace
½ tsp powdered nutmeg

Mix the spices together until well blended, and store in an airtight container.

Curry Paste

Makes sufficient paste for 2 delicious curries, each serving 4 persons

1 cup good (malt or wine) vinegar
2 heaped tbsp coriander seeds
2 level tsp cumin seeds
4 red chillies
1 whole pod fresh garlic, peeled

---

*Recipes in this book that call for the use of 'garam masala', refer to this combination of spices, unless otherwise stated.

A 3" piece fresh ginger, cleaned and chopped
1 heaped tbsp paprika powder
½ tsp turmeric powder
1 level tsp garam masala
½ cup vegetable oil
A few curry leaves (optional)
1 tsp whole mustard seeds (rye)
2 tsp sugar
1 tsp salt, or to taste

Grind the first five ingredients to a paste in the vinegar. Mix in paprika powder, turmeric powder, and garam masala, adding a little more vinegar to form a smooth paste. Place a stainless steel pot over a low flame and pour in oil. Add curry leaves and whole mustard seeds. When the seeds start to sputter, gently lower the curry paste into the pot and fry until the oil separates from the spices. Add in sugar and salt. Continue frying for a further few minutes, or until the spices lose their raw smell. Remove from heat and allow to cool before bottling the paste—use as required. The above ingredients can be doubled or trebled.

This curry paste can be safely stored on the lower shelf of the refrigerator for upto two months.

The method of preparing a curry from the paste is as follows:

Beef or Chicken Curry

Serves 4 persons

¼ cup vegetable oil
2 medium onions, sliced fine

½ the above amount of curry paste
¼ fresh ground coconut, or 2 tbsp coconut powder
3 tbsp curd
1 lb of lean beef or cubed mutton, or 1 medium-sized fryer (700-800 gm), jointed
1 large tomato, chopped fine
2 large potatoes, peeled, cubed and cooked in salt water
Salt to taste
Water

Pour vegetable oil into a heavy-based pot, and place over a moderate flame. Add sliced onions and fry until golden brown. Mix together curry paste and coconut, lower into the pot. Fry the spices, stirring continually until they release their fragrant aroma. Add beef or chicken, and continue frying until the meat is well coated with the spices. Add chopped tomatoes and curd. Test for sufficient salt. Pour in one cup of water, lower heat, cover the pot, and allow the curry to simmer on the top of the stove, stirring occasionally to ensure it does not adhere to the bottom. Add a little water at a time as required.

When the meat or chicken is cooked through and you have a dark, rich gravy clinging to the pieces of meat or chicken, remove from flame and add potatoes. Test once more for sufficient salt. Garnish with chopped green coriander leaves, and serve with white rice, cabbage foogath and papads.

Tandoori Mix

1 heaped tbsp rich red paprika powder
1 level tsp chilli powder

1 level tsp garam masala
½ level tsp powdered red food colouring
1 heaped tsp garlic powder
1 level tsp coriander powder

Mix all the ingredients together until well blended. Store in an airtight container.

Tandoori Chicken

Serves 6-8 persons

2 kg chicken parts—remove skin and excess fat
Tandoori mix as given above
½ cup curd
1 tsp salt, or to taste
1 tsp lemon juice
4 tbsp melted butter

Make a paste of the tandoori powder with the curd and salt. Slit chicken parts all over, using a sharp knife, and rub in the tandoori paste. Allow to marinade overnight in the refrigerator. Preheat oven to 350° F.

Arrange the marinated chicken pieces on a liberally buttered fireproof dish or pan. Sprinkle over lemon juice and remaining butter, and bake uncovered until cooked through, basting frequently with pan juices. Alternately, bake chicken until half done, remove from oven and complete the cooking procedure over an open flame or barbecue.

Serve tandoori chicken with naan/roti, and a cucumber salad.

Vindaloo Paste

To prepare 3 kg pork

1 cup wine or malt vinegar
2 large pods of fresh garlic, cleaned and chopped
2 3" pieces of fresh ginger, peeled and chopped
3 tbsp whole cumin
10 red chillies (remove stems)
2 tbsp paprika powder
½ cup mustard oil and ½ cup vegetable oil
About 10 curry leaves (stalk included)
1 tbsp whole mustard seeds
½ tsp fenugreek seeds
3 tsp sugar
1 tsp salt

Grind the first four ingredients in vinegar to a fine paste. Blend in paprika, using a little vinegar to facilitate the blending. Place a heavy-based saucepan over moderate heat and pour in both mustard and vegetable oil. Throw in curry leaves with stalk. When the oil is hot, place mustard seeds in the saucepan. They will begin to sputter. Lower heat, and add fenugreek seeds to the saucepan, followed by the spice mixture. Fry the spices over low heat for a few minutes, stirring continually to ensure they do not adhere to the bottom of the saucepan. When they begin to release their delicious aroma, and the oil begins to separate from the spices, add sugar and salt. Allow to cook for a further two minutes. Remove from fire, and let the vindaloo paste cool completely before removing the curry leaf stalk. Bottle and store in a cool dark place. To ensure the paste remains fresh, one can also place the bottle on the bottom shelf at the rear of the refrigerator.

Dhania/Jeera Powder

The following is primarily a garnish that adds piquancy to various dishes:

1 level tbsp coriander powder
1 level tbsp cumin powder

Over a low flame roast the two ingredients, combined, in a heavy metal pan, stirring continually. When the mixture is a rich brown colour and gives off a fragrant aroma, remove from fire and use immediately.

Ginger/Garlic Paste

2 whole pods fresh garlic, cleaned and sliced
5" piece of fresh ginger, peeled and sliced

Grind the ginger and garlic to a paste in the blender, using a little cold water to facilitate the blending. Place in a clean glass jar with a tight-fitting lid, and store in the refrigerator. Ginger/garlic paste has a refrigerator life of about two weeks.

Note: When ginger/garlic paste is called for in a recipe, I have counted the above combination as a single ingredient.

Dried, powdered (red) capsicum imparts colour to a dish without making it too pungent. Paprika is now available in India. As an alternative, I have mentioned that Kashmiri chillies may be used.

A Note on Weights and Measures

Correct weights and measures are crucial to the success of a recipe. Therefore, every aspiring cook should have in the kitchen two measuring cups, one for dry ingredients and the other for liquid measure. These are indispensable when baking. For creating confections it is also necessary to have on hand a sugar thermometer, as it eliminates guesswork when making fudge and toffee. Further, a set of measuring spoons ranging from a quarter teaspoon to one tablespoon is a necessity. Given below are equivalents used in this book, that I have found to be indispensable in my culinary endeavours:

Liquid Measure

An American pint is equivalent to 16 fl. ounces. A British pint is equivalent to 20 fl. ounces.

1 fluid oz	=	30 ml		
2 fluid oz	=	60 ml	=	¼ cup
2¾ fluid oz	=	80 ml	=	1/3 cup
5½ fluid oz	=	170 ml	=	2/3 cup

6 fluid oz	= 185 ml	=	¾ cup	
8 fluid oz	= 250 ml	=	1 cup	(½ US pint)

Dry Measure

Standard metric measuring spoons are used in America, Great Britain and Australia; they range from 5 ml to 15 ml. However, an Australian standard tablespoon holds 20 ml, which equals 4 teaspoons.

1 teaspoon	=	5ml—Australia, Great Britain and America
1 tablespoon	=	15 ml—Great Britain and America
1 tablespoon	=	20 ml—Australia

A standard cup, depending on the ingredients, can weigh from two to eight ounces. Listed below are some of the common ingredients measured by cups in this book:

1 cup all purpose flour	=	4 oz	=	125 gm
1 cup wholewheat flour	=	4½ oz	=	140 gm
1 cup butter or margarine	=	8 oz	=	250 gm (2 US sticks)
1 cup grated cheese	=	4 oz	=	125 gm
1 cup dry breadcrumbs	=	4 oz	=	125 gm
1 cup desiccated coconut	=	3 oz	=	90 gm
1 cup cornflakes	=	1 oz	=	25 gm
1 cup mixed dry fruit	=	5-6 oz	=	155-185 gm
1 cup caster sugar	=	8 oz	=	250 gm
1 cup granulated sugar	=	8 oz	=	250 gm
1 cup packed brown sugar	=	6 oz	=	185 gm
1 cup icing sugar (confectioner's)	=	5 oz	=	155 gm

1 cup raw rice	=	7 oz	=	220 gm
1 cup cooked rice	=	4 oz	=	125 gm

Candy Thermometer—° F

230 to 234	—	thread stage
234 to 240	—	soft ball stage
244 to 248	—	firm ball stage
250 to 266	—	hard ball stage
270 to 290	—	soft crack stage
300 to 310	—	hard crack stage

Oven Temperatures

Degrees	Centigrade	Farenheit
Very slow	120	250
Slow	150	300
Moderate	180	350
Hot	200	400
Very Hot	230	450

Mass Weight Conversion

1 ounce	=	28 gm
8 ounces	=	227 gm
16 ounces	=	454 gm
2 pounds	=	907 gm
3 pounds	=	1.4 kg
4 pounds	=	1.81 kg
5 pounds	=	2.27 kg
100 pounds	=	45.4 kg
1 ton (2000 lb)	=	907 kg
1 kilogram	=	1000 gm

Soups

Soups

Then jungles, fakeers, dancing girls, prickly heat,
Shawls, idols, durbars, brandy-pawny;
Rupees, clever jugglers, dust-storms, slipper'd feet,
Rainy season, and mulligatawny.

(From *Curry and Rice on Forty Plates*,
by George Franklin Atkinson, 1859)

Soup is not a prerequisite at dinner in many Anglo-Indian homes, especially during the summer months when the heat diminishes one's appetite for anything more robust than fresh juice, a glass of lassi, or a shandy on weekend afternoons. Most Indian recipe books make just a cursory mention of soups, listing them together with recipes for rasam, pepper water and the like, or in a chapter dealing with tonics and 'pick-me-ups' to nourish the ailing. Soup is actually a European idea, and enjoying a bowl prior to the dinner entrée is understandable in winter climates when one needs to 'keep the chill of', so to speak. The ritual of serving soup before dinner was a habit we inherited from the British, and over time, with the addition of spices, several distinctive Indian soups evolved, that today enjoy universal appeal.

When entertaining friends at home during the winter months, it is a delicious idea to include a hearty mulligatawny or oxtail soup on the menu. Of course, most restaurants offer a variety of different soups on their bill of fare. I was first introduced to soup as a child, at the Officer's Mess in Poona. It was after the War, and my father who had just been posted to that city, had not as yet been allocated any accommodation, and so we took our meals in the Mess. A soup was always served before dinner, generally of tomato, or of mushroom, or a delicious broth with bits of macaroni swimming in it, that my mother called 'bone soup'. I remember searching in vain for the 'bones'.

The basis of good soup is always rich, hearty bouillon, derived from simmering meat, fish or fowl, together with vegetables, in a pot of water, to extract the essence and flavour of the substance. The ensuing broth or bouillon, when clarified, is known as consommé, and consommé is nearly always the foundation of clear light soups. Of course, other herbs and vegetables are infused subsequently, to give distinctive flavours. French tarragon soup, clear tomato soup and onion soup all call for a base of consommé.

Soups made from a base of bouillon, vegetables and herbs, thickened with a roux of butter and flour, may also have a cup of cream stirred into them for added richness. Such soups are often quite filling, and one need only include a loaf of crusty bread and a fresh garden salad to make a really satisfying meal.

No chapter on soup would be complete without mentioning the rich creamy soups made from the broth of fish and shellfish known as bisques. Bisques can be hearty or light, depending on the various ingredients incorporated into the fish broth. The texture of the soup, however, is not as important as the base stock from which it is made. Therefore, it is imperative to start with good stock, and since stock freezes well it can be prepared beforehand. Below I have listed four recipes for basic vegetable, fish, meat and chicken stock, which are indispensable if one is a lover of soup and delights in preparing different varieties on a daily basis. Also are included several soups enjoyed in Anglo-Indian homes, primarily during the winter months.

Fish Stock

Makes 8-9 cups stock

1 kg white fish (meat, bones and trimmings included)
2 large onions, peeled and roughly chopped
A medium bunch of fresh parsley, washed
The juice of 2 limes, or 1 lemon
1 tsp salt, or to taste
½ tsp freshly ground pepper
10 cups water

Place all the ingredients in a stock pot over low heat and bring to a boil. Simmer for half an hour. Remove from flame and allow the stock to cool. Strain through a fine sieve. Makes approximately nine cups of fish stock. Freeze and use as required.

Vegetable Stock

Makes 9 cups stock

3 onions, peeled and roughly chopped
2 tbsp cooking oil
3 onion leeks, washed and chopped
2 carrots, scraped and diced
2 stalks celery, washed and roughly chopped
½ lb fresh mushrooms, washed
2 medium potatoes, wash and cut into quarters
8 flakes of peeled garlic
8 whole peppercorns
1 bay leaf
A medium bunch parsley, washed
¼ cup of masoor dal
10 cups water
1 tsp salt

Place oil and chopped onion in a stock pot on moderate heat and fry until onion is translucent. Add remaining ingredients and allow the stock to simmer on low heat for about two hours, replenishing with hot water as required. There should be about nine cups of liquid in the pot. Allow to cool before straining. Stock freezes well for about three months.

Chicken Stock

Makes 6-8 cups stock

2 kg stewing fowl (include neck and giblets but not liver)
10 cups water
1 large onion, roughly chopped
3 whole cloves
2 whole carrots, scraped and diced
1 stalk of celery, washed and roughly chopped
2 whole onion leeks, washed and chopped
4 flakes of fresh garlic, peeled
2 bay leaves
5 sprigs parsley
1 tsp freshly ground black pepper
½ tsp dried thyme
1 tsp salt, or to taste

Pour ten cups of cold water in a stock pot and place on moderate heat. Add fowl, neck and giblets. Allow the water to come to a boil, skim off the froth. Add remaining eleven ingredients to the pot and simmer for two hours, replenishing water as required. When the chicken is tender and cooked through, transfer the pot to a trivet and allow to cool. Remove chicken, cut away meat and skin from the carcass. Return the carcass to the pot together with chicken skin. Set meat aside for another use. Add two more cups of boiling water to the stock and simmer for a further two hours. Strain stock through a sieve, pressing on the solids in order to extract all the flavourful essence of chicken. Chill stock overnight; the next morning skim off fat that rises to the surface. Freeze and use as required. Chicken stock freezes well for a period of three months.

Beef Stock

Makes 6-8 cups stock

2 kg beef bones or meaty shank bones, cut into 2" pieces
2 tbsp butter
2 onions, roughly chopped
2 carrots, scraped and diced
1 stalk celery, washed and roughly chopped
10 cups hot water
6 sprigs parsley
2 bay leaves
4 garlic flakes, peeled
½ tsp freshly ground black pepper
1 tsp salt, or to taste

Place stock pot over medium heat and add butter. When the butter melts add beef bones, onions, carrots and celery to the pot and brown nicely. Pour in ten cups hot water and remaining five ingredients. Bring the stock to a boil, skimming away froth that rises to the top. Add a further two cups of water if required and allow the stock to simmer for five to six hours continually, replenishing water as required. There should be about eight cups of liquid in the pot at all times. Strain stock into a bowl, pressing on the solids to remove all the essence. Allow stock to chill overnight. The next day remove fat that has risen to the surface.. Freeze and use as required. Beef stock freezes well for a period of upto three months.

Clear Tomato Soup

Serves 6-8 persons

4 cups tomato juice
3 cups beef stock
2 cups hot water
2 whole cloves
1 small onion, diced fine
1 bay leaf
4 whole peppercorns
1 stick celery, washed and roughly chopped
¼ tsp ground basil
1 tsp sugar

Place all the ingredients in a pot and bring to a boil. Allow to simmer for about half an hour. Remove from heat. Strain, add salt to taste and serve garnished with croutons.

Onion Soup

Serves 6-8 persons

2 tbsp butter
2 large onions, thinly sliced
7 cups beef stock
4 egg yolks, beaten
Grated parmesan cheese
Chopped parsley
Salt to taste
½ tsp freshly ground black pepper

Place butter in a pot over moderate flame, add onions and sauté until nicely browned. Lower heat, add beef stock. Simmer for half an hour, or until onions are tender. Mix together egg yolks, cheese and chopped parsley. Stir into hot onion soup, add pepper and salt to taste. Remove from heat, ladle into bowls and serve immediately with thick slices of crusty bread.

Oyster Soup

Serves 6-8 persons

3 cups beef-based stock
3 cups fish stock
1 oz butter
1 tbsp flour
A dozen cleaned oysters
225 ml full cream milk
¼ cup cream
1 egg yolk, beaten
½ tsp grated nutmeg
Salt to taste

Place beef and fish stock in a pot on moderate heat. Make a roux of butter and flour, place in the pot. Lower heat, add oysters and oyster liquor to the pot. Pour in milk. When the soup is hot, pour in cream. Beat in egg yolk and grated nutmeg. Remove from heat immediately. Test for sufficient salt. Ladle into bowls and serve.

Cream of Cauliflower Soup

Serves 8-10 persons

1 kg beef soup bones
10 cups water
1 medium onion, roughly chopped
1 stalk celery, washed and roughly chopped
1 small cauliflower, cut into flowerets
1 tbsp flour
1 tbsp butter
½ tsp freshly ground pepper
2 cups full cream milk
1 cup whipping cream

Place washed bones in a stock pot together with the next four ingredients. Simmer over low heat for two hours. The vegetables should be very soft. Strain and set aside the broth. Discard soup bones. In a blender purée vegetables. Make a roux of flour and butter. Place the broth over low heat and stir in roux. Add vegetable purée to the stock and thicken to desired consistency. Blend in pepper and salt to taste. Pour in milk and whipping cream. Remove from fire. Ladle into soup bowls and serve immediately, garnished with croutons.

Cold Cucumber Soup

Serves 6-8 persons

6 cups chicken stock
4 tbsp fresh dill, finely chopped
1 large onion, minced
4 garlic flakes, peeled and chopped fine
3 tbsp cooking oil
4 cucumbers, peeled, seeded and diced
½ tsp freshly ground pepper
Juice of 1 lime
Salt to taste
1 cup whipping cream
Fresh dill to garnish

Place dill, onion and garlic in a stock pot together with the cooking oil, and fry until the onion is translucent. Pour in stock, lime juice, cucumber and freshly ground pepper. Allow the soup to simmer, covered for about one hour, or until the cucumber is soft and cooked through. Strain soup through a sieve, pressing down on the vegetable mixture to ensure you have all the liquid. Add salt to taste. Chill the cucumber soup. When ready to serve, stir in whipping cream. Ladle into bowls, garnish with dill and serve.

Dal Soup

Serves 4-6 persons

6 oz washed masoor dal
2 whole carrots, scrubbed and diced
3 cups beef stock
3 cups hot water
1 large tomato, diced
5 flakes garlic, peeled and chopped
1 medium onion, roughly chopped
1 tsp salt
½ tsp freshly ground pepper
1 medium onion, minced
2 tbsp butter or ghee

In a stock pot or pressure cooker place the first eight ingredients. Cook until the dal and vegetables are tender. Strain stock through a sieve and set aside. Purée dal and vegetables in blender and return to the stock pot. Add pepper and salt to taste. In a saucepan place minced onion and butter or ghee. Fry until golden and add to the soup. Simmer soup for a further ten minutes, stirring frequently. Ladle into bowls, garnish with chopped fresh coriander, and serve.

Cream of Celery Soup

Serves 4-6 persons

10 cups chicken stock
2 tbsp butter
3 cups celery, washed and roughly chopped
1 large onion, chopped fine
2 large potatoes, peeled and diced
2 flakes garlic, peeled and chopped
Salt to taste
½ tsp freshly ground pepper
1 cup whipping cream

Place butter in a stock pot and fry onion and chopped celery until onion is soft. Stir in potatoes and garlic. Pour in stock. Cover the pot and simmer until the vegetables are tender, replenishing water as required. Remove from heat and allow to cool. Strain through a sieve. Set aside the stock. Purée the vegetable mixture in a blender. Place puréed vegetables in together with stock. Allow soup to simmer on top of the stove until heated through. Add pepper and salt to taste. Stir in cream, and immediately remove from heat. Ladle into bowls and serve hot.

Beef Macaroni Soup

Serves 4-8 persons

1 tbsp butter
1 medium onion, minced

8 cups beef stock
2 cups hot water
100 gm elbow macaroni
½ tsp freshly ground pepper
1 tsp butter
1 tsp flour
Salt to taste

Place minced onion in stock pot and fry until translucent. Pour in eight cups beef stock and two cups hot water. Add macaroni and pepper to the pot. Simmer over low heat until the macaroni is tender. Make a roux with the butter and flour, lower into the pot of simmering liquid. Stir continually until the soup thickens. Test for sufficient salt and remove from heat. Serve beef and macaroni soup with crusty bread or croutons.

Oxtail Soup

Serves 6-8 persons

2 small oxtails, washed and jointed
4 cups hot water
½ tsp freshly ground pepper
½ tsp garam masala
1 tbsp soya sauce
1 tsp salt
6 cups hot water
2 carrots, scraped and diced
1 medium onion, minced
3 onion leeks, washed and chopped
1 large turnip, washed and diced
2 stalks celery, washed and diced

100 gm lean ham, diced
4 flakes garlic, peeled and chopped fine
2 tbsp butter
2 tbsp flour
Salt to taste

Pressure cook oxtail with next five ingredients. Cook until very tender. Strain and reserve oxtail. Place broth in stock pot together with further six cups hot water and next seven ingredients. Simmer over low heat for about two hours, or until the vegetables are tender, replenishing water as required. Make a roux with butter and flour. Add to the pot, and stir until the soup thickens sufficiently. At this point one can either place the cooked joints of oxtail in the pot, or remove the flesh from the joints, discarding the bone. Simmer gently for a further ten minutes. Add salt to taste. Remove from heat and ladle into bowls. Serve immediately.

Oxtail soup is rich and hearty. When served with crusty bread and a salad on the side, it is a satisfying meal.

Mutton Mulligatawny

Serves 6-8 persons

1 kg mutton cut into serving portions (½ kg breast portion, and ½ kg leg or shoulder is ideal)
2 medium onions, chopped fine
1 spray of curry leaves (including stalk)
1/3 cup cooking oil
2 tbsp fresh ginger/garlic paste
1 level tbsp paprika powder

½ tsp chilli powder, or to taste
1 level tbsp cumin powder
1 level tbsp coriander powder
½ tsp freshly ground black pepper
½ tsp turmeric powder
1 cup thick coconut milk
4 cups water
2 medium tomatoes, chopped fine
Juice of 1 lime
2 tsp salt, or to taste
2 level tbsp gram dal, roasted and ground to a paste in water
2 limes, sliced into wedges

Place chopped onion and curry leaves including stalk in a pressure cooker together with cooking oil. Fry over moderate heat until the onions are golden. Make a paste of the next seven ingredients and add to the pot, lower heat and fry until the oil begins to separate from the spices. Stir in mutton and continue frying until the pieces of meat are well coated with the spices. Pour in coconut milk and four cups water. Place chopped tomato in the cooker along with lime juice and salt to taste. Pressure cook the mutton until the meat is tender. Remove from heat and strain the mulligatawny through a sieve, separating the meat from the stock. Add enough cups of water to the stock as portions of soup required, and transfer to a heavy-based saucepan. Discard curry leaves, remove choice morsels of mutton and mutton bone with meat clinging to it. Add to the stock pot. Stir in the gram dal paste. Allow the mulligatawny soup to simmer on the top of the stove until you have a full-bodied soup. A little more water may be added to the soup if required.

To serve mulligatawny soup: Place a cup of cooked white rice in a soup bowl and liberally ladle mulligatawny over it, together with pieces of mutton. The rice should be swimming in the soup. Garnish with a wedge of lime.

On chilly winter nights, mulligatawny makes just the right entrée when accompanied by a side dish of vegetables and papads.

Marrow Bone Soup

Serves 6-8 persons

1¼ kg beef bones with marrow cut into 1" pieces
10 cups hot water
2 medium onions, roughly chopped
2 carrots, scraped and diced
1 large tomato, chopped
6 french beans, top and tail
½ small cauliflower, divided into flowerets
5 garlic flakes, peeled
1 tsp salt, or to taste
Hot water
½ tsp freshly ground black pepper
1 tbsp butter
1 tbsp flour

Wash beef bones and place in stock pot together with the next eight ingredients. Simmer for three hours, skimming the surface occasionally to remove froth. When the marrow and vegetables are cooked, remove from heat. Take the marrow bones out of the pot and set aside to cool. Strain vegetables through a sieve, pressing down to ensure all the stock drains away. There should be as much residual stock as required, but if not, add hot water. Pour stock into a heavy-based saucepan. Place cooked vegetables in blender and grind to a paste. Add paste to saucepan with stock. Simmer soup over low flame. Add pepper to the pot. Make a roux of flour and butter, lower into saucepan and stir constantly until the soup thickens. Test for sufficient salt. Gently remove marrow from bones, and add to the soup. Ladle into bowls and serve hot.

Marrow bone soup is rich and hearty, and makes a most satisfying meal with crusty bread and a fresh garden salad on the side.

Note: This soup is just as excellent when made with mutton bones.

Chicken and Corn Soup

Serves 6-8 persons

2 large chicken breasts
200 gm lean ham
6 cups chicken stock
2 cups hot water
2 cans creamed corn (450 gm each)
Salt to taste
2 tbsp cornflour
Cold water
½ cup dry sherry
1 tbsp Chinese sesame seed oil
1 medium bunch green onions, washed and chopped fine

Skin and bone chicken breasts, chop flesh into fine slices and place in stock pot. Dice ham finely and add to the pot. Pour in the next three ingredients. Simmer chicken/ham/

corn mixture in stock and water over a low flame for about three hours or until the chicken is very soft. Replenish water as required. Add salt to taste. Make a paste of cornflour with a little water, stir into the pot. When the soup thickens sufficiently, add sherry. Stir in one tablespoon sesame oil. Remove from heat. Ladle soup into bowls, and serve garnished with finely chopped green onions strewn over top.

Side Dishes

Side Dishes

The dinner entrée or side dish, as it is more commonly called, generally comprises a meat, fish or fowl savoury. The British introduced side dishes to India, and the Anglo- Indians readily adopted them. With the skilful addition of herbs and spices, they subtly transformed the otherwise bland meat and potatoes into piquant delicacies. Side dishes are generally cooked dry, or with a thick, dark gravy clinging to the succulent morsels of meat. A vegetable dish, salad, bread and butter often serve as accompaniments. To further relish the meal, on the dinner table one is likely to find a cruet stand with vinegar and Worcestershire sauce, together with other condiments like pickles and chutneys, or a pot of pungent English mustard in the event roast is on the menu.

Fillets of meat and fowl are favoured over the tougher cuts when preparing side dishes, mainly because they cook faster, and render a more succulent dish. Of course, one must possess some knowledge of the different cuts when purchasing them, and to this end I have listed below which part of the animal or bird comprises the fillet:

The fillet of mutton is the tender strip of meat which runs down the inside of the saddle under the kidney.

The fillet of beef is the undercut or sirloin.

The fillet of fowl and other game birds is formed by cutting out the whole breast right down to the wing joint. This may be divided into portions.

The hare and rabbit fillet is the long strip of meat running down either side of the backbone.

A fillet of beef, sliced and allowed to marinade overnight in a simple dressing of garlic, olive oil, pepper, with a dash of Worcestershire sauce, into which a roughly chopped onion is mixed, when baked the following day, produces an unbelievably tender roast. Pork fillets marinated in soya sauce with a few slices of fresh ginger, and briefly baked in a moderate oven with a little water and sesame oil, renders a succulent and tender roast.

Every family has their special side dish, but I have always felt beef and potato cutlets (chops) are universal favourites, enjoyed by all, and continue to please no matter how many times a month they are served. Arranged on a platter, beef cutlets surrounded by fried potatoes and served with tomato sauce, a fresh garden salad, bread and butter, create a satisfying meal. In the days before refrigeration, side dishes left over from dinner were often stored overnight in a well-ventilated meat safe. The next morning they appeared once more at the breakfast table. Thinly sliced portions of cold roast beef or cutlets accompanied fried or buttered eggs. At lunch, the remains of the roast were quickly converted to a delicious hash and served together with a simple repast of dal, rice and vegetables.

The meat safe that we today view as a relic of another age was indispensable in the time before refrigeration, or even ice boxes; it had pride of place in every household. In fact, every Anglo-Indian home sported a meat safe in which perishable foodstuff was stored. Covered on four sides with wire gauze for optimum ventilation, the meat safe stood high off the floor with its four legs set in cans of water to prevent ants and roaches from crawling into the food.

Our meat safe at home stood in a corner of the rear veranda. My mother had perfected the art of dishing out just enough provisions to prepare the afternoon and evening meal, and hence there was very little waste. Any food left over from lunch was generally stored in the meat safe and reheated at dinner, where it was served alongside the entrée. Leftovers from dinner were always taken away, except for side dishes seasoned with vinegar, roasts, cutlets and the like. In the hot weather when temperatures soared to 110° F in the shade, the meat safe was often empty with the exception of perhaps a bottle of jam, a can of cheese, or a solitary pat of fresh churned butter standing in a bowl of cold water. Meal planning was carefully executed, without sacrifice to taste, however.

The following recipes are a sampling of the savoury delights served at Anglo-Indian dinner tables.

Chicken Country Captain

Serves 4-6 persons

1 kg frying chicken, skinned and jointed
5 large onions, sliced fine
1/3 cup ghee
3 green chillies, slit
1 tbsp fresh ginger, peeled and minced
1 tsp freshly ground black pepper
1 tsp salt, or to taste
1 cup hot water
2 large potatoes, cut lengthways and cooked in salt water
1 tbsp ghee

In a heavy-based pan over moderate heat put ghee. When hot, add onions and fry until crisp and golden brown. Remove from pan and set aside. Lower heat and place green chillies and ginger in the pan; fry until fragrant. Add chicken and continue frying. Sprinkle over pepper, and salt to taste. Place one cup hot water in the pan, cover and allow the chicken to cook over low heat until tender. This is a dry dish, and there should be little or no gravy in the pan. Remove from heat.

Place skillet over moderate heat and fry potatoes crisp and golden. Place Country Captain on serving dish, arrange potatoes around and garnish with fried onions.

Country Captain is excellent when accompanied by a side dish of cabbage or cauliflower foogath. Chapatis, or a loaf of fresh bread complete the meal.

Chicken Stew

Serves 6-8 persons

1 kg frying chicken, skinned and jointed
¼ cup cooking oil
2 medium onions, sliced
4 slices bacon, finely chopped
2 tbsp fresh ginger/garlic paste
1 tsp garam masala
½ tsp ground black pepper
3 green chillies, slit
1 small bunch green coriander leaves
2 tbsp Worcestershire sauce
2 tbsp soya sauce
1½ tsp salt, or to taste
2 cups hot water
3 whole carrots, scraped and diced
½ cauliflower, washed and broken into flowerets
2 medium potatoes, cubed
½ cup fresh peas
1 large tomato, chopped fine
1 can (284 ml or 10 oz) cream of mushroom soup
1 tbsp cornstarch

Place a large heavy-based pot with lid over moderate heat and pour in oil. When oil is hot, add sliced onions and bacon to the pan. Fry the onion golden. Lower heat and add next five ingredients. Fry spices until they are fragrant. Mix in sauces and salt, pour in two cups hot water and stir. Add next five ingredients to the pot. Cover the pot and allow the stew to simmer until the meat and vegetables are tender. Remove lid and stir in mushroom soup. Mix one tablespoon cornstarch with a little water until you have a smooth paste. Add to the stew a little at a time until the dish is sufficiently thickened, and you have a rich, dark gravy clinging to the chicken. Remove from flame.

Serve with crusty bread or cooked rice. A fresh garden salad on the side makes a fitting accompaniment.

Note: This recipe for stew is equally delicious made with one kg beef undercut, cubed. The only difference to the recipe would be: the beef should be three-quarters cooked before the vegetables are added to the pot.

Chicken Fricassee

Serves 6-8 persons

1½ kg frying chicken, skinned and jointed
3 onions, chopped fine
4 green chillies, chopped fine
1 tsp garam masala
1 stalk celery, washed and diced
2 cups hot water
1 tsp salt, or to taste
3 tbsp butter
2 tbsp flour
½ cup cooking sherry
Yolk of an egg
½ cup cream
GARNISH
A few sprigs of parsley, washed and chopped fine

Place the first six ingredients in a pot together with salt to taste. Cook until the chicken is firm but tender. Strain, and set aside chicken pieces. Place two tablespoons butter in a heavy-based pan and fry the chicken over moderate heat until browned. Remove from pan. Make a roux with remaining butter and flour. Mix in with a cup of chicken stock and stir into the pan. Lower heat and cook until the mixture thickens. Add cooking sherry. Lightly whisk egg yolk into the cream and add to the pan. Stir rapidly and remove from heat. Place chicken pieces in serving dish and pour gravy over. Garnish with chopped sprigs of parsley and serve.

A loaf of crusty bread, butter, a vegetable dish and salad make excellent accompaniments.

Fried Chicken

Serves 6 persons

20 pieces of chicken (legs and thighs), skinned
1 tbsp fresh ginger/garlic paste
1 tsp garam masala
Salt to taste
1 onion, roughly chopped
4 cups hot water
2 eggs, beaten with a pinch of salt
Breadcrumbs
Cooking oil for frying

GARNISH

3 large potatoes, cut lengthways and cooked in boiling salt water

Place first six ingredients in a pot, and cook the chicken

pieces until tender. Strain. Set aside the chicken pieces. Freeze stock, when added to rice, makes a delicious pulao. Dip chicken pieces in egg wash, and roll in breadcrumbs. Place heavy skillet over moderate flame, pour in oil. When oil is hot, fry chicken pieces until crisp and golden. Remove from heat and arrange on a platter. Fry the potatoes golden, and surround the fried chicken.

Serve fried chicken with a vegetable dish, salad and crusty bread. Fried chicken also makes an excellent accompaniment when served along with rice, dal and a cucumber salad.

Note: Fried chicken is excellent picnic fare. Equally delicious served hot or cold!

Chicken Roast

Serves 8 persons

FOR THE ROAST

2 whole frying chickens (700-800 gm) each
2 tsp salt
2 tsp fresh black pepper
1 tsp garlic powder
1 large orange, halved
2 tbsp butter
2 cups water
1 stalk celery, washed and roughly chopped
1 medium onion, roughly chopped
4 large potatoes, peeled and halved
1 tsp cornflour

FOR THE STUFFING

Heart and liver of both birds, chopped
2 tbsp butter
3 strips of bacon, chopped
1 large onion, chopped fine
2 green chillies, chopped fine
1 small bunch green coriander, chopped fine
1 stalk fresh celery, washed and finely chopped
½ tsp garam masala
1 tsp ground pepper
1 tbsp ginger/garlic paste
500 gm breakfast sausage
½ cup breadcrumbs
1 cup hot water
1 tsp salt, or to taste

Preheat oven to 180° C. Mix together salt, pepper and garlic. Cut orange in half, discard seeds. Dip orange half in salt/pepper/garlic mixture, and rub the bird all over, inside and out. Stuff orange in stomach and neck cavity. Grease a roasting pan and set the chickens in the pan. Place half an orange in the stomach cavity of each bird. Arrange celery and onion around the birds. Dot with butter, pour in one cup water and place in preheated oven. Allow the birds to bake uncovered for half an hour. Remove from heat, arrange potatoes around and pour in remaining water. Roast covered until the birds are three quarters done. Remove cover, baste, add more water if required in the interest of making more gravy. Allow to bake until tender. The bird should be tender, with a crisp brown outer skin. Gently lift chicken from the roaster and place on a platter. Arrange potatoes around chicken. Strain the residual gravy into a saucepan and place over moderate heat. Make a paste with one teaspoon cornflour and a tablespoon cold water. Stir into the gravy until thickened sufficiently. Add salt to taste, and pour into a gravy boat.

To make stuffing, place first four ingredients in a saucepan over moderate heat and fry until the onions are translucent. Add next three ingredients and continue frying. Lower heat. Make a paste of the next three ingredients and stir into the giblet mixture. Add chopped breakfast sausage and continue frying until the meat and sausages are nicely browned. Mix in breadcrumbs, pour hot water over the stuffing and allow to cook for a further few minutes. Add salt to taste and remove from heat. Transfer to a dish. Remove orange from chicken cavity and carve into portions. Serve roast chicken with gravy and stuffing.

A fresh garden salad, vegetable dish, and crusty bread and butter make excellent accompaniments.. English mustard complements the roast.

Coq au Vin

Serves 4-6 persons

1 kg frying chicken, skinned and jointed
¼ cup butter
1 tsp fresh garlic paste
8 small onions, peeled
4 carrots, scraped and diced
2 tbsp flour
2 cups dry red wine
1 bay leaf
1 small bunch fresh parsley, chopped
¼ tsp thyme

¼ tsp savoury
200 gm mushrooms, sliced
½ tsp pepper
1 tsp salt, or to taste
¼ cup water (optional)

Place butter in a heavy-based pan with lid. When the butter is hot, add pieces of chicken and fry until browned. Remove from pan and set aside. Place garlic paste in the pan and fry until fragrant. Mix in onions and carrots. Stir in flour and wine, mixing rapidly. When the wine is blended, add bay leaf, parsley, thyme and savoury to the pan. Stir in sliced mushrooms, pepper and salt to taste. Return chicken to the pan, gently spoon sauce over chicken pieces. A quarter cup water, if required, may be added to the pan at this point in the interest of making more gravy. Cover the pan and allow the chicken to simmer until the pieces of chicken and vegetables are tender. Remove from heat.

Serve coq au vin with mashed potatoes, vegetables, salad and crusty bread with butter.

Chicken Pie

Serves 6-8 persons

1 kg boneless chicken breast, cubed
2 tbsp butter
1 onion, chopped fine
1 tbsp ginger/garlic paste
½ tsp garam masala
½ tsp black pepper powder

1 tbsp Worcestershire sauce
1 small bunch fresh parsley, washed and chopped
1 tsp salt, or to taste
½ cup chicken broth
2 medium carrots, scraped, diced and cooked in salt water
1 cup fresh peas, cooked in salt water
1 tbsp butter
1 tbsp flour

FOR THE PASTRY

4 large potatoes, peeled and cooked in salt water
1 tbsp butter
½ tsp pepper
¼ cup cream
1 cup breadcrumbs
2 eggs, beaten to a froth with a pinch of salt

In a heavy-based pan over moderate heat, place butter and chopped onions. Fry the onions till translucent. Lower heat and add in ginger/garlic paste, garam masala and black pepper. Continue frying. Stir in cubed chicken and continue frying until the pieces of chicken are well coated with the spices. Add Worcestershire sauce and parsley, and salt to taste. Pour in half a cup of chicken broth. Cover the pan and allow the chicken to simmer gently until the pieces are tender and cooked through. Remove lid, add the carrots and peas to the pan. Make a roux with butter and flour, add to chicken and stir until gravy thickens. Remove from heat and set aside.

Preheat oven to 180° C. Mash potatoes with next three ingredients. Butter a pie dish and transfer chicken mixture to the dish. Cover with mashed potatoes. Sprinkle breadcrumbs evenly over the potatoes. Pour beaten eggs over breadcrumbs. Bake in preheated oven until the pie is puffed and golden brown on the top. Remove from oven and serve immediately with crusty bread, salad, and a small cauliflower, boiled in salted water and dusted with freshly ground pepper.

Note: For a delicious variation, sprinkle half a cup of grated Cheddar cheese over the mashed potatoes, followed by the breadcrumbs and eggs.

Chicken on Rice

Serves 6-8 persons

2 cups Basmati rice
1½ kg frying chicken parts, jointed and skinned
300 gm butter
1 tbsp freshly ground ginger/garlic paste
1 tbsp curry paste
1 large onion, minced
2 medium capsicum chillies (green peppers), chopped
1 can tomatoes (450 gm)
½ cup raisins
1 tsp crushed thyme
1 tsp salt, or to taste
½ tsp fresh ground black pepper powder

Wash rice, place in a pot with two cups water, a dash of salt and a teaspoon of butter. Cover and place pot over low heat. Parboil until water is absorbed. Remove lid, fluff rice and set aside. Place skillet on moderate flame, fry chicken parts in butter until brown. Drain and set aside. Lower heat, add next four ingredients to the skillet, and fry until the spices are fragrant. Stir in tomatoes, raisins and crushed thyme. Season with salt and pepper to taste. Simmer sauce for ten minutes. Butter oven-proof casserole and layer with parboiled rice. Arrange chicken pieces over rice, and pour over tomato mixture. Cover casserole and bake in preheated (180° C) oven until the chicken is tender and the rice is cooked.

Chicken in Orange Sauce

Serves 4-6 persons

1½ kg frying chicken, jointed and skinned
½ tsp salt
½ tsp freshly ground black pepper
¼ cup flour
1/3 cup cooking oil
½ cup chilli sauce
2 medium capsicum chillies (green peppers), chopped
1 tsp garlic paste
1 tsp prepared mustard
1 cup orange juice
1 tbsp dark brown sugar
2 tbsp soya sauce
2 oranges, peeled and sliced into thin rounds

In a bowl mix flour, salt and pepper. Dredge chicken parts with mixture. Place a heavy skillet over moderate heat. Pour in oil and lightly brown chicken pieces. Arrange fried chicken in a greased oven-proof casserole. Place next seven ingredients in a pot and allow to simmer over low heat for about five minutes, or until ingredients are well blended. Adjust salt. Pour over chicken pieces, cover, and place in preheated (180° C) oven. Bake chicken in orange sauce until tender. Remove from oven. Garnish with orange rounds just before serving.

Chicken in orange sauce is excellent with cooked rice, a garden salad and green bean foogath.

Roast Duck in Orange Sauce

Serves 4-6 persons

1 duck, weighing approx. 2-2½ kg
1 tsp salt, or to taste
1 tsp freshly ground black pepper
1 tsp garlic powder
2 fresh oranges
1 cup consommé
1 cup orange juice
½ cup dry white wine
1 tsp cornstarch

GARNISH

1 large orange, sliced into rings

Preheat oven to 180° C. Wash duck out thoroughly, pat dry and using a fork pierce skin all over. Be careful not to pierce the meat. Mix together salt, pepper and garlic powder. Cut oranges in half, discard seeds. Dip orange half in salt, pepper and garlic mixture and rub the bird all over inside and out. Stuff stomach and neck cavity with the remaining orange halves. Pour consommé over the duck, together with one cup orange juice. Place duck on rack in a greased roasting pan, and roast covered for about one hour. Baste the bird frequently with pan juices. Remove cover and continue basting the duck until the juices run clear when the thigh of the bird is pierced. The bird should be a rich brown colour. Remove duck from oven and set aside.

Pour off all but half a cup of pan juices into a saucepan. Add white wine. Blend cornstarch together with a little water and mix into saucepan. Thicken gravy over low heat, stirring continually. Pour into gravy boat. Carve duckling, garnish with orange slices and serve with gravy alongside.

Stuffing for Roast Duck

Serves 4-6 persons

3 tbsp butter
2 large onions, minced
1" piece fresh ginger, peeled and minced
6 flakes fresh garlic, peeled and minced
2 stalks celery, washed and chopped fine
2 green chillies, chopped
1 tsp fresh ground black pepper
1 tsp garam masala
Liver and heart of duck, wash and chopped
Three rashers bacon, chopped
4 pork sausages, removed from casing and chopped
1 can (284 ml) cream of mushroom soup
½ cup hot water
½ cup breadcrumbs
Salt to taste

In a deep heavy-based pan over low heat place butter and

minced onions. Fry until onions are translucent. Add next four ingredients. Continue frying until fragrant. Mix in pepper and garam masala. Lower heat and stir in chopped giblets, bacon and sausage. Fry until they are nicely browned. Place mushroom soup in the pan together with half a cup hot water. Stir in breadcrumbs. Cook stuffing for a further few minutes. Add salt to taste and remove from heat. Serve stuffing alongside roast duck.

Glace

Serves 6 persons

1 kg fillet of beef or mutton cut into 2" x 3" slices
3 large onions, sliced fine
1/3 cup cooking oil
2 tbsp fresh ginger/garlic paste
1 level tbsp paprika powder
½ level tsp chilli powder
2 tbsp mango chutney
2 large tomatoes, sliced
1½ tsp salt, or to taste
½ tsp sugar

GARNISH

¼ cup cooking oil
3 large potatoes peeled, cut lengthways and cooked in salted water
3 large onions, sliced fine
3 large fresh tomatoes, sliced thick
½ tsp ground black pepper

Place a heavy-based pan with lid over moderate heat and

pour in oil. Fry onions till golden. Make a paste of the next three spices and place in the pan. Lower heat and fry spices until fragrant. Add slices of meat and continue frying until the spices coat the slices of meat. Stir in mango chutney, sliced tomatoes, salt to taste and sugar. Cover the pan and allow the meat to cook in its own juices. Stir frequently. If the meat begins to dry, add a little water to the pan. When the meat is tender, remove from flame. There should be a delicious thick gravy clinging to the slices of meat.

Place a heavy skillet over moderate heat and fry the cooked potato slices crisp and golden. Remove from heat and drain. Place sliced onion in the pan and fry crisp. Put glace on a serving dish, arrange fried potatoes around, and strew fried onions over top. Arrange tomatoes on a platter and sprinkle over with freshly ground pepper. Serve glace with bread, a vegetable dish and a fresh garden salad.

Beef Cutlets

Serves 6-8 persons

1 kg lean ground beef
½ cup fine breadcrumbs
1 egg, well beaten
1 tsp salt, or to taste
1 tsp garam masala
2 large onions, minced
3 green chillies, minced
1 medium bunch of green coriander, washed and chopped fine
2 tbsp ginger/garlic paste

FOR FRYING

2 eggs, well beaten with a pinch of salt
Breadcrumbs
Oil for frying

In a basin place lean ground beef. Mix in next eight ingredients and test for sufficient salt. Shape into flat circular patties about two-and-a-half inches in diameter. Immerse patties in beaten egg, dust with breadcrumbs and set aside.

When all patties have been formed and 'crumbed', place frying pan over moderate heat and pour in oil. When the oil is hot, place as many patties as will comfortably fit into the pan. Fry the cutlets, turning them frequently until they are evenly browned and cooked through. Remove from fire and set on a platter. Add oil as required, until all the cutlets have been fried.

Cutlets are delicious served with fried potatoes and tomato sauce. A fresh vegetable salad on the side completes the meal.

Leftover cutlets, and needless to say this is a rarity, make an excellent accompaniment next morning at breakfast when served with fried eggs. Garnished with a few fried potatoes and tomato wedges.

Potato Cutlets

Serves 6 persons

FOR THE MINCE

500 gm lean ground beef
¼ cup oil

3 large onions, minced
1 tbsp ginger/garlic paste
1 tsp garam masala
2 green chillies, minced
1 medium bunch green coriander, washed and chopped fine
1 tsp lime juice
1 tbsp Worcestershire sauce
1 tbsp soya sauce
½ tsp sugar
Salt to taste

POTATO

1 kg potatoes, peeled and cooked in salted water
¼ tsp pepper
1 tbsp butter

COATING

2 eggs, beaten with a pinch of salt
Breadcrumbs

In a heavy-based pan placed over moderate heat, pour in oil. Add onions and fry till translucent. Stir in next four ingredients and fry until the spices are fragrant. Place ground beef in the pan and continue frying until the meat is evenly browned and mixed with the spices. Pour lime juice over the mince and continue frying; add sauces. The meat should be a rich, dark colour and smell fragrant. Mix in salt to taste, add sugar. Stir once more, remove from heat and set aside.

Mash cooked potatoes, blend in butter and pepper. Take enough mashed potato to make a ball 2" in diameter, form into a shallow cup and place two heaped teaspoons mince inside. Cover with mashed potato to form into a cutlet. Set aside. Continue making cutlets until all the potato has been utilized. Beat eggs with a little salt.

Immerse cutlets in beaten egg and crumbs. Fry to a crisp golden colour. Set on a platter and serve hot. If any mince remains, pass alongside the cutlets. Serve with a vegetable dish and salad.

Pepper Steak

Serves 6 persons

1 kg beef or mutton fillet, cut into 2-2½" x 3" slices
1/3 cup cooking oil
2 medium onions, sliced fine
1 tbsp ginger/garlic paste
2 tsp ground black pepper
½ tsp garam masala
2 green chillies, slit lengthways
2 tbsp Worcestershire sauce
1 tbsp oyster sauce
1½ tsp salt, or to taste
½ tsp sugar
1 cup hot water
2 large capsicum chillies (green peppers), sliced
2 medium tomatoes, chopped
3 large potatoes, cut into thick slices lengthways
1 tsp cornstarch (optional)

Place a large heavy-based pan with lid over moderate heat, and pour in oil. When the oil is hot, add onions slices and fry until transparent. Lower heat, place ginger/garlic paste, pepper, garam masala and green chillies in the pan. Continue frying until the spices release their fragrant aroma. Add meat slices and continue frying until the meat is coated all over with the spices. Pour over sauces. Add salt to taste and sugar. Stir in capsicums, tomatoes and potatoes. Pour over one cup hot water, cover the pot and allow the pepper steak to simmer. Remove lid frequently and stir to ensure the meat does not adhere to the bottom of the pan. The tomatoes and capsicums will release a fair amount of liquid. When the pepper steaks are cooked through, there should be a thick residual gravy clinging to the slices of meat.

In the event the gravy needs to be thickened, do not remove from heat. Make a paste of one teaspoon cornstarch and a little cold water. Stir into the pan. When the gravy is thick enough, remove from heat and place in a serving dish.

Serve accompanied with a loaf of crusty bread and a fresh garden salad.

Rolled Beef

Serves 6 persons

2 large flank steaks—about 700 gm each
2 tsp each, combined salt and pepper
¼ cup cooking oil
2 medium onions, minced
2 slices bacon, chopped fine
1 tbsp fresh ginger/garlic paste
1 level tsp garam masala
1 small bunch parsley, chopped
1 stalk celery, finely chopped
2 green chillies, minced
1 cup cooked peas

1 potato, cooked and diced fine
½ cup breadcrumbs
2 tbsp butter
1 cup water
1 tsp salt

Dust steaks on both sides with one teaspoon combined salt and pepper. Beat with wooden mallet to tenderize and flatten meat. Set aside. In a heavy skillet over a moderate flame, place oil and fry bacon and onion. Lower heat and add next five ingredients. Fry until the spices release their fragrant aroma. Add peas and diced potato. Stir in breadcrumbs and continue frying. Add two tablespoons of water to the skillet and salt to taste. Remove from heat.

Divide the stuffing equally down the centre of the two flank steaks. Fold in edges towards the middle and roll the steak up with the stuffing inside. Tie the rolls securely with kitchen twine (at two ends and in the middle).

Heat oven to 180° C. Place butter in a heavy skillet over moderate flame. Fry the beef rolls until nicely browned. Place in a shallow oven-proof casserole. Pour one cup water over the beef rolls. Add salt to taste. Cover with aluminium foil and bake in preheated oven until rolls are tender.

Remove from oven, cut away string and slice beef rolls; spoon the gravy over top and serve.

Whole cauliflower boiled in a little salted water, drained, and served with a dusting of black pepper makes an excellent vegetable accompaniment. A loaf of crusty bread and a garden salad rounds off the meal.

Mixed Grill

Serves 6 persons

Mixed grill is excellent served as a dinner entrée, but the variety of ingredients that go to make up the recipe also allow it to be served very successfully for breakfast or brunch. The secret of serving a good mixed grill lies not in the ingredients, but rather in the rapid cooking process that allows you to serve it steaming hot and fresh off the skillet. Therefore, it is necessary to have all the ingredients on hand and ready to be fried just prior to the meal. Slices of hot buttered toast and salad make excellent accompaniments. Of course, if the dish happens to be part of a breakfast menu, a dozen eggs should be fried and served alongside, together with tea and coffee.

6 lamb chops
½ tsp salt
1 cup hot water
½ tsp fresh ground pepper
500 gm fresh calf liver, sliced into 2" x 3" slices
1 tbsp ginger/garlic paste
½ tsp salt
½ tsp fresh ground pepper
2 tbsp flour
½ cup cooking oil
6 medium potatoes, cut lengthways and cooked in salted water

4 medium onions, cut into rings
225 gm lean bacon
6 spiced sausages
125 gm butter
250 gm fresh mushrooms, sliced
½ tsp ground black pepper
Salt
3 medium tomatoes, thickly sliced
12 eggs

Cook lamb chops in salt water until tender. Drain, sprinkle over with pepper and set aside. Mix together ginger/garlic paste, pepper and salt. Smear slices of liver with the mixture, dust with flour and set aside. Place a heavy-based skillet over moderate flame and pour in oil. Set a large stainless steel pan on minimum heat beside skillet to receive the various ingredients after they have been fried. Fry potatoes until golden, drain. Place onions in the skillet and fry until soft and translucent. Fry the bacon crisp. Prick pork sausages all over, and fry until golden brown and cooked through. Lower lamb chops into skillet and fry lightly. Place slices of liver in the skillet, and fry, turning frequently until tender and cooked through. Ensure the liver does not get tough. Remove skillet from heat, wash and dry. Place skillet over moderate heat and add in butter. When the butter is hot, fry the mushrooms until tender, add a pinch of salt and pepper to the skillet. Drain mushrooms and place in a separate container. Lastly place tomato rounds in the pan and cook until soft. Arrange all ingredients from large stainless steel pan on to a large serving platter with the liver and lamb chops in the centre, slices of bacon and sausages all around.

Garnish with onion rings, mushrooms and tomato

slices. Fried potatoes may be served on the side. In the event the dish is to be served for breakfast, the eggs should be fried sunny side up and arranged on the platter of mixed grill.

A fresh garden salad makes an excellent accompaniment.

Liver and Onions

Serves 6 persons

225 gm lean bacon
700 gm fresh calf liver, sliced
1 tbsp fresh ginger/garlic paste
½ tsp freshly ground black pepper
1 tsp salt, or to taste
2 eggs whisked together with a pinch of salt
Breadcrumbs
½ cup cooking oil
3 large potatoes, peeled, sliced lengthways and cooked in salted water
3 large onions, cut into rings
2 large tomatoes, cut into rounds

Wash liver and slice into 3" x 2" pieces. Mix together ginger/garlic paste with pepper and salt. Smear slices of liver with the mixture and set aside for two hours. Place oil in a heavy skillet over moderate flame and fry potatoes golden brown. Drain and set aside. Place onions in the pan and fry until translucent. Set aside. Lower slices of bacon into the skillet and fry crisp. Drain and set aside. Immerse slices of liver in egg and coat with breadcrumbs. Fry over moderate heat, turning frequently until the slices are evenly browned and crisp. When all the slices of liver have been fried, skim the surface of the skillet and add tomatoes. Fry tomatoes until soft. Arrange liver and bacon on a serving platter, garnish with fried onions and arrange potatoes around the platter. Tomatoes may be placed on the slices of liver or served alongside.

Serve with cooked greens beans, salad and a loaf of crusty bread.

Pot Roast

Serves 8-10 persons

3 kg chuck or blade roast
2 tbsp flour
1 tsp salt
1 tsp freshly ground black pepper
3 tbsp butter
5 flakes garlic, peeled
½ tsp chilli flakes
3 cups hot water
2 medium carrots, scraped and diced
1 stalk celery, diced
1 large onion, roughly chopped
1 turnip, diced

Mix together flour, salt and pepper. Dust the roast liberally with the mixture. Set aside remaining flour mixture. Place a large heavy-based pot over moderate heat; add butter. When the butter melts, add garlic slices and fry until golden. Place roast in the pot and fry to an even brown colour. Sprinkle over chilli flakes. Add hot water to the pot. Lower heat, cover the pot, and simmer roast until three-quarters cooked. Remove cover and stir in the next four ingredients, adding more water if required. Baste roast frequently. When the meat and vegetables are tender, stir in remaining flour mixture. Allow to simmer until the gravy is sufficiently thickened. Place roast on a cutting board, and carve into thick slices; remove to a large platter. Spoon gravy and vegetables over. Serve, accompanied by crusty rolls, fresh salad and English mustard.

Salted Beef Tongue

Approx. 2 kg dressed cow's tongue
4 limes
1 tsp saltpetre
3 tbsp salt
¼ cup brown sugar

Squeeze limes and mix together with salt, saltpetre and brown sugar. Place the tongue in a glass dish, prick all over with a fork. Rub the salt mixture into the meat . Turn the lime skins inside out and place them over the tongue. Cover with a plate and place a weight on top. Refrigerate tongue. The following morning remove and turn the tongue, forking it well. Continue this practice for a further three days. On the fourth day drain tongue from liquid, wash well, place in a large pot with cold water and cook until tender (a pressure cooker cuts the cooking time by half). Slice the tongue and serve with mashed potatoes and a vegetable dish. Salted tongue makes excellent sandwiches. Place a dab of English mustard on two slices of buttered bread, arrange a few slices of cold tongue on the bread together with shredded lettuce and tomato rounds. Cover with second slice of bread. Cut the sandwich in half and serve.

Sweet and Sour Meatballs

Serves 8-10 persons

This recipe has been a favourite in our family for as long as I can remember. It is a savoury dish that has just the correct amount of piquancy, and makes an excellent addition to a festive menu. Since sweet and sour meatballs keep so well, they are equally delicious warmed and served up the following day, accompanied by a dish of cooked rice or buttered noodles.

2 kg lean ground beef
3 large onions, chopped fine
1 tsp garam masala
1 tsp freshly ground black pepper
2 tbsp fresh ginger/garlic paste
½ cup fresh parsley, chopped fine
2 large eggs, beaten
2 tsp salt, or to taste
Cooking oil
4 cups beef stock
½ cup wine vinegar
½ cup brown sugar
¼ cup soya sauce

2 capsicum chillies (1 each green and red pepper), cut into pieces
1 bottle pickled onions
1 tbsp cornstarch
Cold water
Parsley to garnish

In a large bowl mix together first eight ingredients, shape into balls. Place a heavy-based pot over a low flame and pour in beef stock, vinegar, brown sugar and soya sauce. Allow to simmer for about ten minutes. Pour cooking oil in a skillet over moderate heat, and fry the meatballs in batches to a rich brown colour. Transfer to pot of simmering sweet and sour sauce. Add chopped capsicums, bottled pickled onions with juices, to the pot. Allow the meatballs to simmer in the gravy for a further half an hour. Thicken gravy with cornstarch made into a paste with a little cold water. Adjust flavouring. Remove from heat and set aside.

To serve: Re-heat sweet and sour meatballs with gravy in an ovenproof bowl. Garnish with chopped parsley, and serve with a vegetable dish and salad.

Cold Roast Beef Hash

Serves 6 persons

¼ cup cooking oil
2 onions, chopped fine
1 tbsp fresh ginger/garlic paste
½ tsp garam masala
½ tsp freshly ground pepper

500 gm cold roast beef, cut in strips lengthways
250 gm lean ham, cut in strips
3 strips bacon, chopped
1 stick celery, washed and chopped fine
2 green chillies, chopped fine
1 medium bunch green coriander, chopped fine
3 tbsp roast gravy
Salt to taste

GARNISH

Remaining potatoes from the roast, or
2 large potatoes, peeled, sliced lengthways and cooked in salted water
1 tbsp butter

Place oil in a heavy-based pan over moderate heat and add onions. Fry until golden, add ginger/garlic paste, garam masala and pepper to the pan. Continue frying. Lower heat, and stir in next three ingredients. Fry until the pieces of meat are nicely browned and coated with the spices. Add chopped celery, green chillies and coriander to the pan. Stir in roast gravy. Adjust salt. Allow the hash to simmer over low heat until the liquid dries up and you have a rich, dark gravy. Remove from flame and set aside.

Place a heavy skillet on a medium flame, add one tablespoon butter to the pan, and fry the potatoes from the roast until they are crisp and golden. Or, fry cooked boiled potatoes. Arrange hash in a serving dish, garnish with potatoes, and serve as an accompaniment with eggs at breakfast, or with a dish of dal, vegetable foogath and rice for lunch. Hash also makes an excellent side dish when served at dinner with crusty bread, vegetables and a fresh garden salad.

Masala Fry

Serves 6 persons

1 kg beef or mutton fillet, sliced into 2" x 2" pieces
1 onion, sliced
3 tbsp ghee
1 tsp red chilli powder
2 tsp jeera powder
2 tbsp fresh ginger/garlic paste
1 tsp salt, or to taste
½ tsp sugar
1 cup hot water
2 tbsp thick tamarind pulp

Place a heavy-based pan over moderate heat, and fry sliced onions until golden. Lower heat and stir in next three ingredients made into a paste. Fry until oil separates from the masala paste. Place meat in pan and continue frying until the meat is well coated with the spices. Add salt to taste and sugar. Pour over one cup hot water, cover the pan and allow the masala fry to cook over low heat until tender. Remove lid from pan and pour in tamarind pulp. There should be a piquant dark gravy clinging to the morsels of meat. Remove from heat.

Serve masala fry with chapatis, dal and a vegetable dish on the side.

Chilli Fry—Green Masala

Serves 6 persons

1 kg mutton, washed and cut into bite-sized pieces
¼ cup cooking oil
2 large onions, finely minced
3 green chillies, chopped fine
12 flakes fresh garlic, peeled and chopped fine
2" piece of fresh ginger, peeled and chopped fine
½ tsp turmeric powder
½ tsp garam masala
1 tsp salt, or to taste
2 cups hot water
2 tbsp thick tamarind pulp
2 medium potatoes, peeled, cubed and cooked in salted water
1 small bunch green coriander, washed and chopped fine

Place a heavy-based pan with lid on moderate heat and pour in oil. When the oil is hot add the minced onions and fry until translucent. Lower heat, and add next three ingredients. Fry until fragrant. Stir next two ingredients into the pan. Add meat, and continue frying until nicely browned and covered with spices. Add salt to taste and hot water. Cover the pan and allow the mutton to cook until the meat is tender. Mix in tamarind pulp. Allow the Chilli Fry to simmer until the gravy is reduced. Stir in cubed potato, adjust salt and remove from heat.

Serve Chilli Fry, garnished with fresh coriander leaves. Chapatis, dal and an onion salad make excellent accompaniments.

Meat Loaf

Serves 6-8 persons

Meat loaf can be served in a number of ways. One can bake it in a fancy mould, encase it in flaky pastry, or a savoury potato/cheese crust, and dish it up with a delicious sauce. You have a meal fit for a king! Meat loaves can be made ahead, reheated, or served cold with salad, crusty rolls and butter. The possibilities are endless, and most important of all, meat loaf is inexpensive. Leftover scraps of ham and bacon, when incorporated into a meat loaf, add flavour. The following is a basic meat loaf recipe:

1 kg lean ground beef
1 large onion, minced
½ cup breadcrumbs
2 tsp salt, or to taste
1 tsp garam masala
1 tbsp freshly ground ginger/garlic paste
2 eggs, lightly beaten
1 small bunch fresh parsley, chopped
1 can condensed cream of mushroom soup
6 strips bacon

Grease a loaf pan 9 x 5 x 3, and lay three strips of bacon along the bottom. Combine all ingredients thoroughly, and pack into pan. Lay remaining three strips of bacon on the top. Place the meat loaf in a moderate oven (180° C), and bake until the loaf pulls away slightly from the sides of the pan, and is nicely browned on top.

Remove from oven and serve sliced with a spicy tomato or chilli sauce.

Pork Chops Arthur

Serves 4 persons

These chops are named for my father, Arthur Peters, who developed this unique recipe for making pork chops, and cooked them to perfection. He served them up with fried potatoes, green beans and a salad.

8 pork loin chops, trimmed
1 tbsp ginger/garlic paste
1 tsp salt, or to taste
½ tsp garam masala
½ tsp meat tenderizer
2 tbsp Worcestershire sauce
Cooking oil
3 eggs, beaten with a pinch of salt
Breadcrumbs

Blend together ginger/garlic paste, salt, garam masala and tenderizer. Rub the pork chops with the paste, and pour Worcestershire sauce over them. Prick the chops with a fork. Cover and marinade overnight in the refrigerator. The next day place a heavy skillet over a moderate flame and pour in half a cup of oil. Immerse pork chops in egg and coat with breadcrumbs. Lower heat and fry chops, turning frequently until they are tender and crisp.

Serve pork chops with cooked green beans, salad, fresh rolls and butter.

Pork Fry

Serves 6 persons

1½ kg lean pork, cut into bite-sized pieces
1 tsp turmeric powder
1 tbsp jeera
1 large pod garlic, peeled
2" piece fresh ginger, peeled
1 cup malt vinegar
2 tbsp garam masala
2 tsp salt, or to taste
1 tsp sugar
1/3 cup cooking oil

Wash pork and drain through a colander. Press down on the pieces of pork to ensure all the liquid drains out. Rub pork with turmeric powder and set aside in a glass dish. Grind the next three ingredients in vinegar, and mix with following three ingredients to a smooth paste. Rub pork all over with the masala paste, cover the dish and allow the meat to marinate for at least three hours, or overnight in the refrigerator.

The following day place a heavy-based pot over moderate heat, and pour in oil. When the oil is hot stir in a few pieces of pork at a time, and fry until nicely browned. Adjust salt. Lower heat, add any remaining vinegar to the pot, and cook the pork in its own juices until tender. Pork fry is a dry dish, and there should be only a tablespoon of gravy clinging to the dark, fried morsels of meat.

Serve pork fry with chapatis, dal and a vegetable dish on the side.

Pork Bhoonie

Serves 4-6 persons

The following is a recipe for the most delicious pork bhoonie, given to me by an old friend, Gloria Major.

1 kg pork loin, cut into bite-sized pieces
2 level tsp turmeric
2 cups hot water
1½ tsp salt, or to taste
1/3 cup cooking oil
2 large onions, finely sliced
5 green chillies, sliced lengthways
1 large bunch dill, washed and chopped
2 medium potatoes, peeled, cubed and cooked in salt water

In a pot over moderate heat, place the first four ingredients. Cook the pork until tender. There should be very little water left in the pot. Remove from heat. Place a heavy-based pan on the fire, pour in oil. When the oil is hot, mix in sliced onions, green chillies and dill. Fry over low heat. Add meat and continue frying until the meat is browned all over. Test for sufficient salt and remove from flame. Place a tablespoon of oil in a heavy skillet and fry cooked potatoes crisp and brown. Mix in with the pork.

Serve pork bhoonie with cooked rice or chapatis, dal and cucumber salad.

Pork Assado

Serves 4 persons

The following is a recipe for a succulent pork dish that comes from Goa. I have enjoyed eating it on numerous occasions at the many impromptu dinners given by my friend Tess da'Cunha.

1 kg pork shoulder
1 tbsp fresh ginger/garlic paste
½ tsp turmeric powder
¼ tsp freshly ground pepper powder
1 tsp salt, or to taste
¼ cup cooking oil
1 whole stick cinnamon
5 cloves
3 whole dry red chillies
2 cups hot water

Cut pork into four large pieces, prick all over with a fork. Mix together first three spices and salt. Rub the pieces of pork with the spices, cover, and allow to marinate overnight in the refrigerator. The following day place cooking oil in a heavy-based pan over moderate heat. When the oil is hot, fry the remaining three whole spices. Lower heat and place pork in the pan. Continue frying until the meat is browned all over. Add two cups of hot water to the pan, cover, and allow the pork to cook gently over low heat for about twenty minutes. Remove lid from pan, stir the Assado, and continue cooking until the meat is tender. There should be about half a cup of gravy in the pan. Remove from heat and allow to cool. Slice and serve with crusty bread, a whole cauliflower boiled in salted water, drained and dusted with a dash of fresh ground pepper, green beans, or a vegetable foogath.

Roasted Pork Tenderloin with Egg Noodles

Serves 6 persons

FOR THE ROAST

1 kg pork tenderloin (2 or 3 whole tenderloins), trim and set aside
2 cups water
2" fresh ginger, peeled and slivered
2 tbsp soya sauce
2 tbsp oyster sauce
1 tbsp sesame seed oil
1 tsp cornstarch

FOR THE NOODLES

2 packages fresh chow mein noodles, or instant noodles
2 tbsp fresh ginger/garlic paste
4 strips lean bacon, chopped fine

2 medium onions, finely sliced
2 green chillies, slit
1 tbsp oyster sauce
1 tbsp soya sauce
Half the gravy from roast pork tenderloin
1 cup raw cabbage, sliced fine
2 medium carrots, cut into 2" pieces and slice fine
1 tsp sesame seed oil
FOR THE EGGS
4 large eggs, whisked with salt to taste
3 green onions, minced (set aside green portion)
2 green chillis, minced
1 tbsp cooking oil

Preheat over 180° C. Place tenderloins in greased roasting pan with water. Sprinkle fresh ginger over the meat. Pour soya and oyster sauces over them, and drizzle sesame seed oil all over. Bake in open roaster, basting continuously. When the tenderloin is cooked, take from pan and set aside. There should be about a cup and a half of gravy at the bottom of the roasting pan; add sufficient water to make two cups. Scrape down sides and bottom of pan. Set aside.

Place a large heavy-based pot with cooking oil over moderate heat, and when the oil is hot, add ginger/garlic paste. Fry the spices until fragrant. Add chopped bacon, sliced onions and green chillies to the pan. Continue frying until the onions are translucent. Mix in oyster and soya sauces. Stir noodles into the pot, adding a little at a time until they have all been utilized. Pour half the gravy from roast over the noodles. Mix in sliced cabbage and carrots. The vegetables will sweat and release their liquid, which will be absorbed by the noodles. Lower heat, and toss noodles until well mixed in with the vegetables. Pour over one teaspoon sesame seed oil. Mix well and remove from heat. Cover the noodles and set aside.

Whisk eggs together with a little salt, the white portion of green onions and minced green chillies. Place a heavy skillet over moderate heat and pour in oil; when the oil is hot add egg mixture to the pan. Lower heat and allow the eggs to set until evenly cooked on both sides. Remove from heat. Slice omelette lengthways and stir into noodle dish.

To assemble the dish: Pile noodles on a large serving platter, sprinkle over minced portion of green onions. Slice one tenderloin and place on top of the bed of noodles. Pour the remaining half of roast gravy into a saucepan and place over low heat. Mix a teaspoon of cornstarch with a little water and add to the saucepan. Stir until the gravy thickens. Slice remaining tenderloins, place in a serving dish, cover with gravy and pass alongside the platter of noodles. Serve with stir-fried vegetables.

Baked Ham in Pineapple Sauce

Serves 8-10 persons

1 cup pineapple juice
¾ cup brown sugar
2 tsp powdered mustard
¼ tsp ground cloves
1/8 tsp ground nutmeg
1" piece fresh ginger, peeled and minced
3-4 kg boneless fully cooked ham

8 flakes fresh garlic, peeled
A few whole cloves
½ cup pineapple juice
1 tbsp cornstarch
1 tbsp water

Place the first six ingredients in a heavy saucepan over moderate heat. Bring to a boil. Lower heat and simmer until the sugar is dissolved. Make one-inch cuts all over the ham and insert slices of fresh garlic. Pour the marinade over, refrigerate, and allow the ham to stand overnight in the juices, basting frequently.

The next day, preheat oven to 180° C. Place ham in greased roasting pan and bake for three hours, basting frequently with marinade. Take ham from oven and score all over; stud with cloves. Replace in oven and bake for a further hour. Drain pan drippings into a saucepan and add pineapple juice. Mix together a little pineapple juice and cornstarch, add to the saucepan and cook the gravy over low heat until thickened sufficiently. Serve sauce with ham.

Serve with roasted potatoes, English mustard and accompaniments.

Roast Haunch of Venison

Venison, the edible flesh of the deer, was considered a delicacy by those who loved to hunt. Within the Anglo-Indian community there were scores of hunters, and my grandfather Jim Peters, who lived near the foothills of the Satpura range, knew a great many of them. In the atmosphere of easy hospitality that prevailed at the time, he was continually entertaining one or other of his shikari pals, who would conveniently make a 'stopover' at the farm while in transit to some other destination, just for the opportunity of going for a shoot. They would leave the farm in a group at sunrise, gun bearers and beaters in tow, to spend the day wandering through the jungle visiting various locations where game had been spotted by the local villagers or grass cutters. If their foray proved successful, at dusk one could see them in the distance returning home with the beaters, carrying a deer between them.

Although this way of life has long since disappeared in India, and game is rightly protected, anecdotes and recipes such as these serve to illuminate the past, shedding light on how our ancestors enjoyed their place in time. The following recipe for venison roast is taken from my grandmother's recipe book:

1 haunch of venison (approx. 3 kg)
2 tsp freshly ground black pepper
2 tsp salt
8 flakes garlic, peeled
2" knob of fresh ginger, peeled and cut into slivers
2 cups consommé
½ cup cooking oil
4 whole red chillies
1 large onion, roughly chopped
1 tsp cornstarch

Preheat oven to 180° C. Trim and wash haunch of venison; pat dry. With a sharp knife make slits all over the venison.

Mix together salt and freshly ground black pepper and rub the mixture into the meat, coating it evenly all over. Imbed garlic cloves into slits. Place venison in a well-buttered roasting pan. Pour over consommé and vegetable oil. Strew ginger, whole red chillies and chopped onion around the meat. Cover and place in preheated oven. If potatoes are required, add them to the pan when the venison is three-quarters done, arranging them around the roast. Spoon over pan juices, add water if required.

The flesh of a young buck is tender, with very little fat and, therefore, should be basted frequently with pan juices until cooked through and succulent. Remove lid and allow the roast to brown all over for the last half hour of baking.

Remove from oven. Take roast and potatoes from pan and set aside. Make a gravy with pan drippings, thickened with a teaspoon of cornstarch. Pour into a sauce boat and serve alongside venison roast.

Serve with English mustard, fresh garden salad and crusty bread or rolls. Cold venison roast makes excellent sandwiches, and will keep in the refrigerator for a week.

The Pigman

The Pigman

From my sitting room window I watched him on his rickety bicycle as he rattled down the road and swerved into the driveway. The pigman arrived in a cloud of dust.

'Peeg, memsahib, peegman is here,' he called out in pidgin.

'Who do you think you are, making all this racket in front of the house? Know your place, seller of pigs. First you lose your caste, and now you lose all respect for your betters.' This volley of abuse was followed by the waspish figure of Lourdina the cook as she flew out from behind the bungalow.

Startled, the pigman replied defensively, 'I'll see the memsahib today, vixen, and you are not the memsahib.' Disgustedly, he sprayed the marigold bed with a torrent of bright red paan spittle.

'Oh! Now you have done it,' screeched Lourdina, wagging a finger at him. 'Let Ramesh only see how you have spoiled his most sacred flowers. He will curse you soundly for this. They were his pride and joy. Why, only yesterday he called me out from the kitchen just to take note of them, and now they are spoiled, defiled with your filthy spittle.'

She stopped short and walked quickly away as the ferret figure of Ramesh the gardener darted out from under the grove of papaya trees and hurried towards them. His eyes fell on the desecrated marigolds and rolled upwards to heaven.

'Hai Ram!' he exclaimed aloud, and making for the pigman berated him loudly. It was only my arrival on the front veranda that caused him to scurry back to the papaya grove, muttering imprecations under his breath.

I surveyed the scene with amusement. 'Have you brought us another pig?' I asked, pointing to the squirming bundle tied to the carrier of his bike.

'Ha!' he exclaimed. 'What do you care? I take my life into my hands, bringing this prize animal to your house—riding for more than ten miles in the hot sun, only to be cursed and abused by your servants.'

'Well,' I said, 'are you going to stand there all afternoon, feeling sorry for yourself, or are you going to come around to the back of the house and show us your prize?'

'The vixen is there,' he snorted, 'but I will follow you.' Wheeling his bike around he moved to the rear of the house. I closed the front door behind me and walked to the kitchen.

'Lourdina,' I said with a smile, 'open the back door for your friend, he is coming around.'

'*Vah re vah*!' she replied scornfully. 'Now he has become my friend, that filthy, untouchable seller of pigs. Is this how I am to be repaid for my loyalty to you, by calling me a friend of untouchables and thieves?' Opening the back door she cried out, 'Show us your wares, pig seller.'

Taking the squirming gunny sack off his carrier, he started to untie it. A small white piglet flew out of the bag as he opened it and ran all over the veranda, freely relieving itself. 'A pig like this you will never see again,' he said, looking at me with small, sly eyes. 'I want twenty rupees for this one, not a paisa more, not a paisa less. Take it or leave it.'

Turning, I said, 'I will leave you to settle the price with Lourdina. It is a nice-looking animal though a bit on the lean side. It will have to be fattened for the table.' Leaving the pair to haggle over the price of the pig, I returned to the quiet, cool sitting room to resume my reading. However, I found it hard to concentrate, and instead spent the time eavesdropping on their conversation.

'We all know about you, you devil,' said Lourdina. 'I have a butler friend who works with the superintendent sahib at the mental hospital, and he told me where you get your pigs from.'

Fear that his little operation, whatever it was, had been found out sent the pigman into a further paroxysm of anger. 'Hold your tongue, you lying old witch,' he cried. 'What did you pay the butler for such information? It could not have been much for he fed you lies. Did you allow him to sleep with that slut, your daughter? She is diseased, everybody knows. You are losing your mind, woman. What does anyone know about me and my business? Who is going to give evidence against me, ha? Ha?' he exclaimed angrily.

'Enough of spouting your filth, pig seller. I do not have all day to sit around haggling with you on the price of one miserable animal. How much do you want for this beast?'

'I have already told you,' he replied stubbornly.

'The memsahib will give you twelve rupees, and a cup of tea besides.' She was equally adamant.

'Twelve rupees!' he repeated incredulously. 'Ha! You all want to buy the gunny sack then, that alone costs twelve rupees. No, it will be twenty rupees or nothing. I don't know why I waste my time coming to this household.'

'Leave then,' replied Lourdina, 'for I have work to do and you and your animal are both desecrating the place.'

From the sitting room I could hear his abuse as he shoved the squealing pig back into the gunny sack. From past experience I knew he would be off down the road only to return after a while. I heard the back veranda door slam as Lourdina shut it on his retreating figure.

The house was quiet once more, and lulled by the silence I dozed. The book slipped off my lap and landed with a thud on the floor; I awoke with a start. There was a tapping on the back door, and I decided to answer it myself.

'All this for nothing,' he muttered, looking wretched. He was covered in sweat that poured off him in little rivulets, following the weather-beaten creases of his face.

'I'll take a cup of tea,' he said insolently.

'You'll have a cup of water,' said Lourdina, hearing him, 'and that too from the garden tap. Here, help yourself,' she said, shoving a metal cup into his hands.

'What stingy folk live here,' he muttered, wiping the sweat off his brow with the soiled end of his dhoti. 'Gone are the days of the angrezi memsahibs, when I was greeted at the back door with a cup of tea with plenty of milk and sugar.' Banging the cup down, he once again mounted his bike and was down the road in a trice.

'He'll be back,' I said to Lourdina, matter of factly, 'and this time when he returns, give him thirteen rupees for his pig and a cup of tea besides, just the way he likes it. You can call me when you have made the deal and I will pay him.'

'You are always too good to that wretched man,' muttered Lourdina characteristically. 'That is why he does not know his place, just like those other lowly creatures that you feel pity for and employ. Take, for instance, that baggage Kamala. In any other household she would have been kicked out long ago. Where she lives is like a whorehouse, with all the comings and goings. I tell you, I would not even look in her direction if it wasn't your welfare I was interested in. No wonder she is tired all day, she is up to no good all night. Now if she was my daughter . . .'

'Enough,' I said firmly. 'Whom I employ is none of your business. Besides, your daughter is no paragon of virtue either. I will hear no more. Attend to the pigman when he returns.'

There was a persistent knocking at the back door. I heard Lourdina open the door and gruffly inquire, 'Now what do you want?'

'Where is the memsahib?' asked the anguished pigman. 'I have come to make a deal with her.'

'The memsahib is not here to make a deal with the likes of you,' said Lourdina scornfully. 'You make your deal with me. What will it be ? Here, here is a cup of tea for you, just the way you like it. Drink it, and let us settle on a price for your pig.'

I felt we had had enough of the pigman's shenanigans, and rising from my chair, I walked into the kitchen with the intention of bringing this purchase to a swift conclusion. Entering, I saw him beating his lean belly, asking Lourdina if she couldn't spare him a bit of bread. Cutting a thick slice off a loaf on the sideboard, she silently passed it to him. Cutting a further slice for herself, she joined him in the corner with a cup of tea. Dunking the bread, they enjoyed their tea in companionable silence.

Draining the cup, the pigman wiped his mouth, smacked his lips and said, 'Give me fifteen rupees, this is my final price. Take it or leave it.'

Lourdina cast a withering glance in his direction, and over the top of her cup she muttered, 'Twelve rupees.'

'I am a poor man,' he whined. 'What do you want, to steal the very food from my mouth?'

Memsahib, don't you think I am being reasonable? Hai Ram! What a day this has been.'

'Lourdina, please settle it,' I said. 'Let us conclude this tiresome purchase, once and for all.' Turning, I walked away.

'Twelve rupees and fifty paisa, then,' he said. 'I have no air in my tyres, and they have to be pumped. That alone costs fifty paisa.'

'You have a deal,' said Lourdina amicably. Of course, there was the small matter of change; the pigman had none. He kept the thirteen rupees, and Lourdina dragged the squealing pig in the gunny sack to the outhouse, where it would be fattened for the table.

I heard the pigman pedalling down the gravel path, victoriously ringing his cycle bell.

Roast Suckling Pig

Serves 10-12 persons

1 suckling pig—about 5-6 kg in weight
The pig should be able to fit comfortably into the middle rack of a large roasting oven
1 large head of garlic, peeled and ground to a paste
1 tbsp black pepper powder
2 tsp salt
1 large can pineapple juice
1 cup water
¼ cup cooking oil
Soya sauce
Sesame seed oil
1 can pineapple rings
A few whole cherries

Preheat oven to 170° C. Set aside liver, heart and kidneys of the pigling for stuffing. Wash pigling, including stomach cavity, thoroughly. Pat dry with a tea towel. Set aside. Blend together garlic paste, pepper and salt; rub pigling inside and out with the mixture. Place in a large baking pan, and pour half the can of pineapple juice, basting the inside of the cavity with the juice. Pour over one cup of water, mixed with quarter cup cooking oil. Loosely cover pigling with a sheet of aluminium foil. Set the pan in the oven. Allow pigling to bake for about one hour. Mix half a cup of soya sauce and quarter of a cup sesame seed oil. Remove pigling from oven, spoon over pan juices and brush with soya/sesame oil mixture. Cover and allow to bake for a further half hour. Add pineapple juice to the roast as required. When pigling is cooked through, pierce thigh section with a sharp knife and the liquid will run clear. Remove foil, and allow suckling pig to brown all over, basting continually with pan juices. Remove from oven when the skin is a rich brown colour.

Place pigling on serving platter with an apple in the mouth if desired. Spoon a little gravy over roast to keep it moist. Strain away remaining gravy and thicken with a little cornstarch. Pour into a gravy boat and serve. Garnish platter with halved pineapple rings and cherries.

Roasted potatoes, stuffing, English mustard, a loaf of crusty bread, and a fresh garden salad make excellent accompaniments.

Stuffing for Roast Suckling Pig

250 gm butter
2 large onions, chopped fine
2" piece fresh ginger, peeled and chopped fine
1 large pod fresh garlic, peeled and chopped fine
250 gm sausage meat, chopped
250 gm bacon, chopped
Liver, heart and kidneys of the pig, washed and chopped into small pieces
3 stalks of celery, chopped fine
3 green chillies, chopped fine
1 large bunch green coriander, washed and chopped fine
2 tsp garam masala
½ tsp freshly ground black pepper
2 cups breadcrumbs
2 cans condensed mushroom soup
2 cups hot water
Salt to taste

In a large heavy-based pot over moderate flame place the butter and chopped onions. Fry until onions are translucent. Add the chopped ginger and garlic, and fry until fragrant. Add bacon and sausage meat. Lower heat. When the bacon begins to brown, add the chopped liver, heart and kidneys. Continue frying. Stir in next three ingredients. Sprinkle over garam masala and ground black pepper. Stir well and allow the mixture to cook for about five minutes. Add mushroom soup to the mixture together with hot water, and stir well. Add in breadcrumbs, a little at a time until completely utilized. Test for salt. Continue stirring the stuffing until it is firm. Remove from fire.

Rice

A Note on Rice

Rice is to the Indian what pasta is to the Italian, and noodles are to the Chinese. While Anglo-Indians also enjoy bread and chapatis, rice maintains pride of place. In India, there are almost as many varieties of rice as there are ways of cooking the grain. In South India, parboiled rice is preferred, and Anglo-Indians from that part of the country enjoy cooking and eating it over raw rice. Parboiled rice is treated to preserve the food value lost in polishing.

For the novice I recommend the simpler recipes set down at the beginning of this chapter. One can graduate to the more complicated pulaos and biryanis once the technique has been mastered. Rice has over the centuries become a universal staple because it has that unique quality which allows it to blend in perfectly with any entrée, whether it be vegetarian, meat, fish or fowl.

I advocate the use of raw rice. The long-grain variety suffices. For, besides being cheaper, it is a better-cooking rice. The long-grain variety cooks up to a white, fluffy consistency which is easily digested. For the preparation of biryanis and pulaos, however, it is essential to use 'Basmati' rice of the best quality. For nothing can compare with a platter of fragrant Basmati cooked in ghee, gleaming like a bed of pearls upon which succulent morsels of lamb or chicken lie—adorned with a colourful array of garnishes. Basmati has come into its own with the renewed interest in Indian cuisine all around the globe. A native of the Punjab, Basmati is incomparable for texture and fragrance.

Cooked rice must always be allowed to 'air' uncovered for at least ten minutes before being transferred to a platter ready for serving. This allows the dish of rice to dry out, making for easier separation of the individual grains.

Rice lends itself admirably to garnishing. Fragrant biryanis and rich pulaos offer a never-ending parade of possibilities, capable of firing the imagination of even the dullest cook. In Mogul India, where many of the more exotic dishes were concocted, cooks slaved for hours over platters piled high with mounds of fragrant rice, dressing them with elaborate decorations to please the eye and whet the appetite. Delectable flowers carved from tomatoes, radishes and carrots rested alongside rich, dark koftas and dainty morsels of spiced mutton. Burnished salvers piled high with rice streaked a brilliant orange colour by strands of kesar (saffron), were served up with succulent meats and salad accompaniments.

Garnishes of pistachio nuts, cashewnuts dyed different hues, almonds and raisins, adorned even the simplest of dishes. Varak (beaten silver) was carelessly fluttered over pulaos and also adorned a large array of sweet meats. Even the humble kitcheree of Central India, so loved by the British, served with a simple garnish of fried onions strewn over the top, can take pride of place at any table. Hard-boiled eggs, halved and set on a bed of rice, is a simple eye-catching garnish.

Indeed, there is a veritable variety of ways in which the imaginative cook can dress up a platter of rice. I have tried to suggest suitable garnishes after most of the recipes, but they are interchangeable, and can all be used with confidence.

To Cook Rice

One does not need any special equipment for cooking rice. A deep, heavy-based pot with a tight-fitting lid, a colander and slotted spoon are all that is necessary. 450 gm of rice measure approximately 2½ cups, and rice increases in bulk a little over three times when cooked; therefore, allow one cup of rice for two servings when it is the principal accompaniment to the entrée, and one cup for three servings when it is being served as a side dish along with bread or chapatis.

To boil one cup of rice, wash and drain it in tepid water. Place in a pot and pour in six cups of water together with a teaspoon of salt. Boil the rice over a moderate flame until the water comes to a full rolling boil. Lower heat and allow the rice to simmer for about fifteen to eighteen minutes, after which one should test it for doneness. The easiest way to do this is to scoop out a few grains and press them between the thumb and forefinger to ensure they are not hard in the centre. Grains should be tender, but still firm. When cooked through, strain the rice through a colander and allow it to sit until excess water has drained away. Fluff with a long-pronged fork and pile on a platter before serving.

In order to cook rice by the absorption method which retains all the starch, one needs to bring two cups of water to a boil with half a teaspoon of salt. Place washed rice in the pot, cover and reduce heat to a minimum. Allow rice to cook for about fifteen to eighteen minutes. Remove from stove but keep the lid on the pot for a further ten minutes. Remove lid. The individual grains should be tender. Fluff the rice and serve on a platter.

Rice can also be baked with excellent results. In fact, pulaos and biryanis never fail, and yield perfect results when baked in an oven at 180° C. Every recipe for rice set down in this book, with the exception of plain boiled rice, is baked to complete the cooking process.

Peas Pulao

Serves 4-6 persons

2 cups Basmati rice
¼ cup cooking oil
1 medium cooking onion, sliced fine
2" piece of cinnamon
3 whole green or white cardamoms, split
3 whole cloves
1 tbsp ginger/garlic paste
1 tsp salt
1 cup of fresh green peas
4 cups water or stock

Preheat oven to 180° C. Wash rice in tepid water, drain and set aside. Place a heavy-based pot with tight-fitting lid over moderate flame. Pour in oil. When oil is hot add sliced onions and next three ingredients. Fry until onions are golden brown in colour. Add ginger/garlic paste to the pot. Lower heat, and continue frying the spices until they release their fragrant aroma. Place rice in the pot and continue frying until the grains of rice are covered with the oil/spice mixture. Add salt and green peas. Pour in stock or water. Stir once more. Cover the pot and place in preheated oven. Bake the peas pulao for about twenty minutes, or until the grains of rice are cooked through. Remove from oven and allow the rice to 'air' for about ten minutes. Remove whole spices that rise to the top, fluff rice and pile high on a platter to serve.

To garnish: Slice a large onion fine and fry to a crisp brown. Drain on a paper towel to remove excess oil.

Scatter lightly over mound of rice just before serving.

Peas pulao is excellent with a simple chicken or meat and potato curry, and a plate of fried papads on the side.

Coconut Rice

Serves 4-6 persons

2 cups Basmati rice
¼ cup cooking oil
1 medium cooking onion, sliced fine
2" piece of cinnamon
4 whole cloves
4 whole green or white cardamoms, split
1 tbsp ginger/garlic paste
½ tsp turmeric powder
1 tsp salt
2 cups thick coconut milk
2 cups water

Preheat oven to 180° C. Wash rice in tepid water, drain and set aside. Place a heavy-based pot with tight-fitting lid over a moderate flame. Pour in oil. When the oil is hot, add the sliced onions and the next three spices. Fry until the onions are a golden-brown colour. Blend turmeric powder with ginger/garlic paste. Place the paste in the pot, lower heat, and fry until the spices release their fragrant aroma. Add rice. Continue frying, stirring continually to ensure the grains of rice do not adhere to the bottom of the pot. Pour in coconut milk and water. Add salt to taste. Stir well and cover the pot. Place in preheated oven until the rice is cooked through.

Alternately, if one wishes to cook the rice upon the stove, the flame below the pot may be reduced to a minimum, and the rice allowed to simmer over very low heat until the grains are tender. Remove lid from the pot and allow the rice to 'air' for about ten minutes. Discard whole spices that rise to the top. Fluff rice with a long-pronged fork. Arrange on a platter and serve.

Coconut rice is a fragrant dish that needs very little garnishing, except perhaps, a few crisp fried onions scattered over the top. Excellent when served with kofta curry, a simple cabbage foogath and mango chutney.

Tomato Pulao

Serves 6-8 persons

3 cups Basmati rice
1/3 cup cooking oil
1 large onion, sliced fine
2 2" pieces cinnamon
3 whole cloves
3 green cardamoms split
3 bay leaves
2 tbsp ginger/garlic paste
2 large tomatoes, diced
½ cup of tomato sauce (ketchup)
1 cup of thick coconut milk
4½ cups water
1½ tsp salt, or to taste
1 tsp sugar

Preheat oven to 180° and 50° C. Wash rice in tepid water,

drain and set aside. In a large heavy-based pot over moderate heat, pour in oil. When hot, add sliced onions and next four ingredients. Fry onions and whole spices until the onion are a golden brown colour. Place ginger/garlic paste in the pot and fry until the spices begin to release their fragrant aroma. Add washed rice, lower heat and fry, stirring continuously to ensure the rice/spice mixture does not adhere to the bottom of the pot. Place tomatoes in the pot together with the coconut milk and tomato sauce. Continue mixing until the rice is well blended with the tomato and coconut. Stir in water. Add salt and sugar. Cover the pot and place in preheated oven. Bake tomato pulao until the rice is cooked through. Remove from heat and allow the pulao to 'air' for about ten minutes.

Remove whole spices that come to the surface, and gently fork the rice to separate the grains. Pile high on a platter and serve garnished with a layer of crisp brown fried onions. Set cherry tomatoes and/or halved hard-boiled eggs into the bed of rice.

Serve tomato pulao with a meat curry, vegetable foogath and kachumbur.

Kitcheree

Serves 6-8 persons

Kitcheree or kedgeree, as the British in India liked to call it, is traditionally a rice/lentil mixture. The recipe for 'kedgeree', when prepared for British expatriates in India, reads as follows, and I quote from my Great-Aunt Ethel's hand-written notes:

'Half a teacup of masoor dal, one teacup of fine white rice, half a Bombay onion, a heaped dessert spoon of butter, and a little salt. Wash and clean dal in a deep metal pot with sufficient water. Throw in chopped onion and allow to simmer on medium heat until half cooked; add your washed rice to the pot. The water level should stand one inch above the rice/dal mixture. Cover and allow to simmer over low heat, lifting the lid now and again to stir the dish. Kedgeree may burn if allowed to cook too long without stirring. When all the liquid has been absorbed, stir in the butter. Remove from fire and serve hot for breakfast.'

The actual recipe for kitcheree is a far cry from the above. A staple in Anglo-Indian households, it is often served to patients recovering from lengthy illnesses because of its high nutritional content. Kitcheree can be eaten accompanied by a simple vegetable dish, but it is truly delicious served up with kofta curry, or with a meat and potato curry.

3 cups of Basmati rice
1 cup masoor dal (red lentils)
2 medium onions, sliced fine
½ cup vegetable oil, or the equivalent of ghee
2 2" pieces of cinnamon
5 whole cloves
4 large brown cardamom pods, split
2 bay leaves
2 tbsp ginger/garlic paste
½ tsp of turmeric powder

½ tsp chilli powder
1 cup coconut milk
1 large tomato, diced
2 tsp salt, or to taste
5 cups of water

Preheat oven to 180° C. Wash rice and lentils together in tepid water, drain and set aside. Place heavy-based pot with tight-fitting lid over moderate heat. Pour in oil or ghee and fry onions, cinnamon, cloves, cardamoms and bay leaves, until the onions are a golden brown colour. Make a paste of the next three ingredients, lower heat and add masala paste to the pot. Continue frying for a further few minutes. Add the rice/lentil mixture, and fry, stirring continuously until the mixture is evenly coated with the spices. Add diced tomato. Pour in coconut milk with five cups of water. Stir in salt. Cover the pot and place in preheated oven to bake until the grains of rice and lentils are cooked through.

Take kitcheree from oven and allow to 'air' for about ten minutes. Remove whole spices that rise to the top, and fluff grains of rice and lentils. Allow to cool.

Kitcheree has a mealy consistency that lends itself beautifully to the simplest of garnishes. A few fried onions strewn over top, or a couple of halved, hard-boiled eggs set in the mound of rice suffices. Serve kitcheree with a simple curry of chicken or meat. A side dish of cauliflower foogath and kachumbur salad make excellent accompaniments.

Green Masala Pulao

Serves 4-6 persons

2 cups Basmati rice
¼ cup vegetable oil
1 medium onion, sliced fine
2 2" pieces of cinnamon
4 whole cloves
4 whole green or white cardamoms, split
8 flakes of garlic, peeled and chopped
2" piece of fresh ginger, peeled and chopped
1 medium bunch fresh coriander, washed and chopped
2 green chillies, chopped
½ level tsp turmeric powder
2 cups stock
½ cup beaten curd
1 tsp salt, or to taste
1½ cup water

Preheat oven to 180° C. Wash rice in tepid water, drain and set aside. Place a heavy-based pot over moderate flame and pour in oil. When the oil is hot, add sliced onions and the next three ingredients. Fry until the onions are a golden brown colour. Grind the next four ingredients to a paste and mix with turmeric powder. Lower heat, place the masala paste in the pot and fry, stirring frequently to ensure the spices do not adhere to the bottom of the pot. Add rice, and continue frying until the grains of rice are well coated with the spice mixture. Add two cups of stock and beaten curd. Add salt. Pour in water. Stir the rice/stock mixture once more to blend. Cover the pot and place in preheated oven. Bake green masala pulao until the grains of rice are cooked through. Remove from oven and allow the pulao to 'air' for about ten minutes. Remove whole spices that rise to the top. Fluff the rice to separate the grains. Pile high on a platter and serve.

To garnish green masala pulao, scatter chopped green coriander leaves over top and place halved cherry tomatoes at intervals around the platter.

Serve with dry fried meat, or masoor dal, potato sabzi and kachumbur.

Chicken Pulao

Serves 4-6 persons

2 cups Basmati rice
1 kg chicken parts, remove skin
1 tsp garam masala
1 tsp salt
4½ cups water
¼ cup vegetable oil
1 medium onion, sliced fine
2 2" pieces cinnamon
4 whole cloves
4 whole green or white cardamoms, split
1 tbsp ginger/garlic paste
½ tsp turmeric powder
1 tomato, chopped fine
Salt to taste

Preheat oven to 180° C. Wash rice, drain and set aside. Place next four ingredients in a pot and parboil chicken over moderate heat. Chicken should be firm. Strain and separate chicken from stock. Place a large heavy-based pot over moderate heat and pour in vegetable oil. When the oil is hot, add sliced onions and next three spices. Fry the onions a golden brown colour. Add turmeric powder to ginger/garlic paste and place in the pot. Lower heat, and continue frying until the spices release their fragrant aroma. Place chicken parts in the pot and fry, coating the chicken pieces with the spice mixture. Stir in rice. Fry rice/chicken mixture for a further few minutes. Add chopped tomato. Pour in stock. Stir well and test for sufficient salt. Cover and place in preheated oven to bake until the rice and chicken is cooked through. Remove from oven and allow to 'air' for about ten minutes. Remove whole spices that rise to the top. Gently fluff the chicken pulao to separate the grains of rice. Pile on a large platter and serve.

To garnish chicken pulao: Strew crisp fried onions over top, and set masala fried potatoes into the bed of rice at regular intervals.

Masala fried potatoes: Select six medium-sized potatoes, peel and boil in salted water until cooked through. Drain and set aside. Mix together half a teaspoon turmeric powder, half a teaspoon salt, and one teaspoon chilli powder. Lightly dust potatoes with this mixture. Fry in hot oil until evenly browned. Remove from oil and set in the bed of chicken pulao.

Chicken pulao is a meal in itself and needs very little accompaniment. A dish of raita and papads suffice.

Chicken Biryani

Serves 6 persons

3 cups Basmati rice
1 medium fryer (750-800 gm, skinned and jointed)
10 tbsp butter
4 onions, peeled and finely sliced
2" piece fresh ginger, peeled and chopped fine
8 garlic cloves, peeled and chopped fine
8 whole cloves
6 2" pieces of cinnamon
2 tsp turmeric
2 tsp garam masala
1 tsp chilli powder
4 cups chicken stock
1½ cups hot water
2 tsp salt, or to taste
½ cup heavy cream
1 tsp saffron threads

GARNISH

4 onions, sliced fine
4 oz raisins, plumped in a little water
4 oz cashewnuts
Masala fried potatoes

Preheat oven to 180° C. Wash rice in tepid water, drain and set aside. Place three tablespoons butter in a large heavy-based pot over moderate heat. Add chicken pieces and fry until golden. Remove and set aside. Add a further four tablespoons butter to the pot and fry the four sliced onions together with chopped ginger and garlic. Add next three ingredients and continue frying until onions are golden in colour. Make a paste of the next three ingredients with a little stock, and lower paste into the pot. Fry until the spices begin to release their fragrant aroma. Add in rice and chicken pieces. Stir continually to ensure the mixture does not adhere to the bottom of the pot. Add four cups chicken stock, one-and-a-half cups hot water and salt. Cover, and allow the biryani to simmer on very low heat. Heat table cream, crush saffron threads and add to the cream. Stir into biryani, replace lid and place the biryani in preheated oven. Bake until the rice and chicken is cooked through. Take the biryani from oven and allow it to 'air' for ten minutes. Remove whole spices that have risen to the top. Gently fluff the biryani before arranging on a large platter, ready for garnishing.

To garnish: Fry four sliced onions crisp and brown in three tablespoons butter. Drain on a paper towel. Place cashewnuts in the pan and fry together with plumped raisins. Strew onions on top of the biryani, and sprinkle over with cashewnuts and raisins.

Masala fried potatoes (recipe given as garnish for chicken pulao) may also be used to garnish chicken biryani.

Biryani is a meal in itself. Excellent accompaniments are raita, cucumber salad and papads.

Mutton Biryani

Serves 10 persons

5 cups Basmati rice, washed twice
5 cups water
1 cup ghee

2 kg mutton, cut into serving portions
6 large potatoes, cut in half and cooked in salted water
1 cup ghee
6 large onions, sliced fine
½ tsp clove powder
1 tsp freshly ground pepper
½ tsp cardamom powder
2 tsp cinnamon powder
2 tbsp cumin powder
2 tbsp coriander powder
1 tsp chilli powder
1 medium bunch green coriander, washed and chopped fine
1 medium bunch fresh mint, washed and chopped fine
2 cups curds
Salt to taste
½ cup heavy cream
½ tsp saffron (kesar) strands

Wash rice and place in a large pot with a teaspoon of salt, five cups water and a tablespoon ghee. Cover and allow to cook on minimum heat until the water has been absorbed. Remove lid, fork rice and set aside. Place half the ghee in a heavy-based pot over moderate heat, add sliced onions and fry till golden brown. Remove and set aside. Grind quarter the amount of fried onions to a paste. Add remaining ghee to the pot. With a little water make a paste of the next four ingredients. Stir into the pot and fry until the spices release their fragrance. Lower heat. Add mutton and continue frying until the morsels of meat are well coated with the spices. Mix together cumin, coriander and chilli powders. Sprinkle over mutton mixture and continue frying. Add quarter cup curd to the pot. Continue frying the mutton, adding curd a little at a time until one cup has been utilized. Add salt to taste. Lower onion paste into the pot and mix well. Sprinkle over chopped green coriander and mint. Cover the pot and allow the mutton/spice mixture to cook over low heat until the meat is tender, but not falling off the bone. There should be about five cups of gravy clinging to the succulent pieces of meat.

Heat cream and crush saffron threads. Mix together.

Assembling the biryani: In a heavy-based pot with a tight-fitting lid, place one-third portion of mutton mixture. Cover with one-third portion of remaining curd, and a third of fried onions. Top with one-third portion of rice. Continue layering, meat, curds, onion and rice. The top layer should be of rice. Pierce biryani right through to the bottom of the pot with a long pronged fork. Pour saffron mixture over. Cover the pot and place in a preheated (180° C) oven. Bake biryani for forty minutes, or until the rice/meat mixture is cooked through. Remove from oven, but do not remove lid for a further fifteen minutes.

To garnish: Masala fried potatoes as given in chicken pulao recipe.

Biryani lends itself to any number of garnishes, and is equally delicious served with fried onions and halved hard-boiled eggs set into the rice at intervals, or an elaborate garnish comprising all the former ingredients together with fried cashewnuts, almonds and raisins.

Junglee Pulao

Serves 8 persons

Junglee pulao is a typical Anglo-Indian dish that came into being, I believe, during the turn of the century; at any rate, before iceboxes and refrigerators were invented. In the searing heat of the Indian summer, lethargy and a loss of appetite often resulted in a large amount of curry and rice being left over from lunch, and the prospect of serving it again for dinner was a most unappetizing thought. Rice could always be converted into pudding and served as dessert, but a dish of curry posed a different problem.

Faced with this dilemma, the thrifty mistress of the house placed the dish of curry in her meatsafe, and the following day added a few vegetables to it, together with a cup of curd. Frying an onion, she sautéed a cup or two of rice in a pot and blended the curry and vegetable mixture in with the rice. She then covered the pot and cooked the mixture until the grains of rice had absorbed all the curry sauce and curd. Viola! She had created junglee pulao. Today, in India and abroad, Anglo-Indians enjoy a refined version of this dish, concocted by an inspired cook.

3 cups Basmati rice
1 kg beef (cubed and cooked in 6 cups of water with 1 tsp garam masala and 1 tsp of salt)
½ cup cooking oil
1 large onion, finely sliced
2 2" pieces cinnamon
4 whole cloves
4 whole white or green cardamoms, split
3 bay leaves
1 tbsp coriander seeds
1 tbsp cumin seeds
3 whole red chillies

2 tbsp fresh ginger/garlic paste
½ tsp turmeric powder
1 small bunch fresh green coriander, stalks removed and chopped
2 green chillies, slit lengthways
1 cup beaten curd
1 large tomato, chopped
½ cup of fresh peas
1 medium potato, cut into 8 pieces
1 medium carrot, diced
4 cups beef broth
Juice of 1 lime
1 tsp salt

Preheat oven to 180° C. Wash rice in tepid water, drain and set aside. Over moderate heat place a heavy-based pot and pour in cooking oil. When the oil is hot add sliced onions, cinnamon, cloves, cardamom and bay leaves. Fry until the onions are a golden brown colour. Lower heat. Grind the next three ingredients to a paste and blend together with the ginger/garlic paste and turmeric powder. Place spice paste in the pot together with chopped green coriander and chillies. Fry, stirring continually until the spices begin to release their fragrant aroma. Drain stock from the cooked beef and set aside. Place the cubed beef in the pot and fry with spice mixture until the pieces of meat are well coated. Add Basmati rice to the pot and continue frying. Mix in beaten curd, followed by the tomatoes, peas, potato and carrot. Pour in beef broth and lime juice. Test for sufficient salt, and if required, add salt to taste. Mix all ingredients together. Cover the pot and place in preheated oven to bake until the rice and vegetables are cooked through. Take from oven, remove the lid and allow the junglee pulao to 'air' for at least ten minutes. Remove whole spices that surface. Gently fluff the pulao and serve piled high on a large platter.

Junglee pulao needs very little garnishing. A small bunch of green coriander, washed and chopped fine, may be strewn over the top, or a few cherry tomatoes may be set in the bed of rice. A dish of raita, together with a plate of papads, make excellent accompaniments.

Another excellent accompaniment is devil chutney, whose fiery, hot/sweet taste complements this dish. Junglee pulao is a good 'keeper', and tastes even better when served the next day. Cover remains of the dish, and store in the refrigerator. Reheat in the oven before serving.

Yakhni Pulao

Serves 4-6 persons

FOR THE MEAT

1 kg mutton, cut into bite-sized pieces
1 whole onion
2 green chillies, slit
6 flakes garlic, peeled
1" piece fresh ginger, peeled and roughly chopped
1 tbsp coriander seeds
1" piece of cinnamon
4 whole cloves
3 green or white whole cardamoms, split
1 tsp salt
5 cups of water

FOR THE RICE

2 cups Basmati rice
4 oz butter

1 large onion, sliced fine
2 2" pieces of cinnamon
4 large brown cardamoms, split
4 cloves
2 tbsp ginger/garlic paste
1 tsp kala jeera
1 cup curd
1 tsp salt

Preheat oven to 180° C. Wash rice in tepid water, drain and set aside. Place the mutton in a deep pot. Place the next eight ingredients in a small square of muslin, gather the top together to form a pouch, and tie with string. Drop the pouch into the pot with mutton. Add five cups of water and a teaspoon of salt to the pot. Allow the mutton to cook over moderate heat until tender, but not falling off the bone. Strain through a colander. Set aside the broth, of which there should be three cups. Add hot water if necessary to make four cups of liquid. Separate mutton, and discard muslin pouch and spices. Place a heavy-based pot with the butter over moderate heat. Add sliced onion, whole cinnamon, cardamoms and cloves. Fry until the onions are a golden colour. Add ginger/garlic paste and kala jeera, and fry until the spices release their fragrant aroma. Place the meat in the pot and continue frying for a further few minutes. Stir in two cups rice, and a cup of beaten curd. Mix well. Pour in four cups of liquid. Test for sufficient salt. Cover the rice/meat mixture and place in preheated oven to bake until the rice is cooked through. Remove from oven and allow the pulao to 'air' for about ten minutes before removing whole spices that have risen to the top. Fluff the rice, gently separating the grains.

Pile high on a large platter and serve garnished with

crisp, fried onions and halved hard-boiled eggs set in the platter of rice.

Serve with raita, dal and a vegetable side dish.

Brown Fried Rice

Makes 6 servings

This is a deviation of the Parsi recipe that is traditionally served with Dhansak. I have cooked it on many occasions, serving it alongside a dal curry, accompanied by a dish of beef cutlets and fried potatoes.

3 cups Basmati rice
2 tsp sugar
2 tbsp butter or ghee
1" piece of cinnamon
4 whole cloves
4 green cardamoms, split
6 cups beef broth
1 tsp salt

Preheat oven to 180° C. Wash rice in tepid water, drain and set aside. Place a heavy-based pot over low heat and sprinkle sugar evenly on the bottom. Allow it to caramelize. Lower heat and add the next six ingredients to the pot together with the rice. Stir. Cover the pot and place in preheated oven to bake until the rice is cooked through. Remove from oven and allow the rice to 'air' for about ten minutes. Remove spices that rise to the top. Fluff gently to separate the grains. Serve piled high on a platter.

Garnish with fresh green coriander leaves, washed and chopped fine, or strew sliced onions, fried a crisp brown in a little butter, over top.

Serve as suggested above.

Prawn Pulao

Serves 6 persons

3 cups Basmati rice
1 kg fresh prawns (peel and devein prawns, placing the skins in a separate pot. Add five cups water and a teaspoon of salt to the skins. Cook over high heat until the water reaches a full rolling boil. Strain through a colander. Discard skins.)
1/3 cup of vegetable oil
1 large onion, sliced fine
2 2" sticks of cinnamon
3 green cardamoms, split
2 bay leaves
2 tbsp ginger/garlic paste
1 large tomato, diced
1 cup thick coconut milk
1 tsp salt, or to taste
1 tsp sugar

Preheat oven to 180° C. Wash rice in tepid water, drain and set aside. Place a heavy-based pot with oil over moderate heat. When the oil is hot add next four ingredients and fry until the onions are golden. Lower heat, and place ginger/

garlic paste in the pot. Continue frying until the oil rises to the surface and the spices smell fragrant. Add rice and fresh prawns. Fry rice/prawn mixture, stirring continually to ensure the grains of rice do not adhere to the bottom of the pot. Stir in tomato, coconut milk, salt and sugar. Mix well. Pour in five cups of prawn liquor. Stir once more. Cover and place in preheated oven. Bake prawn pulao until the grains of rice are tender. Remove from heat and allow the pulao to 'air' for at least ten minutes. Fluff and pile high on a platter to serve.

This delicate pulao has an incredible fragrance, and actually needs no enhancement, but if one would like to garnish it, a sprinkling of crisp brown fried onions would suffice.

Serve prawn pulao with a few simple accompaniments such as vegetable foogath, dal, raita, with papads to round off the meal. A good mango chutney also complements the dish.

Tina's Lime Rice

Makes 6 servings

3 cups Basmati rice
1 tsp salt
4 cups water
½ freshly grated coconut
½ cup fresh lime juice
1 level tsp turmeric
¾ cup pure ghee
1 level tsp mustard seeds
1 cup chopped cashewnuts

A few fresh curry leaves, chopped
5 whole green chillies, chopped
1 medium bunch green coriander leaves, washed and chopped

Preheat oven to 180° C. Wash rice, drain and place in a pot with salt and four cups water. Cover and parboil over low heat until the rice has absorbed all the liquid. Remove from heat and set aside. Mix together the next three ingredients and add to the rice, gently forking the grains to mix in the coconut/turmeric/lime mixture. Melt the ghee in a frying pan and add mustard seeds. When they start to sputter add fresh curry leaves, cashewnuts and chopped green chillies. Remove from flame, add chopped green coriander to the pan. Stir the mixture into the rice, cover with a tight-fitting lid, and bake in the oven until the grains of rice are tender. Remove from oven and allow the rice to 'air' for about ten minutes. Gently fluff to separate the grains. Serve piled high on a platter.

To garnish lime rice: Strew chopped green coriander over the platter. Lime rice complements a fish moley, or a delicately spiced mutton korma. Serve with a fresh onion salad and papads on the side.

Chinese Fried Rice

Serves 4-6 persons

The following is a rather unorthodox recipe for Chinese fried rice. However, it is an excellent way of utilizing leftover roasted chicken, ham and cooked white rice. Cooked white rice, stored overnight in the refrigerator, renders the grains firm and separate. Combined with a few vegetables and served together with a stir fry, this dish makes an excellent impromptu dinner.

3 cups cooked long grain rice
2 tbsp vegetable oil
2 tbsp Chinese sesame seed oil
5 flakes garlic, peeled and minced
1" piece fresh ginger, peeled and minced
2 rashers bacon, chopped fine
1 cup leftover chicken roast, shredded
1 cup raw prawns
5 whole green onions, chopped fine
2 green chillies, chopped fine
2 medium-sized carrots, scraped and cut into matchsticks
1 cup of finely shredded cabbage
½ cup of cooked peas
2 tbsp soya sauce
2 tbsp oyster sauce
4 eggs, beaten
1 onion, chopped fine
1 green chilli, chopped fine
2 tbsp sesame seed oil

Place a large heavy-based pot over moderate heat. Add vegetable oil and two tablespoons Chinese sesame oil to the pot. When the oil is hot, add minced ginger and garlic to the pot and fry briskly, stirring continuously. Add next three ingredients, and continue frying until the prawns turn a rosy colour. Stir in following five ingredients. Continue frying. Pour sauces over meat/vegetable mixture.

Mix well, ensuring the meat and vegetables are coated with sauces. Stir rice into the pot a little at a time. When all the rice has been incorporated with the meat and vegetables, remove from heat. Cover and allow to sit for at least five minutes. Meanwhile, beat four eggs with a little salt, add in chopped onion and green chilli. Place two tablespoons sesame seed oil in frying pan and when hot, add the egg mixture. Lower heat. Rotate pan and spread egg mixture to form a thin omelette; flip and cook top side. Remove from heat. Cut into strips. Set aside. Remove lid from fried rice and gently separate the grains. Pile on a platter, garnish with chopped green onion and omelette strips. Serve with Chinese accompaniments.

Curries and Masala Fries

A Note on Curries

'Every grain must be covered, or it is simply boiled rice,' my grandfather once observed, while on his plate the mighty mound of rice grew. He topped it with a liberal portion of meat and potato curry.

Curries are prepared in India of every type of meat, fish, fowl and vegetable. The ingredients vary from north to south. In northern India curries are often cooked in ghee. These savoury concoctions made from a subtle blend of spices are often thickened with curd, cream or ground almonds. The curries of northern India are milder than their counterparts in the south. South Indian curries are often a fiery blend of spices with an abundance of chillies. The milk and meat of fresh coconut is incorporated to give them body and flavour.

Anglo-Indian curries, generally speaking, try to hit the happy medium, and are neither too hot, nor too mild. I rather like to think of them as fricassees, rich with the nutty juices of coconut or almond, and flavoured with an assortment of spices.

The following points are worthy of note when preparing curries:

Because powdered spices lose their freshness and aroma within a very short period of time, it is important to purchase only small quantities, which should then be stored in airtight containers on a cool, dark kitchen shelf, away from direct sunlight. In the interest of convenience, I advocate the use of powdered spices, except in those cases when it is absolutely necessary to grind together certain combinations, without which one would lose the unique taste associated with particular dishes.

Curries can be successfully cooked in the oven. A stainless steel pot with a good-fitting lid, or a deep flame-proof casserole is all that is required. Slow, even baking allows the meat to cook in its own juices, with water, coconut milk or curd being added at the end of the cooking process to produce a rich and flavourful gravy. Besides, very little attention need be paid to the curry as it cooks to perfection in the oven.

Most curries keep well. In fact, they often taste better when served the following day. Curried dishes that have been cooked in spices blended with vinegar, without the addition of any vegetable, can be refrigerated for up to a month. But when fresh coconut meat or milk has been incorporated into the dish, it is best not to keep it for more than three days in the refrigerator, after which time it is likely to spoil. The same is true of curries made with curd. Fish and shell fish curries keep well for up to two days in the refrigerator.

Masala paste should always be fried in hot oil or ghee over low heat until the oil separates from the spices, and the raw smell disappears. When ready, masala paste gives off a fragrant aroma. This is one step in the making of curries that should not be hurried. Take the time to ensure that spices are fried properly. Everyday curries need very little in the way of garnishing. Chopped green coriander leaves, or a sprinkling of crisp fried onions strewn over the dish are quite adequate.

In this chapter I have endeavoured to cover methodically every step in the preparation of the various types of curries. Mutton and beef are interchangeable, and either meat can be successfully used.

Pepper Water and Dry Fry

Pepper water, liberally ladled onto a mound of steaming white rice, accompanied by a generous portion of dry fry, served with a kachumbur salad and papads on the side, has all the makings of a satisfying lunch.

As the pungent aroma of pepper water wafts through the air, I am unwittingly transported to a different place in time. This delicious combination of spices, redolent with the aroma of curry leaves, never fails to stir up memories of my childhood. Standing over the pot, stirring the simmering spices immersed in a bath of stock, I recall the carefree days of my youth, and the many visits we made during the summer holidays to my Great-Aunt Ethel's home. She lived not far from the railway station, and while swinging from the limbs of the guava tree, or playing 'tea party' with my sister Tina, one could hear in the distance the whistle of the great 'puffing Billies' (coal engines), as they chugged in and out of Burhanpur station.

Great-Aunt Ethel's pepper water and dry fry was by far the best I have ever tasted. 'A man would walk miles for this stuff,' my father once observed, helping himself, filling his cup brimful of pepper water for the second time; all the while mopping his copiously sweating brow with a large white handkerchief.

'Eat up,' Aunty Ethel urged. 'Puts hair on your chest.' We needed no encouragement.

Any pepper water remaining after lunch was reheated and served up in a soup tureen at the dinner table. On occasion, it even appeared at lunch the following day. Ladled out over mounds of rice, it was equally delicious served with a savoury dish of meat or chicken, with a vegetable foogath to round off the meal.

Pepper Water

Serves 6 persons

1 kg beef, cut into bite-sized pieces (pressure-cook beef in 8 cups of water, together with salt to taste, 2 or 3 stalks of fresh curry leaves, and ½ onion, chopped. When the meat is tender, discard curry leaves, strain and set aside. There should be 8 cups of broth.)
2 tbsp cooking oil
½ tsp rye (mustard seed)
1 small onion, chopped fine
2 stalks fresh curry leaves
½ tsp cumin powder
½ tsp coriander powder
¼ tsp chilli powder, or to taste
1 tbsp fresh ginger/garlic paste
1 tbsp whole coriander seeds
1 tbsp whole cumin seeds
4 whole dried red chillies
2 tbsp tamarind purée
Salt to taste

Place a deep stainless steel pot over medium heat and pour in cooking oil. Add mustard seeds. When they begin to sputter, place chopped onion and curry leaves including stalks into the pot. Lower heat. Allow the onions to brown before adding the next four ingredients, made into a paste. Fry the masala, stirring continuously until it begins to release its fragrant aroma. Pour in eight cups of beef stock. Add the remaining five ingredients to the pot. Cover and allow to simmer on very low heat for approximately half an hour. Add a little water to the pot as required. The blended spices will release their fragrance, and the essence of curry leaves will predominate. Remove from heat. The pepper water should be pungent and slightly sour. Strain into a soup tureen. Serve hot with dry fry.

Dry Fry

Serves 6 persons

1 kg cooked beef, cut into bite-sized pieces (see pepper water)
1/3 cup cooking oil
1 large onion, chopped fine
1 stalk curry leaves
2 tbsp fresh ginger/garlic paste
1 tbsp cumin powder
1 tbsp coriander powder
1 tsp chilli powder, or to taste
1 tsp Kashmiri chilli powder (optional)
1 large ripe tomato, chopped fine
2 large potatoes, cubed and boiled in salted water
1 tbsp tamarind purée
Salt to taste

Place a stainless steel pot over medium heat and pour in oil. When the oil is hot, throw in the curry leaves together with chopped onion. Fry the onions golden brown. Lower heat. Make a paste of the next five ingredients and place in the pot. Fry the masala paste, stirring continuously. When the spices release their fragrant aroma, add the pieces of cooked meat. Fry meat and spices together for a few minutes until the pieces of meat are well coated with the spices. Add chopped tomatoes and cooked potatoes.

Place tamarind purée in the pot, add salt to taste. Cover the pot and allow the dry fry to simmer for about twenty minutes upon the stove, stirring occasionally. As the liquid evaporates, a residual thick, dark gravy will remain clinging to the morsels of meat and potato. Remove from fire.

Serve pepper water and dry fry with plain white rice, papads and a kachumbur salad on the side.

A Simple Meat and Potato Curry

Serves 6-8 persons

Meat and potato curry is standard fare in Anglo-Indian homes, where it is often eaten at lunch with white rice, dal, a vegetable dish and papads.

1 kg beef steak, or lamb cut into bite-sized pieces
1/3 cup cooking oil
2 medium onions, sliced fine
5 or 6 curry leaves with stalk
2 tbsp fresh ginger/garlic paste
1 heaped tbsp Kashmiri chilli or paprika powder
½ tsp chilli powder, or to taste
1 tbsp cumin powder
1 tbsp coriander powder
2 large potatoes, peeled and cubed
1 large tomato, chopped fine
½ cup beaten curd
1 cup thick coconut milk
1 cup hot water

Salt to taste
1 cup cooked green peas

Place a heavy-based pan with a tight-fitting lid over a moderate flame, and pour in oil. Add sliced onions and curry leaves. Fry the onions golden brown. Lower heat. Make a paste of the next five ingredients, using some of the beaten curd to facilitate the blending. Place in the pan and fry over low heat until the oil separates from the spices. Add meat to the pan and continue frying for a further five minutes, or until all the pieces of meat are well coated with the spices. Mix in chopped tomato and curd. Pour in coconut milk and hot water. Stir in salt. Cover the pan and allow to simmer on the top of the stove until the meat is three-quarters cooked. Remove lid and add cubed potatoes to the pan, together with a little more water if required. Cover and allow to simmer until both meat and potatoes are cooked through. Stir in one cup cooked peas.

Alternately, the water and curd can be omitted from the curry, which is baked in its own juices in the oven (180° C), until the meat is three-quarters cooked. Remove from oven, add potatoes and remaining curds. Replace in oven until meat and potatoes are cooked through. Lastly, add cooked peas to the curry.

Allow the curry to cool for about ten minutes, uncovered, before serving with any or all the above accompaniments.

Gram Dal and Meat Curry

Serves 6-8 persons

1 kg beef undercut or mutton, cut into bite-sized pieces
½ cup of gram dal, washed and soaked for 2 hours in hot water
1/3 cup cooking oil
2 medium onions, sliced fine
A few curry leaves with stalk
1 tbsp coriander powder
1 tsp cumin powder
1 tsp chilli powder
2 tbsp ginger/garlic paste
1 tsp Kashmiri chilli, or paprika powder
½ level tsp turmeric powder
2 green chillies, slit
1 cup coconut milk
1 large tomato, chopped
2 tbsp tamarind purée
Salt to taste
Hot water

Place a heavy-based pan over moderate flame. Pour in oil and add curry leaves. When the oil is hot, add sliced onions and fry till golden brown. Make a paste of the next six ingredients, using a little coconut milk to facilitate the blending. Lower heat, and place masala paste in the pan. Fry for about three minutes, or until the spices release their fragrant aroma. Add meat and gram dal. Fry the spices together with the meat and gram dal, stirring continuously to ensure the mixture does not adhere to the bottom of the pan.

Place next four ingredients in the pan together with two cups of water. Add salt to taste. Stir, cover the pan and allow the curry to simmer gently on the top of the stove for about half an hour. Remove lid and add more water if required. Stir once more and replace the lid. Allow to cook until the meat and dal are both tender. When the curry is ready, there should be a thick, dark lentil gravy with a suggestion of coconut, clinging to the morsels of meat.

Serve gram dal and meat curry, garnished with a few chopped green coriander leaves strewn over top. A platter of cooked rice, papads and a vegetable foogath make excellent accompaniments.

Green Masala Mince

Serves 6-8 persons

1 kg lean ground beef or mutton
1/3 cup cooking oil
4 large onions, chopped fine
A few fresh curry leaves
1 pod garlic, peeled
2" piece of fresh ginger, peeled and chopped
1 large bunch green coriander, washed and chopped
3 green chillies, chopped
1 tsp garam masala
1 tbsp cumin powder
1 level tsp turmeric powder
1 tbsp lime juice
1 tbsp sugar
Salt to taste
2 large potatoes, cubed and cooked in salted water
1 cup of cooked green peas

In a heavy-based pan over a moderate flame heat oil. Add curry leaves and chopped onion. Fry onions until translucent. Grind the next four ingredients into a paste and mix with garam masala, cumin and turmeric powder. Lower heat and place in the pan. Fry the spices until they release their fragrant aroma. Add ground meat and continue frying. Stir in the next three ingredients. Cover the pan and allow the mince to cook in its own juices, stirring from time to time to ensure the spices do not adhere to the bottom of the pan. When the mince is cooked through, add potatoes and peas. Gently simmer the mince for a further ten minutes before removing from the fire.

Place masala mince in a serving dish. Cut one large firm tomato into thick rounds and arrange around the dish. Serve together with cooked rice, dal and mango chutney.

Kofta or 'Ball' Curry

Serves 6-8 persons

On Sundays, our kitchen was a hive of activity as more often than not guests were invited for lunch. Kofta, 'ball' curry was generally on the menu, it being a particular favourite of my father. As the balls were being fried in the kitchen at the rear of the house, the delicious aroma of blended spices wafted through the air, followed by the sweet succulent fragrance emitted by the bath of coconut milk in which the 'balls' were simmered. Friends arrived, and while waiting for lunch, many tankards of beer were consumed. The atmosphere was light and breezy; jokes and laughter filled the air. Finally, we sat down to a lunch of 'ball' curry, served along with a large platter of brilliant yellow coconut rice, cabbage foogath, papads and masoor dal. Fresh fruit salad, served with custard sauce, made a delicious dessert.

FOR THE KOFTAS

1 kg lean ground beef
1 large onion, chopped fine
A few fresh curry leaves, chopped fine
2 green chillies, chopped fine
1 small bunch green coriander, washed, stalks removed and chopped fine
Salt to taste
Oil for frying the koftas
1/3 portion of masala paste as given below

MASALA PASTE

3 tbsp cumin powder
3 tbsp fresh ginger/garlic paste
2 tbsp Kashmiri chilli, or paprika powder
1½ tsp chilli powder
2 tbsp fresh ground coconut, or coconut powder
1½ tsp garam masala

INGREDIENTS FOR CURRY

1/3 cup cooking oil
1 medium onion, sliced fine
A few curry leaves
1 medium tomato, chopped fine
1 can of coconut milk
½ cup beaten curd

1 tbsp tamarind pureé
Salt to taste
1 cup hot water
1 medium bunch green coriander leaves, washed and chopped fine
2 large potatoes, cubed and cooked in salted water

Mix together first six ingredients together with one-third portion of the masala paste, using a little curd if required to facilitate the blending. Set aside.

To make the curry: In a deep pot over moderate heat, pour in oil followed by curry leaves and sliced onion. Fry the onions a golden brown colour. Lower the heat and add the remaining two-thirds of the masala paste. Fry the spices until fragrant. Add the chopped tomato. Pour in the can of coconut milk, beaten curd and hot water. Stir in tamarind purée, salt to taste and half the bunch of green coriander leaves. Allow the curry to simmer on low heat.

Form the ground beef into koftas about the size of large walnuts. Place a heavy skillet with oil over a moderate flame and fry the koftas a rich brown colour. Drain and transfer to the pot of simmering curry gravy. When all the koftas have been fried and added to the curry, place cooked potatoes in the pot, cover and simmer the assembled curry for a further fifteen minutes.

Garnish with remaining green coriander leaves.

Serve kofta curry with coconut rice, vegetable foogath and papads.

Frithath Curry

Serves 6-8 persons

The following is a very pungent curry, although the spices mellow when refrigerated overnight. In our home frithath curry was often cooked the day prior to serving, allowing the spices to permeate the meat.

1 kg beef or pork shoulder, cut into bite-sized pieces
2 medium onions, sliced fine
1/3 cup cooking oil
3 green chillies, chopped fine
1 whole pod garlic, peeled and chopped fine
2" piece of fresh ginger, peeled and chopped fine
¼ cup malt vinegar
1 tsp cumin powder
1 tsp chilli powder
1 tbsp Kashmiri chilli, or paprika powder
½ tsp turmeric powder
1 tsp garam masala
2 tbsp tamarind purée
Salt to taste
2 tsp sugar
2 cups hot water

GARNISH

4 large potatoes, sliced lengthways and cooked in salt water
3 medium onions, sliced fine

Place a heavy-based pan with oil over moderate heat. Add onions and fry until transparent. Add green chillies, garlic and ginger to the pan, and fry for a further few minutes. Lower heat, place meat in the pan and fry, stirring continuously for about ten minutes. The meat should be nicely browned. Make a paste of the next five ingredients with vinegar and add to the pan. Stir the mixture until the spices release their fragrance, and the pieces of meat are well coated with the spices. Add salt to taste, sugar and tamarind purée. Cover the pan and place in a preheated oven until the meat is cooked through. If cooking upon the stove, pour two cups hot water into the pan, cover, and allow the meat to simmer gently until it is cooked through and the oil rises to the surface. There should be a pungent, dark gravy clinging to the morsels of meat.

Drain potatoes and fry golden in a little oil. Remove from heat. Add sliced onions to the oil and fry crisp. Place Frithath curry in a serving dish and arrange fried potatoes around. Sprinkle fried onions over top. The very pungency of the dish lends itself beautifully to a simple accompaniment of cooked white rice, a creamy raita and papads on the side.

Maharashtrian Curry (Roasted Masala)

Serves 6-8 persons

1 kg beef or mutton, cubed
1/3 cup cooking oil
ROAST AND GRIND
1 medium onion, peeled and roughly chopped
½ fresh coconut, roughly chopped

1 tsp kala jeera
1 tsp aniseed
4 whole red chillies
1 tbsp coriander seeds
1 tsp whole cumin

MIX WITH

½ tsp turmeric powder
1 tsp garam masala
1 tbsp fresh ginger/garlic paste

FOR THE CURRY

1 medium onion, sliced fine
2 green chillies, slit
Hot water
½ cup coconut milk
Salt to taste
2 potatoes, peeled, cubed and cooked in salted water
1 small bunch green coriander, washed and chopped fine

Place a frying pan with a tablespoon of oil over moderate heat. Roast the first seven ingredients until they give off their fragrant aroma. Grind to a paste, using a little water to facilitate the grinding. Blend with next three ingredients. Place a heavy-based pan over moderate heat and brown the onion. Lower heat and place the masala paste in the pan. Fry until the oil separates from the spices. Add beef or mutton to the pan, and continue frying until the pieces of meat are well covered with the spices. Stir in green chillies, hot water and coconut milk. Add salt to taste. Cover the pan and allow the curry to simmer gently on the stove until the meat is cooked through and you have a thick residual gravy clinging to the morsels of meat. Stir in cooked potatoes. Strew chopped green coriander over the curry. Remove from flame.

Serve Maharashtrian curry with cooked white rice, kitcheree or chapatis, a mango salad, cabbage or cauliflower foogath, and papads on the side.

Beef or Mutton Buffath

Serves 6-8 persons

1 kg beef or mutton, cut into bite-sized pieces
1/3 cup ghee
½ whole fresh garlic, peeled and chopped fine
2" piece fresh ginger, peeled and chopped fine
2 green chillies, slit
Malt vinegar
1 tsp mustard powder
1 tsp cumin powder
1 tsp garam masala
½ tsp chilli powder
1 tbsp Kashmiri chilli, or paprika powder
½ tsp turmeric powder
2 cups hot water
Salt to taste
1 tsp sugar
3 potatoes, peeled and cubed
3 carrots, scraped and diced
1 medium white radish, scraped and diced
1 bunch green onions, chopped
1 cup cooked peas

GARNISH

3 large onions, sliced fine, and fried a rich brown colour in 2 tbsp ghee

Place ghee in a heavy-based pan over a moderate flame, and fry chopped ginger and garlic. Add green chillies and meat to the pan. Lower heat, and continue frying until the meat is nicely browned all over. Make a paste of the next six ingredients with a little vinegar and lower into the pan. Fry spices together with the meat until they give off a fragrant aroma. Add salt and sugar to taste. Pour in half a cup of vinegar and two cups of hot water. Cover the pan and allow the buffath to simmer over low heat for about half an hour. Remove lid and stir in next four vegetables. Add a little more hot water if required, remembering the vegetables will also release their liquid. Test for sufficient salt. Continue cooking until the meat and vegetables are tender. Stir in half a cup of cooked peas. Remove from heat and allow the buffath to cool completely.

Place ghee in frying pan and fry sliced onions until crisp and brown. With a slotted spoon separate the morsels of meat from the vegetables in the buffath. Place the meat in the centre of serving dish. Remove vegetables from gravy and arrange around the meat. Pour the gravy over the buffath. Garnish with crisp fried onions.

Buffath is excellent when served with crusty white bread and a fresh garden salad on the side.

Snake Gourd Curry with Mince Meat

Serves 4-6 persons

Although this curry is time consuming, the results are delicious.

1 medium snake gourd, or zucchini
½ kg lean ground beef or mutton
2 medium onions, chopped fine
2 tbsp cooking oil
1 tsp red chilli powder
½ tsp turmeric powder
1 tsp Kashmiri chilli, or paprika powder
1 level tsp cumin powder
2 tbsp fresh ginger/garlic paste
1 tsp coriander powder
¼ cup cooking oil
1 medium onion, sliced
2 cups coconut milk
Salt to taste

Scrape surface of gourd clean, cut into 2" lengths. Place in a saucepan of salted water and boil rapidly for ten minutes. Strain through a colander and set aside. In a heavy-based saucepan over moderate heat, pour in two tablespoons cooking oil. Add chopped onion and fry golden. Make a paste of the next six ingredients. Lower half the amount of paste into the saucepan, and fry until fragrant. Add the lean ground meat and fry to a rich brown colour. Add salt to taste. Carefully remove insides of snake gourd or zucchini, and pack ground meat mixture firmly into cavity. Set aside.

In a heavy-based pan over moderate heat place a quarter cup cooking oil. When the oil is hot, fry one medium onion, sliced. Place remaining spice mixture in the pan, and continue frying until the spices are fragrant. Gently lower stuffed gourd pieces into the pan and fry until well coated with spice mixture. Pour over two cups coconut milk, add salt to taste. Allow snake gourd curry to simmer over very low heat for a further ten minutes.

Serve with cooked white rice, dal and kachumbur.

Ceylon Curry

Serves 6-8 persons

1 kg beef, cut into bite-sized pieces
½ tsp chilli powder
1 tsp freshly ground black pepper
1 tbsp ground coriander
1 tsp ground cumin
½ tsp turmeric powder
2 cups coconut milk
1 cup hot water
1 medium onion, sliced fine
12 flakes garlic, peeled and chopped fine
1 stalk curry leaves
¼ tsp fenugreek seeds
2 tbsp tamarind purée
Salt to taste
4 or 5 curry leaves
Juice of 1 lemon
2 tbsp cooking oil
1 medium onion, chopped fine

Make a paste with the first five ingredients and place in a pot together with the meat. Pour in one cup of coconut milk and one cup hot water. Stir in next eight ingredients. Place the pot over a moderate heat and allow the curry to simmer, stirring frequently until the meat is tender and you have a thick dark gravy. Stir in the second cup of coconut milk and the juice of a lime. Adjust salt. Simmer for a further five minutes.

Place frying pan over moderate heat and pour in oil. Add chopped onion to the pan and fry to a golden brown colour. Add to the simmering pot of curry. Remove from fire and serve.

A platter of cooked white rice, pickles and papads make excellent accompaniments.

Mutton Korma

Serves 6-8 persons

1 kg lean mutton, trim and cut into bite-sized pieces
2 large onions
3 whole Kashmiri chillies
1 tbsp poppy seeds
10 blanched almonds
2 tbsp fresh ginger/garlic paste
1 tsp garam masala
1 tbsp cumin powder
1 tbsp coriander powder
3 tbsp ghee
1 cup curd
A few saffron threads (¼ tsp), pounded and soaked in 2 tbsp hot water
Salt to taste
2 cups hot water

GARNISH

1 small bunch fresh green coriander, chopped fine

Grind to a paste one onion with the next three ingredients. Mix together with following four ingredients. Place a large heavy-based pot with a tight-fitting lid on a moderate flame. Add ghee to the pot with remaining onion, sliced fine. Fry onions until golden brown. Lower heat and stir in masala paste. Fry until ghee rises to the surface and the spices are fragrant. Add cubed meat to the pot and stir until the pieces of meat are well coated with the spices. Blend in curd and saffron. Add salt to taste. Pour over one cup hot water. Cover the pot and allow korma to cook slowly, stirring, and replenishing water as required. When ready, there should be a rich, delicious gravy clinging to the tender morsels of meat. Stir in freshly chopped green coriander leaves, and serve korma with a peas pulao, creamy raita and a vegetable accompaniment.

Mr Johnson's Chicken Curry
The Story

This story has been doing the rounds since I was a child. Anglo-Indian men very seldom bothered with culinary tasks, preferring to relegate such duties to the cook, with their wives acting as overseer. However, on occasion, in the interest of making an impression, they have been known to take the credit in company for the excellence of certain dishes. The following story perfectly illustrates this trait:

After Sunday Mass, the parish priest came over to greet Mr and Mrs Johnson. During the course of the conversation, Mr Johnson, who was trying to ingratiate himself with the good Father, boasted of how good a cook he was. Father promptly seized the occasion to invite himself to lunch, thus avoiding another badly cooked meal prepared by the parish sacristan, who also doubled as his cook-cum-bearer. They set the time for one o'clock in the afternoon, and Father went on to greet other parishioners, while the Johnsons made their way home.

Donald Johnson was no cook; he couldn't even boil a pot of water. On the way home he casually mentioned to his wife, as if she hadn't been present, that the padre was going to be joining them for lunch. He thought they should serve chicken curry and rice.

'I heard you,' she replied irritated, 'boasting about your cooking skills. Cannot even boil an egg.'

'Girlie, I just said it for appearances' sake,' he replied soothingly. 'You will help me, won't you? Do we have a fowl, by the way?'

'Have you gone daft?' she retorted. 'There's plenty in the back. You can catch one and wring its bloody neck.'

Mr Johnson shuddered inwardly. He was not a violent man, and, furthermore, the sight of blood made him weak in the knees. It was obvious he was not going to get any help with the chicken curry.

Upon reaching home he called at once to his manservant Govind and instructed him to catch and kill the biggest fowl in the coop. Govind had never received such instructions before, and he looked at his employer dumfounded. He was a timid man, afraid of his own shadow, but being more afraid of his master's temper, he hurriedly entered the coop amidst the squawking fowl and seizing one, emerged victorious. Killing the bird was quite another matter, but Sahib Mr Johnson was already there, standing over him in the back veranda. Hurriedly Govind grabbed a sharp knife and cut the poor fowl's throat. The beheaded bird danced all over the compound, and fell jerking frantically in the dust before finally expiring. He triumphantly presented the dead bird to Donald. Now what, thought Mr Johnson—ah!—feathering the bird was the next step. 'Girlie, we need a pot of hot water!' he called out plaintively.

'Here is a pot, and there is the tap,' Mrs Johnson stated flatly, shoving a large metal container in his direction.

'Shanti,' cried Mr Johnson loudly, calling for their kitchen maid. He felt quite helpless and abandoned. She came to his rescue, filling the pot with water and setting it on the stove to boil. As soon as it was done, she grabbed the bloodied bird, plunged it into the boiling water, and feathered it expertly. 'Ah!' exclaimed Mr Johnson. 'That was done quite nicely.'

He next busied himself with the ingredients needed for the curry. Surveying the pantry shelves and their assortment of spices, he shook his head in dismay. 'Girlie,' he wailed once more—she was there at his elbow. She looked at him pityingly, and silently proceeded to remove the spices required for the curry, blending them skilfully. The onions were sliced by Shanti, who also ground the coconut and diced the tomatoes.

'Could you cut up the chicken?' Mr Johnson asked hesitantly as Shanti completed her last task. It was jointed in a trice.

The stove was lit, and a large cooking pot was

placed on it. Mrs Johnson poured cooking oil into the pot and added onions. Mr Johnson watched the onions fry, stirring them with a wooden spoon. When they were browned, Mrs Johnson instructed him to add the spices. He did, and as they fried, the kitchen was filled with their fragrant aroma. The jointed pieces of the bird were next placed in the pot. 'Shanti, where is the salt?' he inquired. She showed him, but he hesitated, not knowing quite how much to add. Taking the container from him, she quickly threw some in. The chicken and spices were sizzling at the bottom of the pot, and there was the distinct possibility they might burn if some water was not quickly added. Mrs Johnson's keen nose smelled the curry 'catching', and she swiftly poured in the water, thus averting a disaster. Tomatoes were thrown in, and Mr Johnson proudly stirred the curry once more.

The fire was lowered by Shanti, who covered the pot and proceeded to cut up a few potatoes for the curry. The clock struck eleven, and it was stifling hot in the kitchen. Time for a beer, thought Mr Johnson. Going to the refrigerator, he poured himself a glass of the cold frothy brew and returned once more to the kitchen. He took the lid off the curry pot and peered in with satisfaction. Giving it a quick stir, he sat down on the kitchen stool to enjoy his beer. The curry simmered and the chicken cooked as Mr Johnson drank his beer. When the bird was three-quarters done, Shanti added the potatoes and completed the cooking process.

Father arrived on time and lunch was served. The

chicken curry was dished up with coconut rice and various accompaniments. Father pronounced the meal delicious, and complimented Mr Johnson on the excellence of his curry. Mr Johnson, sipping his beer, grew expansive and enlarged on the topic of his culinary skills; he invited Father for lunch once more the following Sunday. The priest readily accepted.

Mrs Johnson glowered at her husband and silently ate her meal.

The Curry

Serves 8 persons

2 medium roasting chickens (700 gm each), skinned and jointed
3 large onions, sliced fine
A few curry leaves
1/3 cup cooking oil
2 tbsp fresh ginger/garlic paste
2 tbsp cumin powder
2 tbsp coriander powder
1 tbsp Kashmiri chilli powder
1 tsp chilli powder, or to taste
1 tsp garam masala
3 green chillies, slit
1 small bunch green coriander, washed and chopped fine
1 large tomato, chopped fine
2 cups thick coconut milk
Hot water
3 large potatoes, peeled and cubed
1 cup beaten curd
2 tsp salt, or to taste

Place a deep pot over moderate heat. Pour in oil and curry leaves. When the oil is hot, add sliced onions and brown them. Make a paste of the next six ingredients, using a little curd to facilitate the blending. Lower heat and add to the pot. Fry the spices until they release their fragrant aroma. Place jointed chicken in with the spice mixture, and continue frying until the spices evenly coat the pieces of chicken. Stir in green chillies, coriander and chopped tomato. Pour in two cups coconut milk, one cup hot water and beaten curd. Add salt to taste. Cover the pot and allow the chicken to simmer for about half an hour before adding the potatoes to the curry. Stir well, cover, and cook until the chicken and potatoes are tender. Remove from heat. The succulent joints of chicken should be swimming in a richly spiced coconut gravy.

Serve chicken curry with peas pulao, raita and a green mango salad. Any remaining curry can be stored overnight in the refrigerator. The taste improves immeasurably when warmed and served the next day.

Chicken Shakuti

Serves 6-8 persons

Chicken Shakuti is Maharashtrian in origin, but the Goan and Anglo-Indian community having developed a great affinity for this dish, serve it regularly. The rich blend of roasted spices that include coconut and poppy seeds, when cooked together with chicken, creates a dish that is distinctive in flavour and delicious in taste.

2 medium roasting chickens (700-800 gm), skinned and jointed
½ cup cooking oil
1 large onion, roughly chopped
½ level tsp whole fenugreek (methi) seeds
½ cup dried coconut (copra), desiccated
2 tbsp khus khus (poppy seeds)
1 tbsp ground coriander
1 tsp ground cumin
1 tsp garam masala
1 tbsp Kashmiri chilli powder
1 tsp chilli powder
1 tsp ground turmeric
2 tbsp ginger/garlic paste
3 large onions, finely sliced
1 cup thick coconut milk
2 cups hot water
2 tbsp tamarind purée
2 tsp salt, or to taste

Place a pan over moderate flame, and individually dry roast each one of the ingredients, starting with the chopped onion, and ending with the chilli powder. Grind fenugreek, coconut and poppy seeds to a fine paste, combine with ground spices and ginger/garlic paste.

Place a deep, heavy-based pot over a moderate flame. Pour in oil and sliced onion. Fry onions to a golden brown colour. Lower heat, place masala paste in the pot and fry until the oil begins to separate from the spices. Add chicken pieces and continue frying until the chicken is well coated with the spice mixture. Add coconut milk and two cups hot water to the pot. Stir in tamarind purée together with salt to taste. Cover the pot and allow the chicken to simmer over low heat until tender. There should be a rich brown gravy clinging to the morsels of tender chicken. Serve with rice and a side dish of vegetables.

Note: Shakuti is equally delicious when prepared with duck.

Hyderabadi Chicken Curry

Makes 4 servings

1 medium roasting chicken (700-800 gm), skinned and jointed
¼ cup cooking oil
1 medium onion, sliced fine
1 tbsp ginger/garlic paste
1 tsp garam masala
1 tsp ground cumin
½ tsp turmeric powder
2 large tomatoes, diced
2 cups thick coconut milk
1 cup hot water
1 tsp salt
1 tsp fresh lime juice
1 small bunch green coriander leaves, chopped

Place a heavy-based pan over moderate heat. Pour in oil. When the oil is hot, place the sliced onion in the pan and fry to a golden colour. Lower heat, make a paste from the next four ingredients, add to the pan and fry until the spices release their fragrant aroma. Stir chicken parts into the pan and continue frying until the pieces of chicken are coated with the spices. Add diced tomatoes. Pour in coconut milk, hot water and salt to taste. Cover the chicken and allow to cook over low heat until tender.

During the cooking process occasionally stir the curry to ensure the chicken/spice mixture does not adhere to the bottom of the pan. When cooked remove from heat. Stir in lime juice. Strew chopped green coriander over top and serve.

This is a delicate, flavoursome curry that improves with keeping. The gravy should be rich with the subtle infusion of coconut milk, and tangy with the taste of lime and tomato.

Serve Hyderabadi Chicken with rice or chapatis.

Tomato Chicken

Serves 4-6 persons

1 kg roasting chicken, skinned and jointed
¼ cup oil
2 medium onions, sliced
1 whole star anise
2" piece cinnamon
1" piece fresh ginger, peeled and chopped fine
1 tsp chilli powder
½ tsp turmeric
1 cup tomato purée
1 cup hot water
Salt to taste
1 tsp sugar

Place pan over moderate heat. Pour in oil. When the oil is hot add first four ingredients to the pan, and fry until they release their fragrant aroma. Stir in chicken pieces, and continue frying for a further few minutes. Make a paste of chilli powder and turmeric, and mix in with chicken. When the spices have coated the pieces of chicken, add tomato purée and one cup hot water. Add salt to taste and one teaspoon sugar. Cover the pan and allow tomato chicken to simmer until tender. There should be a rich red gravy clinging to the pieces of chicken. Remove star anise and cinnamon.

Serve tomato chicken with bread or chapatis. A vegetable side dish, mango chutney and salad make excellent accompaniments.

Chicken Jal Frezi

Makes 4 servings

1 kg roasting chicken, skinned and jointed

MARINADE

½ tsp turmeric powder
1 tbsp ginger/garlic paste
1 tsp ground coriander
1 tsp ground cumin
1 tsp red chilli powder
Salt to taste
1 tsp garam masala

FOR FRYING

3 tbsp ghee or ¼ cup oil
3 medium onions, sliced fine
¾ cup beaten curd
½ cup hot water

Make a paste of the first seven ingredients with a tablespoon of curd. Rub the chicken all over with the spices and set aside for two hours.

Place the ghee or oil in a pan over moderate heat, and fry the onions golden brown. Drain and set aside. Remove chicken pieces from marinade and add to the pan, frying until the pieces of chicken are nicely browned. Stir in curd, residual marinade and half a cup of hot water. Test for sufficient salt. Cover the pan and allow to cook, stirring frequently until the chicken is tender. Blend in fried onions.

Serve chicken jal frezi with chapatis, raita and a vegetable dish.

Duck Vindaloo

Makes 8 servings

2 large ducks, jointed; remove excess fat from the birds but do not remove skin
½ cup mustard oil
2 large onions, sliced fine
8 curry leaves with stalk
½ tsp fenugreek seeds
1 tsp whole mustard seeds (rye)
2 cups malt vinegar
1 large pod fresh garlic, peeled and sliced
1 3" piece fresh ginger, peeled and sliced
½ level tsp turmeric powder
2 tbsp cumin powder
2 tbsp Kashmiri chilli powder
1 tsp chilli powder, or to taste
1 tbsp sugar
2 tsp salt, or to taste

DRY ROAST
1 tbsp cumin powder
1 tbsp coriander powder

Place a large heavy-based pot over a moderate flame. Pour in mustard oil and allow to heat. Add fenugreek and mustard seeds to the pot. When the seeds start to sputter, stir in curry leaves and onions. Fry until onions are nicely browned. Grind ginger and garlic to a paste with a little vinegar, and mix with next five ingredients, using more vinegar to facilitate the blending. Lower heat and add masala paste to the pot. Fry the paste, stirring continuously until the oil separates from the spices. Stir in pieces of duck and continue frying until they are well coated with the spice mixture. Pour in a cup of vinegar and salt to taste. Cover the pot and allow the duck to cook over low heat. During the cooking process remove lid from time to time and stir vindaloo, adding a little more vinegar if required, until the pieces of duck are tender. Dry roast cumin and coriander powder until fragrant, being careful not to burn the spices. Mix into the duck vindaloo.

Duck vindaloo should always be cooked a day or two prior to serving. This allows the dish to mellow and the portions of duck to absorb the spices. Besides, duck being a fatty bird, on the following day, when the vindaloo has sufficiently cooled, one is able to skim off the extra fat that rises to the surface. Duck vindaloo keeps well, and has a refrigerator life of over a week. In fact, the taste improves with keeping.

To serve duck vindaloo, gently warm the dish over low heat until heated through. Serve with rice or chapatis.

Chicken Korma

Serves 6 persons

The following recipe was given to me by a good friend, Gloria Major, who happens to be an excellent cook.

1 kg roasting chicken, skinned and jointed
½ cup ghee
2 onions, sliced fine
2" stick cinnamon
3 whole cloves
3 green cardamoms, split
1 tsp red chilli powder
2 tbsp ginger/garlic paste
1 tsp garam masala
2 cups beaten curd
1 cup hot water
Salt to taste
2 large potatoes, cubed and cooked in a little salted water
1 tbsp ghee
GARNISH
2 medium onions, sliced fine and fried a crisp brown in 1 tbsp of ghee

Place a heavy-based pan over moderate heat and pour in the ghee. When the ghee is hot add onions and the next three ingredients. Fry onions a golden colour. Make a paste of the next three ingredients, using a little curd to facilitate the blending. Lower heat and stir masala paste into the pan, frying continuously to ensure the spices do not adhere to the bottom of the pan. When the spices release their fragrant aroma, add chicken pieces to the pan and continue frying until the pieces are well coated with the spices. Pour in one cup hot water and curd. Add salt to taste. Stir the mixture. Cover and allow the korma to simmer until the chicken is cooked through. There should be a dark, rich gravy clinging to the pieces of chicken. Fry the cooked potatoes until crisp and golden in a tablespoon of ghee. Remove from heat and add to the korma curry.

Garnish with fried onions. Serve with peas pulao, a creamy raita and papads on the side.

This korma is equally delicious when made with mutton.

Stella's Chicken Korma

Serves 6-8 persons

No chapter on curries would be complete without the inclusion of the following recipe for chicken korma, which was prepared in our home at least once a week, generally for lunch on Saturday. It was brought to the table swimming in a rich coconut gravy, accompanied by a platter of peas pulao, vegetable foogath, papads and green coriander chutney. Any korma remaining after the meal was placed in the meatsafe, and appeared once more at the dinner table together with the dinner entrée. Having soaked in a bath of spicy gravy all afternoon, the pieces of chicken were succulent and pungent. Often forgetting the dinner, we savoured the portions of tender chicken, chewed on the bones, and sopped up the delicious gravy with thick slices of crusty bread.

I call it Stella's Korma after my mother, because it was she who first fed it to me. When she passed away, I hunted high and low for the recipe, but could not find the ingredients written down in any one of her many books. It was destined to be found, however, for one day as I thumbed through an old notebook that belonged to her, I discovered it, safely tucked in between the pages. Placed there for safekeeping, or for me.

2 medium chickens (700-800 gm each), skinned and jointed
10 oz curd
3 tbsp fresh ginger/garlic paste
1 tsp turmeric
1 tsp salt

GRIND TO PASTE

3 tbsp poppy seeds or khus khus
4 red chillies
2 tbsp coriander seeds
1 tbsp cumin seeds

MIX WITH

1 tsp garam masala

FOR FRYING

½ cup ghee
4 large onions, sliced fine
3 green chillies, slit
2 cups thick coconut milk
Salt to taste

Mix half the curds with 1 tablespoon ginger/garlic paste, turmeric and salt. Rub the chicken pieces all over with the mixture. Place in a glass bowl, cover and marinade overnight in the refrigerator. On the following day grind the next four spices in water, and mix with remaining fresh ginger/garlic paste and garam masala. Set aside. Place a heavy-based pan over moderate heat and add ghee to the pan. When the ghee gets hot, add in sliced onions and fry until crisp and brown. Remove half the amount of onions and grind to a paste. Lower heat and add masala paste to the pan. Fry until the spices release their fragrant aroma. Drain chicken from marinade and stir into spice mixture. Fry for a further few minutes, or until the chicken pieces are well coated with the spices. Pour in marinade juices, remaining curd, two cups coconut milk and sliced green chillies. Add salt to taste. Blend in ground onions. Stir once more, cover the pan and allow the chicken to cook until tender. Remove from flame.

Serve chicken korma with a dish of masala fried potatoes on the side. Tomato pulao, raita and papads make excellent accompaniments.

Pork Specialities

Pork is considered a great delicacy, and is specifically enjoyed by the Christian community and the Coorgs of South India. There are a number of highly spiced recipes unique to each, but regardless of where they originate, each community enjoys the delicious creations of the other.

Preserving pork in the tropics when there was no refrigeration required a lot of care in the preliminary dressing of the meat, and thereafter in the preserving of the cooked dishes. Pork dishes are generally heavily spiced and cooked in vinegar if they are to be preserved. In some instances, the pork, before it is cooked, is washed in vinegar. When the cooking process is completed, pickled pork vindaloo is allowed to cool before being transferred to a stone jar or 'burnee' in which it is stored, covered with a layer of oil. The different methods of preparing and preserving pork, like time-honoured traditions, are often handed down in families from generation to generation.

Pickled Pork Vindaloo

Serves 8 persons

Even during the lean days when game was scarce, one could always hunt wild boar in the jungles around my grandfather's farm. Fires were stoked well into the night, keeping cauldrons of water on the boil as the animal was shaved and gutted. A division of spoils followed, with friends and field hands each receiving their share.

In the kitchen, great quantities of spices were ground to a paste, awaiting the dressed meat. The air was redolent with the smell of masala and vinegar. Choice portions of meat were brought in, rinsed once more in vinegar, and cut into chunks. From my post on the lowly milking stool, I watched in awe as Granny and Sevanti, my grandparents' old cook and faithful retainer, deftly trimmed, chopped, and boned the meat.

An ancient aluminium degchee, blackened with the smoke of ages, was then placed over the wood fire, and the cooking process began. A bottle of bright yellow mustard oil streamed into the pot and was allowed to get hot. Sevanti tossed in a handful of mustard and fenugreek seeds that sputtered and spit as they hit the hot oil. She then lowered the masala paste and commenced stirring vigorously with a large wooden spoon. Pungent vapours arose from the depths of the cauldron, permeating every corner of the kitchen—stinging the eyes and nostrils. Undaunted, she continued with her frantic stirring, ensuring the masala paste, as it fried, did not burn or adhere to the bottom of the vessel. Her attentive, hovering figure, like one of the witches out of *Macbeth*, cast a giant shadow on the wall.

Granny passed the portions of pork that were then slowly added, a little at a time into the frying masala. Reaching for the old cigarette tin that held rock salt, Sevanti threw a handful into the meat/ masala mixture. Granny passed the sugar and the bottle of vinegar. Skilfully she added portions of each. Without exchanging a single word, the women worked in unison, each one knowing exactly what was expected of her. Finally, Sevanti placed a heavy lid on the pot; removing a few logs of wood from the fire, she lowered the flames. Beating the logs on the earthen floor, she extinguished them before casting them into the corner for later use. Drenched with perspiration, the two women moved away from the fire. The pork simmered gently, and it was frequently stirred and tasted until a perfect balance of salt, vinegar and spices had been achieved. When the vindaloo was finally cooked through, it was allowed to cool. The lid, however, was never removed in case a gecko fell from the ceiling into the pot and spoiled the entire effort.

When completely cooled, the pickled pork was spooned into large earthen 'burnees'. A one-inch layer of mustard oil covered the meat and gravy. The 'burnees' were then stored in a cool dark place (under Granny's bed), where they lay undisturbed for at least a fortnight as other cuts of the wild boar were cooked and served up as chops, roasts and fries. When the lean days came, and they inevitably did, portions of this pickled meat were carefully taken from the jar by Granny herself, using a clean, slotted serving spoon that allowed the excess oil to drain back into the 'burnee'. The vindaloo was then gently reheated, and served accompanied with masoor dal, rice and a vegetable side dish.

2 kg boneless pork butt or shoulder, cut into bite-sized pieces
½ cup of mustard oil
A few curry leaves
½ tsp whole fenugreek seeds
1 tsp mustard seed (rye)
1 large onion, sliced fine
1 whole pod garlic, peeled and chopped

2" piece fresh ginger, peeled and chopped
Malt vinegar
1 tbsp cumin powder
1 tsp chilli powder, or to taste
1 tbsp Kashmiri chilli powder, or paprika powder
2 tsp sugar
2 tsp salt, or to taste

Place a heavy-based pot over moderate heat and pour in oil. Throw in the curry leaves. Allow the oil to get hot before adding the fenugreek and mustard seeds. When the seeds begin to sputter, place the sliced onion in the pot. Fry until golden brown. Lower heat. Grind garlic and ginger to a paste in a little vinegar. Add next four ingredients to the paste, using more vinegar to facilitate the blending. Place the masala paste in the pot and fry, stirring continually until the oil separates from the spices. Stir in pieces of pork, and continue frying for a further ten minutes. Season with vinegar, stir to ensure spices do not stick to the bottom of the pot. When the meat is well coated with the spices, add salt to taste and a further cup of vinegar. Cover the pot and allow vindaloo to cook. From time to time remove lid and stir. Add more vinegar if required, until meat is cooked through.

There should be a thick, red gravy clinging to the succulent morsels of pork. Allow to cool. Cover, and allow the vindaloo to soak for at least twenty-four hours before serving. The taste of the dish improves as the meat absorbs the spices, that mellow to a delicious pungency. Vindaloo is even more delicious when aged for a week or ten days.

Serve with parathas or rice, and a side dish of dal.

Note: If the vindaloo is to be stored for longer than a week, the sliced onion should be omitted from the recipe.

Pork Sorpotel

Serves 6-8 persons

1 kg pork
250 gm pork liver
½ cup cooking oil
1 large pod fresh garlic, peeled and finely minced
3" piece of fresh ginger, peeled and finely minced
6 green chillies, chopped fine

GRIND TO A PASTE IN MALT VINEGAR

6 red chillies
12 peppercorns
2 tsp whole cumin

MIX TOGETHER WITH

½ tsp turmeric powder
2 tsp garam masala
1 tbsp sugar
Salt to taste

Parboil pork and liver separately in salt water. Drain and reserve stock and meats separately. Set aside to cool, after which cut pork and liver into very small pieces. Place a heavy-based pot over moderate heat and pour in oil. When the oil is hot, lightly fry the pork and liver together. Remove and set aside. Lower heat and in the same oil fry the next three chopped ingredients. Grind the next three ingredients in vinegar and mix with turmeric, garam masala and sugar. Place the masala in the pot and fry until the oil begins to separate from the spices, that give off a fragrant aroma. Add the pieces of pork and liver once more to the pot and continue frying. Once the meats are well coated with the spices, pour in a quarter cup vinegar and two cups stock to the pot. Add salt to taste. Allow the sorpotel to simmer covered until the pork is cooked through and the gravy thickened. At this point one can add extra salt or sugar according to taste.

Sorpotel should be prepared at least a week ahead of time. Traditionally, this dish is not stored in the refrigerator but in a cool, dark place. Every day until the day of serving, place the sorpotel over low heat and allow to simmer until heated through. This allows the spices to consistently permeate the meat. Serve sorpotel when required as a side dish with rice or chapati, vegetables and dal.

Pork Indad

Serves 6 persons

1 kg pork cut into bite-sized pieces
¼ cup cooking oil
¼ cup malt vinegar
½ large pod fresh garlic, peeled
1 medium onion, peeled
1 tbsp Kashmiri chilli powder, or paprika powder
½ tsp chilli powder
½ tsp turmeric powder
1 tsp garam masala
2 tbsp tamarind purée
1 tbsp sugar

Salt to taste
1 cup hot water
1 tbsp brandy
2 large potatoes, peeled, cubed and cooked in salted water

Grind the onion and garlic to a paste in vinegar, and blend with next four ingredients. Pour oil into a heavy-based pan and place over moderate heat. When the oil is hot, add masala paste to the pan and fry briskly, stirring continually to ensure the spices do not adhere to the bottom of the pan. Stir in pieces of pork. Continue frying until the meat is well coated with the spices. Add tamarind purée, sugar and salt to taste. Pour in remaining vinegar and hot water. Stir the meat and gravy together. Cover the pan and allow indad to simmer over low heat until the meat is cooked through and there is a dark pungent gravy clinging to the morsels of pork. Stir in potatoes and brandy. Cover and allow the indad to cool.

The taste of this dish improves immeasurably with keeping, and one can safely store it in the refrigerator for a few days. However, omit the potatoes. Just before serving, reheat indad together with potatoes. Pork indad is excellent with chapatis, dal and a salad of fresh tomatoes, cucumber and onion rings on the side.

Masala Pork Chops

Serves 6 persons

12 pork loin chops (trim excess fat)
1/3 cup cooking oil
A few curry leaves

½ tsp fenugreek seeds
2 large onions, sliced fine
1 tbsp Kashmiri chilli powder, or paprika powder
½ tsp chilli powder
½ tsp turmeric powder
2 tbsp fresh ginger/garlic paste
2 tbsp tomato sauce (ketchup)
2 large tomatoes, sliced
1 tsp salt, or to taste
1 tsp sugar
1 cup hot water

GARNISH

3 large potatoes, peeled, cut lengthways and cooked in salted water
3 tbsp cooking oil
1 small bunch fresh, green coriander leaves, washed and chopped

In a heavy-based pan with lid, pour oil and place over moderate heat. Throw in curry leaves and fenugreek seeds. When the seeds begin to brown, lower heat. Add sliced onions to the pan and fry until they begin to colour. Make a paste of the next five ingredients and mix into the oil and onions. Fry the spices until they are fragrant. Add pork chops and continue frying until the meat is well coated with the spice mixture. Stir in next four ingredients, cover the pan and allow the masala pork chops to simmer over low heat until they are cooked through and tender. Remove from heat.

To serve, remove the individual pork chops onto a platter and pour the thick red gravy over them. Fry potatoes golden brown. Strew chopped green coriander leaves over top, and place fried potatoes around. Masala pork chops are excellent served with crusty bread and a fresh garden salad on the side. A cabbage foogath or a small whole cauliflower cooked in salt water, drained and served with a dusting of fresh ground pepper, make excellent accompaniments.

Note: When I make masala pork chops, I omit the hot water. Instead, I place the lid on the pan and bake the chops in the oven at 180° C until they are tender. In this way the meat cooks in its own juices, and the flavour is vastly improved.

Coorgi Pork Pickle

Serves 6-8 persons

2 kg pork butt, cut into bite-sized pieces

GRIND TO A PASTE

3" piece of fresh ginger, peeled and chopped
1 large pod garlic, cleaned and chopped
1 tbsp mustard seed

DRY ROAST

1 tsp chilli powder
1 heaped tsp Kashmiri chilli powder
½ tsp turmeric powder
2 tbsp coriander powder

FOR PICKLE

½ cup mustard oil
A few curry leaves
½ tsp whole fenugreek seeds
1 small bottle malt vinegar
5 green chillies, slit
2 tbsp tamarind purée
Salt to taste
1 tbsp sugar

Grind first three ingredients to a paste in vinegar and set aside. Dry roast next four ingredients in a heavy skillet over a moderate flame. Remove from heat and set aside. Place a heavy-based pot with a lid over a moderate flame. Pour in mustard oil. When the oil is hot, add curry leaves with stalk and fenugreek seeds. The seeds will turn brown. Lower heat and add the spice paste to the pot. Fry the spices until they begin to release their fragrant aroma. Add pieces of pork to the pot and continue frying until browned and coated with the spice mixture. Place green chillies in the pot together with the tamarind purée. Stir in sugar and salt to taste. Continue frying the meat and spices for about five minutes. Sprinkle roasted spices over the meat, mix and pour in one cup vinegar. Cover and allow to simmer over low heat. Remove lid from time to time and stir the pickle to ensure that the meat and spices do not adhere to the bottom of the pot. Add a little more vinegar in the event the pickle begins to dry out. When cooked, remove from heat and adjust the salt and sugar to taste. Allow the pickle to cool completely before storing in an earthen or glass jar.

This pickle must age for at least three days before it can be served as an accompaniment along with rice, dal and a vegetable dish.

Pork Curry

Serves 6 persons

1 kg pork shoulder, cut into bite-sized pieces
½ cup malt vinegar

GRIND TO A PASTE

3 large onions, peeled and chopped
6 whole red chillies

1 tbsp whole cumin
1 tbsp coriander seeds
1 tsp garam masala
1 tbsp freshly ground ginger/garlic paste
1 tsp salt, or to taste
1 tsp sugar
2 cups hot water

GARNISH

2 tbsp cooking oil
2 large potatoes, peeled and sliced lengthways, cook in salted water
2 large onions, sliced fine

Grind the first four ingredients to a paste in a little vinegar, and mix with the next four ingredients. Mix together meat and spices. Place in a heavy-based pot with remaining vinegar and two cups hot water. Cover, and allow the meat/spice mixture to cook over low heat until the pork is tender, and the gravy reduced. This is a dry curry and, therefore, only one cup of gravy should be left in the pan, clinging to the morsels of meat. Allow the pork curry to cool. Reheat before serving.

In a heavy skillet fry potatoes a golden brown colour in two tablespoons oil. Remove and set aside. Add sliced onions to the same pan and fry crisp. Place curry in an open serving platter and arrange fried potatoes around. Strew fried onions over top and serve with chapatis, dal and vegetables.

Favourite Fish Recipes

In the late 1960s, my husband and I lived with our three young sons in Versova, a suburb of Bombay, in one of the many apartments that stood along the Seven Bungalows Road. It was a period in my life, of which I have the most pleasant memories. Our apartment was very near the beach, and from the balcony one could watch the tide as it swept in and out, leaving behind that strong fish smell that I always associate with Bombay.

The fish market was within walking distance of the apartment, and every morning I ventured forth to haggle with the sharp-tongued fisherwomen over the price of fresh pomfret, or a pound of prawns. The fish lay on beds of crushed ice, gleaming silver in the morning sun. Huge live prawns with twitching whiskers, and crabs that crawled over one another, lay in baskets alongside the stalls—smelling of brine and the sea from which they were taken. The seafood brought home from that market was firm and fresh, and as I laid out my purchases on the kitchen counter, the fish fairly leaped out at me from the shopping basket. I would toss them slithering into the sink, and begin deftly scaling and gutting them, in readiness for the meal I was about to cook.

Versova spoiled us, and it was a long time before we got used to frozen fish, or flash-frozen fish, whatever that means; nothing satisfied, after experiencing the taste of the real thing. However, when cravings for a bit of fish come to the fore, they must be appeased, and one learns to compromise, making do with frozen fillets, salted or canned fish.

Fish is a very important part of the Anglo-Indian diet, and those who live in northern India, or other land-locked regions of the country, soon become adept at preparing salted fish and shrimp in diverse ways. It is not uncommon to enter an Anglo-Indian home at lunch time, and be greeted with the overpowering aroma of salt fish curry being cooked with tomatoes and brinjals. Dried Bombay duck, roasted and made into sambal, is another favourite lunchtime accompaniment. Prawn balchow made from dried shrimps is universally enjoyed by all. Eating fish on Friday was mandatory for Roman Catholics at one time; in our house, however, far from being considered a sacrifice, fish was eaten with relish, and we looked forward to enjoying a good curry at lunch, and fried fish or cutlets for dinner on Friday night.

The way fish is prepared and served differs from province to province. Along the coast, pungent curries infused with coconut milk are poured over portions of boiled rice, and served together with vegetables and sambals. In Bengal, slices of hilsa and bekte are often smeared with a fiery paste of chilli and garlic before being fried in mustard oil. In Maharashtra, the pomfret is often served in a delicately-flavoured moley, or stuffed with a blend of green masala and baked to perfection in the oven. In North India, baking fish in a tandoor is quite common. The brilliant red of the spices smeared over the fish owe their colour more to food dye than to chilli powder. Whatever the preference, it is safe to say that the waters which lie on three sides of the subcontinent have greatly influenced the way we look at fish.

Goa Fish Curry

Serves 6 persons

1½ kg firm fresh fish (pomfret), cut into ½" steaks
1/3 cup cooking oil (mustard oil is preferred)
1 large onion, sliced fine
A few curry leaves with stalk
2 tbsp fresh ginger/garlic paste
1 heaped tbsp cumin powder
½ level tsp turmeric powder
1 heaped tbsp Kashmiri chilli, or paprika powder
1 level tsp chilli powder, or to taste
2 large tomatoes, chopped fine
2 cups thick coconut milk
2 green chillies, slit
2 tbsp tamarind purée
1 tsp of salt, or to taste
1 cup hot water
2 large potatoes, cubed and cooked in salted water
A small bunch of fresh coriander leaves, washed and chopped fine

Place a heavy-based pan over moderate heat. Pour in oil, and add curry leaves with stalk to the pan. When the oil is hot, lower sliced onion into the pan and fry until translucent. Make a paste of the next five ingredients, lower heat and place the masala paste in the pan. Fry masala until the oil separates and the spices release their fragrant aroma. Lower slices of fish into the pan and fry, gently spooning the spice mixture over the pieces of fish. Pour in coconut milk, chopped tomatoes, and green chillies. Add salt to taste, cover the pan and allow the fish to simmer on the stove until barely tender. Remove lid from the pan and add tamarind paste, salt, and cooked potato. At this point a cup of hot water may be added if required, in the interest of creating more gravy. Gently simmer fish and potato in curry gravy until the slices of fish are firm and tender. Take care not to overcook the fish, or it will break up, making it difficult to serve. Remove curry leaf stalk.

Garnish with chopped green coriander leaves, and serve with rice, vegetables and papads.

Note: The above curry is equally excellent when made with fresh crabs or prawns.

Fish Moley

Serves 6

1½ kg fresh fish, cut into steaks
1/3 cup cooking oil
A few curry leaves
1 medium onion, sliced fine
2 tbsp ginger/garlic paste
1 tbsp cumin powder
½ tsp turmeric powder
2 green chillies, slit lengthways
2 cups coconut milk
Salt to taste

2 tbsp lemon juice
1 small bunch green coriander, washed and chopped

Pour oil into a heavy-based pan and place over moderate heat. Add curry leaves. When the oil is hot, stir in sliced onion and fry until translucent. Make a paste of the next three ingredients and place in the pan. Lower heat. Fry the spices until they release their fragrant aroma. Add green chillies, followed by the slices of fish. Fry the fish, gently spooning the spice mixture over the slices. Pour in two cups of coconut milk, add salt to taste, and cover the pan. Allow the moley to simmer until the fish is firm and tender. Pour in lemon juice, and sprinkle over chopped, fresh coriander. Gently stir the moley. Remove from heat.

Serve fish moley with rice, cucumber salad and papads.

Fish Balchow

Serves 6 persons

1½ kg fresh fish, cut into ½" steaks
½ tsp turmeric powder
½ tsp salt
½ cup malt vinegar
1 large onion, chopped
2 tbsp fresh ginger/garlic paste
1 heaped tbsp Kashmiri chilli, or paprika powder
1 level tsp chilli powder, or to taste
1 level tbsp cumin powder
1/8 tsp ngapi*
1/3 cup mustard oil
A few fresh curry leaves

½ tsp fenugreek seeds
1 tsp sugar
Salt to taste

GARNISH

2 large potatoes, cubed and cooked in salt water
2 tbsp cooking oil

Rub salt and turmeric over slices of fish and set aside. Grind onion in vinegar and blend in with the next five ingredients, using a little more vinegar to facilitate the blending. Place a heavy-based pan over moderate heat and pour in oil. Fry fish slices golden. Remove from oil and set aside. Add curry leaves and half a teaspoon fenugreek seeds to the oil. When the seeds start browning, lower heat and stir in masala paste. Fry spices until the oil begins to separate and the spices release their fragrant aroma. Place slices of fried fish in the pan and continue frying, gently spooning spice mixture over the fish. Add in salt and sugar together with remaining vinegar. Cook balchow until the slices of fish are firm and tender. Remove from heat and allow to cool.

The taste of fish balchow improves with keeping. Cover and store in refrigerator for a day or two. Before serving balchow, fry cooked potatoes in oil until crisp and brown. Reheat balchow and transfer to a serving dish; arrange potatoes around. Serve with rice, dal and vegetables.

Note: *Ngapi is a preparation made from dried prawns, and comes packed in small containers. Only a pinch is required to give optimum flavour. Ngapi has an indefinite shelf-life, and should be stored in a cool dark place.

Masala Fried Fish

Serves 6-8 persons

18 fillets of fish, fresh or frozen
2 tbsp fresh ginger/garlic paste
1 tbsp Kashmiri chilli, or paprika powder
1 tsp chilli powder, or to taste
½ tsp turmeric powder
Salt to taste
1 tsp sugar
Malt vinegar
2 eggs, beaten with a little salt
Breadcrumbs
Cooking oil for frying

GARNISH

4 large potatoes, cut lengthways and cooked in salted water
3 tbsp cooking oil
2 medium tomatoes, thickly sliced

Thaw fillets. Pat dry and set aside. Blend the next six ingredients to a paste, using vinegar to facilitate the blending. Test for sufficient salt. Rub masala paste all over the fish fillets and set aside. To fry fish, dip in beaten eggs and coat with breadcrumbs. Place a heavy skillet over moderate heat, pour in cooking oil, and allow to get hot. Lower fish fillets into the pan a few at a time and fry, turning frequently, until they are crisp and cooked through. Fillets should be a rich golden colour.

To fry potatoes: Place oil in skillet, and when hot, add in potato slices. Fry crisp and golden. Arrange fish on a large open platter and surround with potatoes and slices of tomato.

Salt Fish Curry with Tomatoes

Serves 6 persons

6 oz salted mackerel, or any other fish (wash fish 3 or 4 times and allow to soak in water for about 2 hours. Drain, pat dry and cut into 2" slices. Set aside)
¼ cup cooking oil
A few curry leaves with stalk
1 large onion, sliced fine
1 tbsp fresh ginger/garlic paste
1 tsp chilli powder
1 tbsp Kashmiri chilli, or paprika powder
1 tbsp cumin powder
2 large tomatoes, diced
1 cup thick coconut milk
½ cup hot water
1 tbsp tamarind purée
Salt to taste

Pour cooking oil in a pan and place over moderate heat. Throw in curry leaves and stalk. When the oil is hot, add onions and fry a golden colour. Lower heat, make a paste of the next four ingredients, and place in the pan. Fry the spices until they release their fragrant aroma. Stir in pieces of fish and continue frying until the fish is well coated with the spices. Add chopped tomatoes and coconut milk. Pour in half a cup of hot water. Cover pan and allow the salt fish curry to simmer gently for about twenty minutes. Remove lid and add tamarind purée. Test for salt, and if required, add to taste. Remove from heat. Serve salt fish curry with cooked white rice, dal and a vegetable side dish.

Note: A medium-sized brinjal (eggplant) may be cubed and added to the curry for a tasty variation.

Masala Fried Bombay Duck

Serves 6 persons

10 large dried Bombay Ducks (trim the fish and remove centre bone, wash thoroughly and drain. Set aside)
¼ cup malt vinegar
4 red chillies
1 tsp mustard seeds
1 tbsp cumin seeds
12 flakes garlic, peeled
2" piece of fresh ginger, peeled and chopped
½ tsp sugar
Salt to taste
¼ cup cooking oil

Grind first five ingredients in vinegar, add sugar and salt to taste. Smear the masala paste all over the fish and set aside for an hour. Heat the oil in a frying pan and fry the dried Bombay Duck gently on both sides, being careful not to burn. Drain and place on a serving platter.

Serve fried Bombay Duck immediately as an accompaniment, together with dal, rice and vegetables.

Pomfrets in Tomato Curry

Serves 6-8 persons

3 fresh pomfrets—combined weight about 2 kg (gut and trim each fish, cut in half)
454 gm fresh prawns, peeled and deveined

1 tsp turmeric powder
½ tsp salt
1/3 cup cooking oil
3 large onions, chopped fine
3 green chillies, slit lengthways
2" fresh ginger, peeled and chopped fine
½ garlic pod, peeled and chopped fine
3 bay leaves
2 large tomatoes, scalded and peeled and diced fine
2 tbsp malt vinegar
1 tsp sugar
Salt to taste
1 tsp flour
1 small bunch green coriander leaves, washed and chopped

•

Mix together turmeric powder and salt. Rub the pomfrets all over with the mixture and set aside. Place oil in a pan over moderate heat and fry the pieces of fish. Remove from pan and set aside. Add chopped onions to the pan and fry until translucent. Stir in next four ingredients and fry until the spices begin to release their fragrant aroma. Lower peeled prawns into the pan and fry together with the spice mixture. When the prawns are coated with the spices, add diced tomatoes to the pan. Mix well. Pour in vinegar, sugar and salt to taste. Add fish and cover the pan. Allow the curry to simmer until the prawns and fish are firm and cooked through. Make a paste of flour and water. Blend into the curry, stirring continually until the curry thickens sufficiently. Sprinkle over chopped green coriander. Remove the pan from heat, and take the bay leaves out of the curry.

Serve tomato fish curry with cooked white rice, coriander chutney and papads.

Fish in Sweet and Sour Sauce

Serves 4 persons

The following is a Parsi recipe that is a family favourite. It has a delicious piquant flavour that may have over time been altered to suit Anglo-Indian tastes. I therefore extend my apologies to the purists within the Parsi community, who may frown on the deviations.

1 kg fresh pomfret, or any other firm white fish (trim and gut fish before cutting into ¾" slices)
¼ cup vegetable oil
1 large onion, sliced fine
1 tbsp fresh ginger/garlic paste
1 tsp cumin powder
1 small bunch green coriander, washed and chopped fine
3 green chillies, slit lengthways
1 medium tomato, chopped fine
1 tbsp vinegar
1 tbsp Worcestershire sauce
1 tsp sugar
1 tbsp flour
1 cup hot water
Salt to taste

Place a heavy-based pan with lid over moderate flame and pour in oil. When the oil is hot, add the onions to the pan and fry until translucent. Lower heat, make a paste of the next two ingredients and stir into the pan together with the chopped green coriander and green chillies. Fry the spices until they are fragrant. Place fish in the pan and fry, gently spooning the spiced mixture over the slices of fish. Add chopped tomato. Blend together next four ingredients and stir into the fish/tomato mixture. Stir in one cup hot water. Test for sufficient salt. Cover the pan and allow the fish to simmer gently over very low heat until firm and tender. There should be a piquant, thick gravy clinging to the slices of fish. Adjust seasoning if required, remove from heat.

Serve sweet and sour fish with thick slices of crusty bread, a vegetable side dish , and a fresh garden salad.

Fish Rissoles

Serves 6 persons

1 large can mackerel, salmon, or any other fish, drained
3 cups mashed potatoes
½ cup breadcrumbs
1 egg, slightly beaten
1 tbsp cooking oil
1 large onion, peeled and chopped very fine
2 green chillies, chopped fine
1 large bunch of green coriander leaves, washed and chopped fine
4 or 5 curry leaves, chopped fine
1 level tsp garam masala
2 tbsp ginger/garlic paste
Salt to taste

FOR FRYING

2 eggs, beaten
Breadcrumbs
Oil for frying

Drain fish and mix together with mashed potatoes. Blend in breadcrumbs and egg. Set aside. Place a frying pan over moderate heat and pour in oil. When the oil is hot, fry chopped onion until translucent. Add next three ingredients to the pan and continue frying. Stir in garam masala and ginger/garlic paste. When the spices release their fragrant aroma, add salt to taste. Remove from flame and blend with the fish/potato mixture. Allow the mixture to cool. Form into rissoles about two-and-a-half inches long. Dip in egg wash and coat with breadcrumbs. Place half a cup of cooking oil in a heavy skillet and allow it to get hot. Lower rissoles into the skillet and fry until crisp and golden.

To serve fish rissoles, arrange on a bed of lettuce and garnish with sliced fresh tomatoes. Crusty bread, butter, a vegetable side dish and fresh garden salad make excellent accompaniments.

Masala Prawns

Serves 6 persons

The following is a highly spiced dish, but if you wish to make it less hot, slit green chillies and discard seeds. Rinse and pat dry before placing in the pan.

1 kg prawns, shelled and deveined
¼ cup cooking oil
A few fresh curry leaves
½ tsp whole fenugreek seeds

1 large onion, minced
¼ cup malt vinegar
2 tbsp ginger/garlic paste
1 tbsp Kashmiri chilli, or paprika powder
1 tsp chilli powder
½ tsp turmeric powder
1 tbsp brown sugar
3 green chillies, slit lengthways
1 medium bunch of fresh green coriander leaves, washed and chopped fine
Salt to taste
3 tbsp tomato sauce (ketchup)

Place a heavy-based pan over a moderate flame. Pour in oil and add curry leaves. When the oil is hot, place fenugreek seeds in the pan, and as soon as they begin to brown, stir in chopped onion. Fry until the onions are a light golden colour. Make a paste of the next five ingredients with vinegar and stir into the pan. Fry the masala until it begins to release its fragrant aroma. Add prawns and continue frying until the prawns are well coated with the spices. Place slit green chillies and chopped green coriander in the pan together with salt to taste and remaining vinegar. Simmer masala prawns until they are firm and cooked through. Blend ketchup in with prawn/spice mixture. Adjust salt if required before removing from flame. There should be a delicious red gravy clinging to the prawns.

Serve masala prawns with cooked white rice or chapatis, dal and a side dish of vegetables.

Prawn Vindaloo

Serves 6-8 persons

1½ kg fresh or frozen prawns, peeled and deveined
1/3 cup mustard oil
A few curry leaves
½ tsp fenugreek seeds
2 onions, minced fine
½ cup malt vinegar
2 tbsp ginger/garlic paste
1 tbsp cumin powder
½ tsp turmeric powder
1 tbsp Kashmiri chilli, or paprika powder
1 tsp chilli powder, or to taste
1 tbsp sugar
2 green chillies, slit
1 tsp salt, or to taste

In a heavy-based pan over moderate flame, pour in mustard oil. Throw in curry leaves. Place fenugreek seeds in the pan, and when they start to brown, add onions and fry until they begin to colour. Make a paste of the next six ingredients with vinegar. Lower heat and place masala paste in the pan. Fry until the oil rises to the top and the spices smell fragrant. Mix in the cleaned prawns, stirring continually to ensure the spices do not adhere to the bottom of the pan. Add salt to taste, green chillies, and remaining vinegar. Cover the pan and allow the vindaloo to simmer gently on low heat. The prawns will release their liquid, adding to the gravy.

When the prawns are firm and cooked through, remove from heat and allow the vindaloo to cool. Prawn vindaloo should always be cooked the day prior to serving. The delicious taste is even more pronounced when the spices permeate the prawns. Reheat prior to serving. This dish is excellent with parathas or white rice, and a dish of masoor dal on the side.

Note: Fresh crabs, when prepared using the above masala, are equally delicious.

Clam Fry

Serves 4 persons

I asked my friend Tess da'Cunha to share with me her recipe for clam fry, which she cooks to perfection.

500 gm fresh clams, or a 10-oz can, drained
2 tbsp cooking oil
2 large onions, minced
½ tsp ground cumin
½ tsp ground black pepper
½ tsp turmeric powder
4 flakes garlic, peeled and chopped fine
½" fresh ginger, peeled and chopped fine
2 green chillies, chopped
1 medium tomato, diced
2 tbsp fresh grated or desiccated coconut
1 tbsp vinegar or lemon juice
Salt to taste

In a saucepan place cooking oil and fry onions until transparent. Make a paste of the next three ingredients, add to the pan. Stir in ginger, garlic and green chillies. Fry the spices until fragrant. Blend in diced tomato and clams. Continue frying. Add coconut and one tablespoon vinegar or lemon juice to the pan. Add salt to taste. Remove from heat.

Serve clam fry as an accompaniment to rice, dal and vegetables.

Breaded Shrimp

The following recipe for breaded shrimp was always served at home as a snack. It was a particular favourite of my son Andrew, whose face would light up as he entered the house and smelled the shrimp being fried. No matter how many pounds of shrimp were purchased, they never proved to be enough to satisfy the hearty appetites of my four sons. I say this in the past tense because we lost our Andrew suddenly and under tragic circumstances a few years ago. Since that awful day, I have not had the heart to prepare this dish. Nevertheless, it is quite delicious, and needs no particular culinary skills to be cooked to perfection.

1 kg jumbo shrimps (prawns), peeled and deveined
¼ cup malt vinegar
2 tbsp fresh ginger/garlic paste
1 tsp chilli powder, or to taste
1 tbsp Kashmiri chilli, or paprika powder
½ tsp turmeric powder

1 tsp sugar
1 tsp salt, or to taste
2 eggs, slightly beaten with a little salt
Breadcrumbs
Cooking oil for frying

Wash shrimp and drain off excess water. Make a paste of the next six ingredients with the vinegar, and rub the masala into the shrimp. Set aside to marinade for a couple of hours. Place a heavy skillet over a moderate flame and pour in cooking oil. Dip individual shrimp in egg wash and roll in breadcrumbs. When the oil is hot, fry the shrimp until golden brown and crisp. Drain onto a paper towel. Serve immediately.

Vegetables, Lentils and Eggs

A Note on Vegetables

A large part of the Indian subcontinent is vegetarian, preferring soft, spicy vegetable creations and lentil curries to meat, fish or fowl. In fact, it would not be presumptuous to say that no Indian meal is complete without at least one side dish of vegetable. When the monsoons are 'good' and the harvest plentiful, markets in urban areas and remote villages are a sight to behold. They abound with an immense variety of fresh vegetables; pumpkin, radish, tomatoes, bitter gourd and okra spill over the vendor's stalls in a cornucopia of abundance. Mounds of green chillies, fresh coriander, mint and leafy greens, damp and aromatic, lie piled high on sacks of jute. A veritable feast for the senses, their colour and aroma tempt shoppers to linger at every stall, undecided on what to purchase and what to save for another day.

Vegetables are cooked in an assortment of spices into which curd, coconut milk or cream is incorporated, each addition lending a subtle difference to the dish. Cauliflower, pumpkin and brinjals lend themselves admirably to fries and savouries. Cooked in cream or fried in a batter of chick pea flour, their tantalizing aroma and delicious taste are enough to satisfy even the most fastidious palate.

Everyday vegetables such as carrots, peas and potatoes can be concocted into the most delectable creations with a hint of ginger and garlic, or a spoon of aromatic cumin. Half a cup of shredded coconut, when added to the homely ash pumpkin, yields a fitting accompaniment to any meal.

In South and Central India, vegetables are often fried in oil with green chillies, curry leaves and mustard seeds, into which is infused the rich milk or meat of the coconut. In northern India, there is a distinct preference for ghee, which imparts a subtle difference in taste to the end result. Paneer, ground almonds and cream are also added along with other spices, to create a variety of dishes.

In Anglo-Indian homes, foogaths dominate. Foogaths are generally served at lunch, and nearly every type of vegetable can be successfully prepared in this way. An apt description of the foogath would be, a delicately spiced stir fry of vegetable made with oil, onions, mustard seeds, green chillies, ginger and garlic.

For the evening meal, however, vegetable dishes may be selected to compliment the main course, especially if there are to be guests for dinner. They may consist of mashed potatoes, baked cauliflower in cheese sauce, or green beans. On festive occasions, there may be two or three vegetable side dishes to choose from, but they generally tend to be simple, all the better to showcase a delicious entrée.

Cauliflower in Cheese

Serves 4-6 persons

1 large cauliflower
3 tbsp butter
3 tbsp flour
2 cups milk
½ cup whipping cream
1 cup grated cheddar cheese
4 eggs, separated
1 tsp sugar
½ tsp pepper
Salt to taste

Trim cauliflower and break into flowerets. Cook cauliflower in salt water until barely tender, drain and set aside. Place a saucepan over low heat and add butter. As the butter melts, stir in flour, and do not allow it to brown. Add milk, stirring continually, until blended in with the roux. Pour in cream and grated cheddar cheese. Separate eggs, beat egg yolks with sugar, pepper and salt to taste. Add to the white sauce. Beat egg whites stiff and fold into sauce. Place cooked caulifloweretts in a greased baking dish and pour the cheese sauce over. Bake in preheated 180° C oven for about twenty minutes, or until puffed and golden. Serve immediately.

Roasted Carrots and Potatoes

Serves 6 persons

6 medium potatoes, each cut lengthways into 8 pieces
6 large carrots, scraped and cut into 3" sticks lengthways
6 tbsp butter
Salt to taste
½ tsp fresh pepper
2 cups chopped parsley

In a deep dish toss together potatoes, carrots, salt, pepper and parsley. Transfer to a greased baking dish. Melt six tablespoons butter and pour over the vegetables until they are evenly coated. Cover and roast, stirring occasionally until the vegetables are tender. Remove from oven and serve garnished with fresh parsley.

Stuffed Tomatoes

Serves 6 persons

6 large tomatoes
2 tbsp butter
1 large onion, minced
2 green chillies, minced
2 tbsp chopped, fresh parsley
2 tbsp chopped ham
1 tbsp Worcestershire sauce
½ tsp ground black pepper
Salt to taste

½ cup breadcrumbs
1 egg, beaten

Preheat oven to 180° C. Wash tomatoes and wipe dry. With a sharp knife remove the top slice from each tomato and scoop out the insides. Set aside tomato meat and top slices. Drain liquid from tomato cases. Place a skillet over moderate heat and melt butter. Add next four ingredients to skillet, together with the chopped centres from the tomatoes. Cook until onions are translucent. Stir in next four ingredients. Add breadcrumbs and egg to the skillet, fry briskly and remove from heat. Fill the tomato cases with the mixture, top with a dot of butter, and replace top slices. Bake in preheated oven for about twenty minutes. Serve hot.

Note: If preferred, grated cheddar cheese may be used instead of ham.

Potato Croquettes

Serves 4-6 persons

500 gm potatoes cooked in salted water
1 tbsp butter
1 large onion, minced
2 tbsp chopped parsley or green coriander
1 green chilli, finely minced
½ tsp garam masala
½ tsp pepper
1 tsp salt, or to taste
2 eggs, beaten
½ cup fine breadcrumbs
Cooking oil

Peel cooked potatoes, mash and set aside. Place butter in a heavy skillet, and fry next three ingredients. Add garam masala, pepper and salt to taste. Remove from heat and mix in with mashed potatoes. Whisk eggs. Form potato mixture into croquettes. Immerse in egg bath, and roll in breadcrumbs. Place cooking oil in skillet. When oil is moderately hot, fry the croquettes golden. Drain on absorbent paper. Transfer to platter and serve garnished with chopped green parsley or coriander. A large ripe tomato cut into thick slices and dusted with fresh ground pepper may be arranged around the platter.

Note: Potatoes croquettes make an excellent accompaniment served with steaks and chops.

Battered Brinjals

Serves 6 persons

2 cups sifted gram flour (besan)
1 tsp salt, or to taste
1 tbsp fresh ginger/garlic paste
½ tsp chilli powder
½ tsp turmeric powder
½ tsp baking powder
Cold water
2 large brinjals, cut into 1/8" thick rounds
Cooking oil for frying

Make a smooth thick paste of the first seven ingredients and coat brinjal slices. In a heavy skillet over moderate heat place half a cup of cooking oil. When the oil is hot lower the coated brinjal slices into the skillet and fry to a crisp golden-brown colour. Remove from skillet and drain on absorbent paper. Serve battered brinjals for lunch, with rice, curry and dal.

Mushrooms and Capsicum Fry

Serves 6 persons

3 tbsp butter
1 large onion, sliced
1 tbsp fresh ginger/garlic paste
2 green chillies, slit
500 gm mushrooms, washed and sliced
3 green capsicum chillies (green peppers), washed and sliced
2 tbsp oyster sauce
½ tsp fresh ground black pepper
Salt to taste

Place butter in a heavy-based saucepan over moderate heat. Add sliced onions and fry until translucent. Stir in next two ingredients. Fry until the spices are fragrant. Place sliced mushrooms and capsicums in the pan and continue frying until the vegetables are well coated with the spices. Stir in oyster sauce and sprinkle over pepper. Continue frying until the vegetables are crisp and tender. Add salt to taste. Remove from heat.

Mushrooms and capsicum fry makes an excellent accompaniment when served with steak, roast and beef cutlets.

Cabbage Foogath

Serves 6 persons

1 medium cabbage, shredded fine
1/3 cup cooking oil
1 medium onion, sliced fine
1 tsp whole mustard seeds
2 green chillies, slit
1 tbsp fresh ginger/garlic paste
Salt to taste

GARNISH

1 tbsp fresh coconut (optional)

Place oil in a heavy-based saucepan over moderate heat. Add mustard seeds to the pan. When the seeds start to sputter, mix in sliced onions and green chillies. Fry until the onions are golden. Add ginger/garlic paste to the pan, and continue frying until the spices are fragrant. Stir in cabbage a little at a time. Continue frying cabbage until it is crisp and tender. Add salt to taste.

Remove from heat and serve garnished with a tablespoon of grated fresh coconut.

Cauliflower Foogath

Serves 6 persons

1 large cauliflower separated into flowerets (parboil in salted water, drain and set aside)
¼ cup cooking oil

A few curry leaves
1 tsp whole mustard seeds
1 tsp whole cumin
1 medium onion, sliced fine
1 tbsp fresh ginger/garlic paste
1 medium tomato, chopped fine
2 green chillies, chopped fine
Salt to taste

Place cooking oil in a heavy-based pan over moderate heat. Throw in curry leaves. Add mustard and cumin seeds to the pan. When mustard seeds start to sputter, add onion slices and fry golden. Lower heat, stir in ginger/garlic paste and green chillies. When the spices are fragrant, add the cauliflower and chopped tomato. Stir, cover and allow the cauliflower foogath to simmer gently for about ten minutes, stirring occasionally. Add salt to taste. Remove from heat.

Serve cauliflower foogath with cooked rice or chapatis, curry and pickles.

Foogath of Red Pumpkin

Serves 4-6 persons

½ kg red pumpkin, seeded and cubed
1/3 cup oil
A few curry leaves
1 tsp mustard seeds
1 large onion, minced
2 green chillies, slit
1 tbsp fresh ginger/garlic paste
2 tbsp fresh grated or dried coconut*
Salt to taste

In a saucepan over moderate heat pour in oil. Throw in curry leaves and mustard seeds. When the seeds start to sputter, add minced onion. Fry until the onion begins to colour. Place green chillies and ginger/garlic paste in the pan. Continue frying. Stir in pumpkin and grated coconut. Lower heat and fry the vegetable mixture, stirring continually, until the vegetable is tender and much of the water has been absorbed. Add salt to taste. Remove from heat.

Serve pumpkin foogath as an accompaniment, together with rice, chapatis, curry or a side dish.

Note: *Fresh grated coconut when available is ideal, but dried coconut (copra) or desiccated, unsweetened coconut serves just as well.

Foogath of French Beans

Serves 4-6 persons

½ kg French beans (Top and tail, cut in half)
1/3 cup cooking oil
1 large onion, sliced fine
1 tbsp fresh ginger/garlic paste
2 green chillies, sliced lengthways
2 tbsp fresh or dried coconut, scraped
2 tbsp water
Salt to taste

Place a saucepan with lid over moderate heat. Pour in oil. Add sliced onions and fry until translucent. Place ginger/ garlic paste and green chillies in the pan and fry until fragrant. Stir in green beans together with coconut. Sprinkle over two tablespoons water, add salt to taste. Lower heat, cover the saucepan and allow the green beans to cook gently, stirring occasionally. When green beans are tender, remove from heat and serve as an accompaniment at lunch or dinner.

Masala Brinjal

Serves 6 persons

2 large brinjals (wipe with a damp cloth and cut in half lengthways. Cut each half into strips. Sprinkle with a tsp of salt and set aside)
1 tsp fenugreek seed
1/3 cup mustard oil
A few curry leaves with stalk
1 pod fresh garlic—grind to a paste in a little vinegar
2" piece of fresh ginger—grind to a paste in a little vinegar
1 tsp Kashmiri chilli, or paprika powder
½ tsp chilli powder
3 green chillies, slit
2 tbsp tamarind purée
2 tbsp sugar
1 tbsp vinegar
Salt to taste

Place a heavy-based pan over moderate heat. Pour in mustard oil and curry leaves. When the oil is hot add fenugreek seeds. Make a paste of the next four ingredients and stir into the pan. Lower heat and fry the spices until they are fragrant. Place slices of brinjal in the pan and continue frying until the vegetable is well coated with the spice mixture. Add green chillies, tamarind and sugar to the pan. Pour over a tablespoon of vinegar. Cover and allow the brinjals to cook until soft. Add salt to taste. Remove from heat and serve together with rice, chapatis, curry or dal.

Note: Masala brinjal keeps for a few days in the refrigerator, and the taste improves with keeping.

Peas and Potato Sabzi

Serves 6 persons

5 large potatoes, peeled, cubed and cooked in salt water (drain and set aside)
1 cup cooked peas
1/3 cup cooking oil
A few fresh curry leaves
1 tsp mustard seeds
2 large onions, minced
2 tbsp fresh ginger/garlic paste
½ tsp turmeric powder
1 medium bunch fresh coriander leaves, washed and chopped
3 green chillies, chopped
Salt to taste
2 tsp fresh lime juice

Place a heavy-based pan over moderate heat, pour in oil. Throw in curry leaves and mustard seeds. When the seeds begin to sputter add minced onion and fry until translucent. Lower heat. Make a paste of ginger/garlic paste and turmeric powder. Stir into the pan and fry until fragrant. Add the next two ingredients, together with potatoes and peas. Rapidly stirring, fry the potato/peas mixture until well coated with the spices. Pour over fresh lime juice. Stir in salt to taste, and remove from heat.

Serve peas and potato sabzi with puris as a snack, or as a vegetable accompaniment at lunch or dinner.

Curried Ladies Fingers (Okra)

Serves 4 persons

250 gm ladies fingers (wash and wipe dry. Top and tail)
¼ cup oil
A few curry leaves
½ tsp mustard seeds
1 large onion, minced
1 tsp fresh ginger/garlic paste
½ tsp turmeric powder
2 green chillies, slit
1 cup thick coconut milk
Salt to taste

Place a heavy-based pan with lid over moderate heat. Pour in oil. Throw in curry leaves and mustard seeds. When the seeds begin to sputter, stir in minced onion and fry golden. Combine ginger/garlic paste with turmeric powder. Stir into the pan, and fry until fragrant. Add ladies fingers and green chillies to pan, and fry until the vegetable is well coated with the spices. Pour over coconut milk. Add salt to taste. Cover pan. Allow vegetable to simmer over low heat until tender. Serve as an accompaniment at lunch or dinner.

Methi Bhajee with Prawns

Serves 4 persons

¼ cup cooking oil
1 large onion, minced
1 tbsp fresh ginger/garlic paste
3 green chillies, chopped fine
250 gm shelled and deveined prawns
1 medium bunch methi leaves (remove stalks, wash and set aside)
1 large potato, peeled, diced and cooked in salt water
Salt to taste

Place oil in a heavy-based pan over moderate heat and fry onions until translucent. Add ginger/garlic paste and green chillies to the pan; continue frying until fragrant. Stir in prawns and cook for a few minutes until firm. Mix in the methi leaves and diced potato. Add salt to taste. Fry the mixture on low heat, stirring continuously, until the prawns are cooked through. Remove from heat.

This is an incredibly fragrant dish that is excellent served with chapatis, or rice, dal and chutney.

Masoor Dal

Serves 6 persons

> And Esau said to Jacob, 'Let me eat some of that red pottage for I am famished!'
>
> And thus he sold his birthright to his brother Jacob.
>
> —*Genesis 25; 29-34*

The 'pottage' referred to was made from red lentils or masoor dal, as it is commonly called. One of the oldest legumes known to man, lentils are mentioned repeatedly in the Bible, and may indeed have been cooked and served as regularly in those times as they are in this day and age.

Dal is a staple and integral part of Indian cuisine. Since it is the chief source of protein in a vegetarian's diet, its importance can hardly be exaggerated. Whether it comprises the main meal, or is served as an accompaniment along with other dishes, no Indian meal is complete without a dish of dal.

Masoor dal has to be the most favoured of lentils as far as Anglo-Indian cuisine is concerned, and gram dal comes in a close second. Served with white rice, a dish of vegetable foogath and chutney on the side, masoor dal rounds off a simple, delicious meal. The recipe given below is one I learned from an old cook, who prepared it nearly every day in our household. I serve it to this day at least once a week, for besides being highly nutritious, it is an excellent-tasting dish.

1 cup of masoor dal, rinsed in cold water
2 cups of water
A few curry leaves
1 tsp salt, or to taste
½ cup of vegetable oil, or 3 tbsp ghee
1 tsp mustard seeds
1 large onion, sliced fine
1 tbsp ginger/garlic paste
½ tsp turmeric powder
2 green chillies, slit
1 small bunch green coriander, washed and chopped
1 large tomato, chopped
½ cup of hot water

Cook dal until soft in two cups water together with curry leaves and a little salt. Remove from heat and set aside. In a heavy-based pan over moderate heat, pour in oil or three tablespoons ghee. Add mustard seeds to the pot, and when they begin to sputter add in sliced onions. Allow onions to fry until golden brown in colour. Mix together turmeric powder and ginger/garlic paste. Place the paste in the pan and fry for a few minutes, or until the spices release their fragrant aroma. Stir in chopped green coriander, green chillies and chopped tomato. Lower heat and fry the mixture until the oil separates from the spices. Pour in cooked dal and stir well. Test for sufficient salt. Pour over half a cup of hot water. Cover the pan and simmer dal for a further fifteen minutes. Remove from heat.

For variation, two tablespoons tamarind purée may be stirred into the dal together with a teaspoon of sugar, and a little extra hot water. This will infuse a sour/sweet taste that is pleasing to the palate. Garnish masoor dal with chopped, fresh green coriander leaves and serve as a side dish together with rice, curries and other vegetable accompaniments.

Vegetable Sambar

Serves 4-6 persons

½ cup toovar dal
½ tsp turmeric powder
½ tsp salt
DRY ROAST
1 tbsp coriander powder
1 tsp red chilli powder
A pinch of asafoetida
FOR SAMBAR
¼ cup cooking oil
A few curry leaves
1 large onion, sliced fine
1 small brinjal, cubed
1 medium potato, peeled and cubed
1 drumstick, clean and cut into 2" bits
6 whole small onions, peeled
2 tomatoes, peeled and cubed
2 green chillies
2 cups hot water
3 tbsp tamarind purée
1 tsp mustard seeds
1 tsp cumin seeds
Salt to taste

Wash dal and soak overnight. The following day cook dal together with turmeric and salt until soft. Mash dal and pass through á sieve. Set aside. Dry roast coriander, chilli powder and asafoetida. Place a heavy-based pot over moderate heat and pour in oil. Add curry leaves. When the oil gets hot throw in sliced onions and fry until golden. Stir in dry-roasted ingredients together with next six vegetables. Continue frying. Pour in cooked dal. Add water, salt to taste and tamarind purée. Lower flame and simmer the sambar until the vegetables are soft. Add more water as required.

In a heavy skillet place one tablespoon cooking oil, and fry the mustard and cumin seeds. When the mustard seeds start to sputter, remove from heat and add to the sambar. Ladle vegetable sambar over rice and serve with papads and pickles.

Rasam

Serves 6 persons

1 cup toovar dal (Soak in water for 3 hours)
½ tsp turmeric powder

DRY ROAST

A pinch of asafoetida
1 tsp red chilli powder
1 tsp cumin powder
1 tbsp coriander powder
4 whole peppercorns

FOR RASAM

¼ cup cooking oil
A few curry leaves
½ tsp mustard seeds
1 large onion, sliced fine
1 tbsp fresh ginger/garlic paste
2 tbsp tamarind pulp
2 cups water

Cook dal with half teaspoon turmeric powder and a little salt until soft. Mash, pass through a sieve and set aside. Dry roast the next five ingredients. In a heavy-based pot over moderate heat pour in oil, curry leaves and mustard seeds. When the seeds begin to sputter, stir in sliced onions and fry until golden. Place ginger/garlic paste in the pot and fry until fragrant. Stir in roasted spices, followed by the cooked dal and liquid. Pour in two cups of hot water, tamarind pulp and salt to taste. Lower heat, cover and allow the rasam to simmer, stirring occasionally until the spices have blended in with the dal. Remove lid and test for sufficient salt.

Rasam is a thin watery dal with a delicious pungency.

Ladle rasam over cooked rice, and serve with vegetables, papads and pickles.

Amti

Serves 6 persons

Amti is a sweet and sour lentil soup with a suggestion of coconut. This soup is excellent when served with a complementary platter of delicious and satisfying puran polis.

1 cup toovar dal (wash dal and soak for 3 hours in cold water)
½ tsp turmeric powder
Water
Salt to taste

¼ cup oil
A few curry leaves
½ tsp mustard seeds
1 large onion, finely sliced
1 tbsp ginger/garlic paste
3 green chillies, slit
1 cup thick coconut milk
2 tbsp tamarind pulp
2 tbsp brown sugar or jaggery

Place dal with five cups water, turmeric and salt to taste in a pot over moderate heat and cook until soft. Stir occasionally to ensure dal does not adhere to the bottom of the pot, and add more water if required. Remove from heat, mash and strain through a sieve. Set aside. Place a heavy-based pot over moderate heat and pour in oil. Throw in curry leaves and mustard seeds. When the seeds start to sputter, place sliced onions in the pot and fry golden. Stir in ginger/garlic paste and green chillies, fry spices till fragrant. Pour mashed dal into the pot, followed by coconut milk, tamarind paste and brown sugar or jaggery. Lower heat, and allow the amti to simmer for about fifteen minutes. Add more water if the dal is too thick. Remove from stove and serve with puran polis.

Puran Polis

Serves 6 persons

250 gm gram dal
250 gm toovar dal
½ tsp salt

6 oz sugar
¼ tsp cardamom powder
3 cups wheat flour
½ tsp salt, or to taste
8 oz ghee

Soak dals for about two hours and cook in salted water until tender. Strain, discard liquid, and mash until soft. Blend in sugar and cardamom powder. Set aside.

Make a soft pliable dough of the wheat flour with salt, a little ghee and cold water. Roll out dough as for stuffed paratha, place one tablespoon of the dal mixture in the centre of the round. Fold and roll out again. Place a heavy skillet over moderate flame and add one teaspoon of ghee to the skillet. When the ghee is hot, lower the 'poli' into the skillet and gently fry. Brush with more ghee, flip and fry the other side until crisp and golden. Remove from heat to a platter. Continue until all the polis are fried. Serve with Amti.

Egg Curry with Gram Dal

Serves 6 persons

A few simple rules should be observed when using eggs in a curry. It is essential to lower halved, hard-boiled eggs into the curry sauce at the very end of the cooking process. In some cases the hard-boiled eggs are set in a serving dish, and the curry sauce is spooned over. Too much handling breaks up the cooked eggs, which spoils the look of the end product.

Egg curry must be served immediately for optimum taste.

½ cup gram dal (wash and soak for 2 hours in water)
10 hard-boiled eggs, peeled and halved
¼ cup cooking oil
A few curry leaves
1 large onion, minced
1 tbsp fresh ginger/garlic paste
½ tsp red chilli powder
1 tsp Kashmiri chilli powder
1 tsp cumin powder
1 tbsp coriander powder
1 tomato, peeled and diced
1 cup thick coconut milk
2 tbsp tamarind pulp
2 green chillies, slit
Salt to taste

GARNISH

2 tbsp chopped green coriander

Cook gram dal in water until soft; mash and set aside. Place a heavy-based pan over moderate heat, pour in oil and add curry leaves. When the oil is hot add minced onion to the pot and fry until translucent. Make a paste of the next five ingredients and lower into the pan. Fry spices fragrant, and stir in tomatoes. Place cooked dal in the pan together with coconut milk, tamarind pulp and salt to taste. Simmer for a further ten minutes, stirring frequently. At this point one may add a little water to the pot if required, in the interest of making more gravy. Stir in halved eggs.

Garnish with chopped green coriander leaves and serve immediately with rice, vegetables and papads.

Egg Moley

Serves 4 persons

6 hard-boiled eggs, peeled and halved
¼ cup cooking oil
A few curry leaves
1 large onion, minced
1 tbsp fresh ginger/garlic paste
1 tsp ground cumin
½ tsp garam masala
½ tsp turmeric powder
1 small bunch fresh coriander, washed and minced
3 green chillies, chopped fine
1 large tomato, chopped
1 cup thick coconut milk
½ cup hot water
1 tsp salt, or to taste
2 tsp lime juice
½ tsp sugar
1 cup cooked peas
1 potato, cubed and cooked in salted water

Place a pan over moderate heat and pour in oil. Add curry leaves. When the oil is hot, fry minced onions golden. Make a paste of the next four ingredients, stir into the pan and fry until the spices release their fragrant aroma. Mix in green coriander, chillies and tomato. Continue frying. Stir in next five ingredients. Add cooked peas and potatoes to the curry gravy. Cover the pan and allow the curry to simmer over low heat for about ten minutes, or until the spices are well blended. Remove lid and place halved eggs in the pan.

Serve egg moley with rice, chutney and papads.

Omelette

Serves 6 persons

On my grandfather's coffee plantation, deep in the heart of the Nilgiris, breakfast consisted of savoury omelettes served with flaky parathas, followed by copious cups of delicious percolated coffee. Slices of honey-sweet papaya and tiny butter bananas rounded off the meal. The following recipe makes an excellent omelette. For a variation, diced cooked ham may be incorporated into the dish.

12 large eggs, separate whites from yolks
2 medium onions, minced
1 medium bunch fresh green coriander, washed and chopped fine
3 green chillies, chopped fine
½ cup diced lean ham (optional)
¼ tsp freshly ground black pepper
Salt to taste
Cooking oil for frying
3 large tomatoes, cut into thick rounds
Freshly ground black pepper

In a bowl whisk egg whites stiff. Set aside. Beat egg yolks separately, and stir in next four ingredients. Add pepper and salt to taste. Fold egg whites into yolk mixture. Place a heavy skillet over moderate heat and pour in two tablespoons oil. When oil is hot, lower flame and pour in a portion of the egg batter. Cook on one side until set, flip and cook other side until golden brown. Fold in half. Lift omelette out of the skillet. Add oil if required, and repeat process until all the egg mixture has been utilized. Place omelettes on a large platter. Garnish with tomato rounds and dust with pepper. Flaky parathas fried in ghee, or hot buttered toast, make an excellent accompaniment.

Scrambled Eggs

Serves 6 persons

12 eggs
½ tsp freshly ground black pepper
1 tsp salt, or to taste
¼ cup cooking oil
3 medium onions, minced
3 green chillies, minced
1 medium bunch fresh green coriander, washed and chopped
1 large tomato, diced

Whisk eggs with pepper and salt to taste. Place a heavy skillet over moderate heat and pour in oil. When the oil is hot, add minced onions to the skillet and fry until translucent. Add next three ingredients. Lastly mix in beaten eggs, and stir the mixture continuously until the eggs are set. Remove from flame and serve for breakfast with hot buttered toast.

Buttered Eggs

Serves 6 persons

12 eggs
½ tsp black pepper
Salt to taste
½ cup full cream milk
2 tbsp butter
½ tsp freshly ground black pepper

GARNISH

3 medium tomatoes, cut into rounds
Pepper
Crisp fried bacon

Beat eggs with pepper and salt to taste. In a heavy skillet over low heat place milk, and as it heats, stir in beaten eggs. Add butter to the egg/milk mixture, stirring rapidly. When the eggs set, remove from heat. Place on serving platter, surrounded by tomato rounds dusted with pepper, and slices of crisp fried bacon. Slices of buttered toast, hot tea and coffee make excellent breakfast accompaniments.

Cakes, Cookies and Custard

Sweet Treats from Aunt Isabella's Kitchen

Invitations to Aunt Isabella's high teas were much sought after. A gregarious Bombay matron, she loved entertaining and was not above going into the kitchen herself to oversee the baking and 'lending a hand'. Aunt Isabella, however, drew the line at washing up. Washing up was not for her, she proclaimed; it ruined a lady's hands.

As a child, I was fascinated with everything about Aunt Isabella. She owned a large airy bungalow with a veranda running all around, located in suburban Bombay. The garden at the front of the house was overgrown and unruly, with flowers everywhere, growing in a wonderful state of disarray. I liked to think she deliberately planned it that way. However, the truth of the matter was, Aunt Isabella was much too preoccupied with the social whirl, card games, dinner parties and club nights to pay too much attention to her mali, a small squirrelly man called Shankar. I often came across him, fast asleep in the shade of the large mango tree at the end of the garden.

Using his turban for a pillow, he snored in concert with the music of the insect world, while all around him plant life flourished in wild profusion. The back garden was a veritable orchard where sprawling mango, custard apple and guava trees flourished. Birds squawked and fluttered among the branches, with the guava trees being much favoured by the parrots. As the golden fruit ripened, weighing the branches almost to the ground, great flocks would come swooping down, and one could see them with their hooked beaks deeply embedded in the rose-coloured flesh, as they gorged themselves on the harvest.

Whenever my mother came into town on a shopping expedition, I always tagged along. While the two ladies went gallivanting, I was left in the care of the servants, which was as good as being left to my own devices, for they spent the entire time gossiping on the back veranda. I would wander through the garden with a book under my arm, to that particular shady spot beneath the raintree, and here among the beds of nasturtiums and sweet peas, I whiled away the hours, reading. To this day when I smell nasturtiums, I recall that wonderful garden.

Aunt Isabella had three daughters with no husband in sight. I timidly ventured to ask about his whereabouts one time, and she informed me that he had died in the war. She named her daughters after the flowers she loved. There was Rose the eldest, followed by Violet, and her youngest daughter was named Daisy. Being much younger than they, I often watched with wide-eyed fascination as they dressed to go out in the evening in a flurry of chiffon and silk. I gazed in awe at their finery, and inhaled with delight the mingled scents of different perfumes that filled the air. Aunt Isabella spent a lot of time discussing the eligibility of their various suitors with my mother. 'When they are all married,' she would say with a sigh, 'I will at last be at peace.'

When I was older, my mother confided in me that she was not really related to Aunt Isabella, but that they had been friends for ages. Nevertheless, since I had known her all my life, I continued to call her Aunt. I think she sensed my love of cookery, for I was always sneaking into her large dark kitchen, asking if I could help out. At first, no doubt, she considered me a nuisance child, always underfoot, but as time passed I was accepted. 'Here is a stool,' she would say in her no-nonsense way. 'Sit still and remove the capes from these gooseberries for we are going to make some jam.' I always hurried to comply with her wishes.

As the years went by, all her three daughters finally married and left home, and Aunt Isabella came to visit my mother more often. It was during this period that she and I grew closer. She shared many secrets with me, and helped with countless bits of advice, from how to bake the perfect pound cake to the art of flower arrangement. During one of her holidays she presented me with a book of her favourite recipes. Frayed at the edges, the pages were well thumbed. I was startled to receive such a precious gift, and asked what she would do when she had to bake.

Tapping the side of her head with a forefinger, she replied, 'It's all in there.'

The book was a thick note pad with recipes jotted down in her neat hand. Attention to weights and measures had been cast to the wind. Cakes and pastries were concocted with a cup of this, a pinch of that, or a smidgen of something else. But, oh, what a challenge it presented! Over the years I tried all the recipes at one time or another, and I am happy to report that eventually I succeeded in perfecting most of them, using recognized weights and measures.

Recipes that I found to be especially delicious have been prepared time and again, to the delight of family and friends. They have never failed me. I now offer these recipes, together with some of my own that are tried and true.

Seed Cake

Makes 1 loaf

2 cups cake flour
¼ tsp salt
2 tsp baking powder
1 cup butter
1 cup sugar
1 tsp vanilla extract
5 eggs
2 tbsp caraway seeds

Mix together first three ingredients. Set aside. With an electric beater, cream together butter, sugar and essence. Add eggs to the bowl one at a time. Stir in dry ingredients and beat for a further four or five minutes. Lastly, sprinkle over caraway seeds and lightly mix into the batter. Butter and flour a (9" x 5" x 3") loaf pan and pour in batter. Bake in moderate oven (180° C) for about half an hour, or until cake tester, inserted, comes out clean.

Cool cake, slice and serve.

Coconut Cake

Makes 1 loaf

250 gm butter
250 gm sugar
3 eggs
1 tsp vanilla extract

2/3 cup fresh grated or desiccated coconut
1 cup thick coconut milk
2 cups cake flour
2 tsp baking powder

Butter a (9" x 5" x 3") loaf pan, and line base with brown paper. In a mixing bowl cream together butter, sugar, eggs and vanilla extract. Blend in grated or desiccated coconut. Mix together flour and baking powder. Add flour mixture to the bowl, alternating with coconut milk, until both have been utilized and you have a smooth batter. Pour into cake pan and bake in preheated moderate (180° C oven) for about half an hour, or until cake tester, inserted, comes out clean. Remove cake from pan, peel away brown paper and cool coconut cake on a rack.

Slice and serve.

Boiled Raisin Spice Cake

Makes 1 loaf

1 cup firmly packed brown sugar
1 cup raisins
1¼ cups water
½ cup butter
1½ tsp garam masala
2 cups all-purpose flour
1 tsp baking powder
1 tsp baking soda
½ tsp salt

In a saucepan boil together first five ingredients. Chill. Sift together next four ingredients and stir into chilled raisins, butter mixture. Pour into a greased loaf pan (9" x 5" x 3") and bake in moderate oven (180° C) for about forty-five minutes, or until a cake tester, inserted, comes out clean.

Allow to cool, slice and serve.

Note: Boiled raisin/spice cake improves with keeping, and will taste even more delicious the following day. To store, wrap cooled cake in foil or plastic wrap.

Simnel Cake

Makes 1 cake

125 gm butter
125 gm sugar
3 eggs
1 cup cake flour
1 tsp baking powder
Pinch of salt
½ tsp powdered ginger
½ tsp ground cinnamon
¼ tsp ground nutmeg
125 gm currants
125 gm sultanas
125 gm raisins
½ cup chopped mixed fruit
Milk
500 gm almond paste (marzipan)

In a bowl cream together butter, sugar and eggs. Mix flour, baking powder, salt and ground spices. Blend in with butter/sugar mixture, adding a little milk if required to facilitate blending. Add currants, sultanas, raisins and mixed fruit to the batter. Butter a nine-inch springform cake pan and pour in half the batter. Roll out half the almond paste to fit the circumference of the pan. Place over cake batter. Pour the rest of the batter over almond paste. Bake simnel cake in preheated (180° C oven) for about one hour. Remove cake from oven, and when cool, decorate top of simnel cake with remaining almond paste.

Simnel cake is traditionally served at Easter time, and decorations of eggs and chicks set on and around the cake reflect the Easter celebrations.

Orange Pound Cake

Makes 1 cake

3 cups flour
½ tsp baking soda
1½ cups butter
2 cups sugar
6 eggs
1 cup milk
2 tsp orange extract
Grated rind of half an orange
1 cup milk

Grease loaf pan and dust with flour; set aside. Sift flour and baking soda into a bowl. Cream butter and sugar, adding eggs to the batter one at a time. Mix orange extract in with milk. Add flour/baking soda mixture to the creamed batter a little at a time, alternating with milk/essence mixture. Stir in grated orange rind. Turn the batter into loaf pan and bake in (180° C) oven for about one hour, or until a cake tester, inserted, comes out clean. Remove from oven.

Make a glaze from confectioner's sugar, vanilla and milk. Pour glaze over cake.

Note: Orange pound cake improves with keeping. To store, wrap cooled cake in foil or plastic wrap until ready to cut and serve.

Chocolate Cake

Makes 1 cake

1¾ cups unsifted cake flour
2 cups sugar
¾ cup cocoa
1½ tsp baking powder
1½ tsp baking soda
1 tsp salt
2 eggs
1 cup milk
½ cup vegetable oil
2 tsp vanilla extract
½ cup hot water

Combine first six ingredients in mixing bowl. Add next four ingredients. Beat the mixture with electric mixer until well blended. Beat in one cup hot water. Divide the cake batter between two layer pans and bake in preheated (180° C) oven for about half an hour, or until cake tester, inserted, comes out clean. Remove from pans and cool. Spread strawberry jam between layers, frost and serve.

Luscious Chocolate Rum Cake

Makes 3 9" layer cakes

250 gm unsweetened cooking chocolate, melted
2 tbsp hot water
2 cups sugar
1 cup butter
2 tsp vanilla extract
4 eggs, separated
1 tsp cream of tartar
2¼ cups sifted cake flour
½ tsp baking soda
1 cup milk

Mix melted chocolate with hot water. Cream sugar and butter. Mix in chocolate mixture, vanilla extract and egg yolks. Beat egg whites stiff with cream of tartar, set aside. Blend together cake flour and baking soda. Add sifted flour alternately with milk to the creamed batter. Lastly fold in the stiffly beaten egg whites. Pour into buttered layer pans, and bake in moderate (180° C) oven for about half an hour, or until a cake tester, inserted, comes out clean. Cool.

FILLING

½ cup raspberry or strawberry jam
2 tbsp rum

In a saucepan warm jam until soft and runny. Pour in rum and blend well. Pierce cake layers all over with cake tester and pour jam/rum mixture over each layer. Frost the cake with a luscious chocolate/rum frosting.

CHOCOLATE/VANILLA/RUM FROSTING

250 gm semi-sweet cooking chocolate, melted
2 tbsp hot water
½ cup butter
½ cup dark rum
1 tsp vanilla extract
3 cups confectioner's (icing) sugar

Mix together semi-sweet chocolate with hot water. In a mixing bowl place butter, rum and vanilla extract. Add in melted chocolate mixture. Blend until smooth and creamy with electric beater. Add icing sugar to the mixture a little at a time until you have a dark, smooth icing of spreadable consistency. Frost chocolate cake.

Coconut Custard Pie

Makes 1 pie

FOR THE TART SHELL

2 cups all-purpose flour
½ tsp salt
1 cup vegetable shortening
1 egg
2 tbsp cold water
1 tbsp white vinegar

FOR THE PIE

2 tbsp butter
1 cup icing sugar
3 eggs, separated
Pinch of salt
1 tsp vanilla extract

½ cup full cream milk
2 cups freshly grated or desiccated coconut
A pinch of grated nutmeg

Mix flour and salt together, and rub in vegetable shortening, lightly mixing with fingertips until the mixture is crumbly. Beat egg with water and vinegar. Pour liquid evenly over flour mixture, and stir with a fork until dough is moist and holds together. Gather into a ball. Refrigerate for about fifteen minutes. On a lightly floured surface roll dough out into a circle and fit into pie plate, without stretching. Allow dough to overlap about one inch all around. Set aside

For pie: Cream together butter and sugar, add in egg yolks one at a time. Beat egg whites together with salt and set aside. Mix vanilla extract and milk, pour into the butter/sugar mixture. Stir in grated or desiccated coconut. Fold in beaten egg whites and pour the mixture into the pie plate. Sprinkle over grated nutmeg. Trim pastry and place coconut/custard pie in preheated oven (180° C). Bake until the pie is set and golden brown on top. Remove from oven, cool and serve.

Caramel Custard

Serves 4-6 persons

2 cups full cream or evaporated milk
4 eggs
¾ cup sugar, or to taste
1 tsp vanilla extract

Sprinkle two tablespoons sugar over the base of a custard mould with a tight-fitting lid. Place mould over high heat. The sugar will melt and caramelize. Remove from heat. Tilt mould until the base is well coated with the caramel mixture. In a bowl whip together eggs and sugar, blend in milk and vanilla. Pour the mixture into mould. Secure lid, and set in a pan of water that should come halfway up the sides of the mould. Place in preheated (180° C) oven, and bake the custard until set. Remove from oven and allow to cool before inverting on to a dessert plate.

The cooled custard should slip out of the mould easily. Burnt custard swimming in a caramelized sauce is delicious, and will please even the most discerning palate.

Steamed Carrot Pudding

Makes 1 pudding

½ cup butter
1½ cup brown sugar
3 large eggs
3 tbsp lemon juice
2 tsp grated lemon rind
1 cup all-purpose flour
½ tsp baking powder
½ tsp baking soda
¼ tsp salt
½ tsp garam masala
1½ cups grated carrots
Whipped cream

Cream butter and sugar in a bowl. Beat the eggs into the

batter one at a time, add lemon juice. Sift together flour, baking soda, baking powder, salt and garam masala. Add to the batter a tablespoon at a time until utilized. Stir in grated carrots and lemon rind. Transfer the mixture to a buttered pudding mould. Cover the mould with foil and set in a pan. Fill the pan with water, two thirds up the sides of the mould, and bake in a preheated (180° C) oven until a cake tester inserted through the centre comes out clean. Allow to cool.

Invert pudding onto a dish and serve with whipped cream.

Apricot Jam Tart

Makes 1 tart

2 cups all-purpose flour
1 cup butter
1 cup confectioner's sugar
½ cup ground almonds
½ tsp ground cinnamon
½ tsp salt
3 egg yolks
Juice and grated rind of half lime
Apricot jam

Place first eight ingredients in a bowl and work into a crumbly dough. Gather dough into a ball and chill, covered for half an hour. Remove two thirds dough and roll out to fit an eight-inch diameter tart pan with fluted edges. Cover with a half-inch layer of apricot jam. Roll out remaining dough and cut into strips about half an inch wide. Lay on the tart lattice fashion. Bake in preheated oven (180° C), until pastry is flaky and golden. Remove from oven, and when the tart is cool, fill more jam into lattice openings.

Slice apricot jam tart into sections and serve with whipped cream.

Lemon Curd

Makes 3 cups

1 cup sugar
6 eggs
½ cup fresh lime juice
½ cup butter

Lightly beat together sugar and eggs; blend in lime juice. Place the mixture in a heavy-based saucepan over low heat. Add butter to the pan, and stir continually until the mixture coats the back of the spoon. Be careful not to overcook lemon curd, or it will curdle. Remove from heat immediately, and allow the curd to cool. When cool, it will thicken further.

Spoon lemon curd into baked tart shells.

Baked Rice Pudding

Serves 6-8 persons

2 eggs
½ cup sugar
Pinch of salt

1 tsp vanilla extract
2 cups full cream milk
½ cup raisins
1 cup cooked rice (preferably short-grained)
¼ tsp ground nutmeg

In a bowl beat together first four ingredients until well blended. Pour in two cups milk. Add cooked rice and raisins to the bowl. Pour into a buttered pudding dish. Sprinkle nutmeg over, cover and place rice pudding in a pan of water that comes halfway up the sides of the pudding dish. Bake in a preheated slow oven (150° C) for about one hour, or until rice/custard mixture has set. Remove cover, and continue baking until a rich, brown crust forms on the surface of the pudding. Remove from oven and serve warm or chilled.

Lemon Sponge Pudding

Makes 1 pudding

¼ cup butter
½ cup sugar
2 eggs
Grated rind of 1 lemon
¼ cup raisins
3 tbsp fresh lime juice
¼ cup milk
½ cup cake flour
½ tsp baking soda
Dash of salt

LEMON SAUCE

½ cup sugar
2 tbsp cornstarch
2 cups water
¼ cup butter
2 tbsp fresh lime juice
Dash of salt

In a pudding basin cream butter and sugar. Add eggs to the mixture one at a time, after which, stir in grated lemon rind and raisins. Pour in milk. Sift together flour, baking soda and salt. Blend flour mixture into creamed batter until smooth. Generously butter a pudding mould. Pour lemon batter into mould and seal. Place a trivet in a pan of boiling water, and place the mould on the trivet. Water should come halfway up the sides of the pudding mould. Steam lemon sponge for approximately one hour. When the sponge has set, unmould and serve warm with lemon sauce.

To make lemon sauce: In a saucepan mix together sugar and cornstarch. Add water and stir until the mixture is smooth. Place over low heat, stirring continuously until slightly thickened and clear. Remove from heat and blend in remaining ingredients. Serve hot.

Marmalade Pudding

Serves 4 persons

3 eggs
½ cup sugar
2 oz butter

1 tsp orange extract
1 cup breadcrumbs
1 cup full cream milk
½ cup orange marmalade

In a bowl beat eggs, sugar, butter and orange extract until smooth. Stir in breadcrumbs, and pour over milk. Add orange marmalade and blend well. Pour batter into buttered pudding mould. Cover and set in a pan with enough water to come halfway up the sides of the mould. Place the basin in preheated (180° C) oven and bake until firm. Unmould, and serve warm with whipped or clotted cream.

Roly Poly Pudding

Makes 1 pudding

Roly Poly pudding is a suet dough pudding of English origin.

1 cup cake flour
1 cup chopped suet
2 cups breadcrumbs
3 tbsp sugar
1 egg
Cold milk
Thick raspberry or black currant jam

Work the first five ingredients into a soft pliable dough, using as much milk as required. Roll out suet pastry in a rectangular shape and place on a piece of cheesecloth or muslin. Spread a thick layer of jam on the dough to within one inch from the edge all around. Roll up the dough in the cloth as for jelly roll. Tie on both ends. Steam pudding in a pot of boiling hot water for two hours. Remove from heat, untie, slice and serve with heavy cream, or custard sauce.

Custard Sauce

Serves 6-8 persons

½ cup sugar
3 large eggs
1 tsp vanilla extract
2 cups full cream or evaporated milk

Beat together first three ingredients, pour in milk and blend well. Place the mixture in a heavy-based saucepan over low heat and stir until the custard coats the back of the spoon. Remove from heat, chill and serve.

Trifle

Serves 6 persons

1 lb sponge fingers, or stale pound cake (cut into 8 thick slices)
1 cup of port wine
1 cup raspberry jam
Custard sauce

1 cup heavy cream
Whipped cream
Glace cherries

Layer slices of pound cake at the base and up the sides of a trifle bowl. Spoon over half the quantity of port wine and set aside for ten minutes. Place a layer of raspberry jam over the pound cake at the base of the trifle bowl. Blend heavy cream in with custard sauce until smooth and thick. Cover raspberry jam with half the amount of custard sauce. Place the remaining sponge fingers over the custard. Spoon over remaining port wine. Spread with raspberry jam. Pour over the remaining custard sauce. Top with whipped cream. Decorate with glace cherries. Chill and serve.

Gulab Jamuns

I have achieved some measure of success with this recipe. In the interest of cutting calories, I have refrained from frying the gulab jamuns in ghee. They are nevertheless quite delicious, and may be enjoyed without feeling too much guilt.

FOR THE GULAB JAMUNS

1 cup all-purpose flour
1 cup powdered milk (not skimmed)
1 tbsp sugar
A pinch of salt

½ tsp baking powder
2 oz unsalted butter
4 oz heavy cream
Vegetable oil for frying
FOR THE SYRUP
3 cups sugar
4 cups water
Seeds from 5 cardamom pods
A few drops rose essence
1 tbsp butter

Sift the first five ingredients together into a large basin. Work butter into the flour mixture, continuously adding cream until the dough is soft and moist. Cover with a damp tea towel and set aside. Place a wok over low heat, and pour in vegetable oil until three quarters full. Place all ingredients for the syrup in a pot. Cook over moderate heat until sugar is dissolved, lower heat and allow to simmer gently to a heavy syrup. Maintain minimum heat under the syrup.

Uncover dough and roll into balls the size of small walnuts. Lower about twenty balls into the simmering oil. They will sink to the bottom, and then rise to the surface once more. Allow the gulab jamuns to fry until they are increased in size and uniformly a rich, golden brown colour. Gently remove them from the oil with the aid of a slotted spoon, and place in the heavy syrup. Spoon syrup over the gulab jamuns and allow to simmer until they have doubled in size. Remove from the syrup with a slotted spoon and place in a bowl. The gulab jamuns at this point are very fragile and must be handled with a great deal of care. Repeat this process until all the gulab jamuns have been fried and immersed in the syrup. Pour any remaining syrup over cooked gulab jamuns.

Allow to cool completely before serving. Gulab jamuns taste delicious served warm or cold. Gulab jamuns should be allowed to cool completely prior to serving. If preferred warm, individual servings should then be gently reheated.

Dodol

Makes approx. 1 kg

2½ cups sifted rice flour
¼ tsp salt
3 cups thick coconut milk (fresh or canned)
300 gm jaggery (gur), melted
4 tbsp butter
250 gm chopped cashewnuts

Place rice flour and salt in a bowl together with coconut milk. With an electric mixer beat mixture until smooth. Stir in melted gur. Place all the ingredients in a heavy-based pot or saucepan, and cook over low heat, stirring continually until the dodol begins to thicken. Add butter and chopped cashewnuts. Continue stirring. When the mixture begins to leave the sides of the pan, remove from heat and turn out on a flat buttered platter. Cool and cut into diamonds.

Fried Vermicelli

Serves 6 persons

250 gm ghee or butter
500 gm fine vermicelli
10 cardamom seeds
1¼ cup sugar, or to taste
3 cups water
¼ tsp salt
¼ cup slivered almonds
¼ cup raisins

Place ghee or butter in a heavy-based pan over moderate heat. Stir in raisins and almonds. Fry until the almonds are golden. Remove with a slotted spoon and set aside. Lower heat, and place cardamom seeds in the pot. Fry a few minutes. Add vermicelli. Fry vermicelli until golden brown. Stir in sugar, and pour over one cup water and salt. Cover, and allow the vermicelli to simmer for a few minutes; the water will be absorbed. Remove lid and stir in a little more water. Continue stirring, adding water as required until the vermicelli is cooked. Remove from heat. Turn vermicelli onto a buttered platter. Garnish with raisins and almonds.

Vermicelli is excellent served warm, or at room temperature.

Phirni

Serves 6-8 persons

¼ cup Basmati rice
1 tbsp water
4 cups full cream or evaporated milk
½ tsp saffron threads
1 cup sugar
1/8 tsp salt
½ tsp cardamom powder
2 drops rose essence
½ cup coarsely crushed pistachio nuts

Soak Basmati rice in water for half an hour. Grind to a paste with a tablespoon of water. Set aside. Heat two tablespoons milk. Crush saffron threads and stir into heated milk. Set aside. Pour remaining milk into a heavy-based saucepan, and blend in ground rice. Place saucepan over moderate heat and stir in sugar and salt. Reduce heat and continue stirring until the mixture thickens and coats the back of the spoon. Remove from heat, blend in saffron mixture, cardamom powder and rose water. Chill phirni. Just before serving add crushed pistachio nuts to the phirni. Serve phirni in individual pudding bowls.

Jalebi Pudding

Serves 6 persons

6 large jalebis, cut in half
½ cup sugar, or to taste
4 eggs
3 cups full cream or evaporated milk
6 whole cardamom seeds

Arrange halved jalebis on the base of a buttered pudding dish. Beat together sugar and eggs, pour in milk. Mix until well blended. Stir in cardamom seeds. Pour the milk mixture over jalebis. Cover and place the pudding dish in a pan with enough water to come halfway up the sides of the dish. Bake in preheated (180° C) oven until the custard is set. Remove cover, and continue baking until a golden crust covers the surface of the pudding. Remove from oven and serve warm.

Banana Fritters

Serves 6 persons

1½ cups all-purpose flour
1 tsp baking powder
¼ tsp salt
2 eggs, beaten
¾ cup sugar, or to taste
2 tsp vanilla extract
4 large overripe bananas, mashed

A little milk
2 limes cut into wedges
Vegetable oil for frying

Sift together flour, baking powder and salt. In a deep bowl beat eggs, sugar and vanilla. Add mashed bananas, and gradually stir in flour mixture a tablespoonful at a time. Pour in enough milk to make a thick smooth batter. Place a frying pan over moderate heat and pour in one cup of oil. When the oil is hot, reduce heat and drop fritter batter a tablespoonful at a time into the pan. Fry on both sides until puffed and golden brown in colour. When fritters are firm in the centre, remove from pan and drain onto a paper towel.

Once all the fritters have been fried, arrange on a platter, and sprinkle over with a little sugar and lime juice. Garnish with lime wedges and serve.

Carrot Halwa

Makes approx. 3 lb

800 gm carrot (scrape carrots and grate)
1½ cups sugar
½ tsp salt
½ cup water
250 gm butter
10 whole cardamom seeds, crushed
½ cup golden raisins

Place the first six ingredients in a heavy-based pot over moderate heat. Stir the carrot mixture continuously until the sugar melts and the grated carrots release their juices. Reduce heat and continue stirring until the halwa starts to dry out. Stir in raisins. The mixture will get stiff and start to leave the sides of the pot. Remove from flame and turn onto a large well-buttered plate. Cut cooled carrot halwa into diamonds.

Carrot halwa is a rich, moist delicacy.

Pancakes

Makes 24 pancakes

The French call these delicate creations made from flour, milk and eggs, crêpes, while we call them pancakes. But what's in a name? Regardless of what they are called, when cooked to perfection, crêpes or pancakes are delicious. Unsweetened crêpes in Europe are stuffed with cheese, seafood or vegetables, while Crêpes Suzette, the most famous of European crêpes, are folded in quarters and served accompanied with a flaming Grand Marnier liqueur sauce.

Anglo-Indians serve crêpes or sweet pancakes stuffed with a delicious combination of fresh grated coconut, raisins, sugar and vanilla extract. These are a particular favourite on Shrove or Pancake Tuesday. Unsweetened pancakes or pan rolls are prepared stuffed with a savoury or masala mince, and served as a dinner entrée. The secret of making good pancakes lies in their preparation. In order to achieve a delicate, tender pancake, one needs to have the proper utensils.

A good electric beater, heavy frying pan or skillet about eight inches in diameter, a spatula and pastry brush are prerequisites.

FOR THE PANCAKES

4 eggs
½ cup full cream milk
½ cup cold water
2 tbsp ghee
1 tsp vanilla extract
2 tbsp sugar
½ tsp salt
1 cup cake flour

FOR THE STUFFING

The meat of 1 fresh coconut, grated and soaked in a tbsp of coconut milk, or 2 cups desiccated coconut, soaked in 3 tbsp coconut milk
1 tsp vanilla extract
4 tbsp sugar, or to taste
½ cup golden raisins

GARNISH

2 sour limes, cut into wedges
Lime juice

Place first seven ingredients in a large bowl, and with an electric beater blend until smooth. Add flour to the mixture a little at a time until you have a thin, smooth batter. Set aside for an hour. Mix together all ingredients for the stuffing into a delicate blend of sweetly scented coconut, sugar and raisins. Place heavy skillet on high heat and allow the pan to get very hot. Pour a further two tablespoons warm ghee into a saucer. Dip pastry brush in saucer of ghee and brush the skillet. Pour in two tablespoons batter. Working rapidly, turn the pan so that the batter forms a thin film that sets almost immediately. Turn, and allow the pancake to cook on the other side for a further fifteen seconds. With spatula remove the pancake to a warm plate. Repeat this procedure, brushing the skillet with ghee before making each pancake. When all the pancakes have been made, stuff them with coconut filling and serve garnished with a sprinkling of fresh lime juice, with a wedge of lime on the side.

Note: To make savoury pancakes, omit sugar and vanilla. Stuff with mince, and serve garnished with a sprig of green coriander.

Christmas Baking

The following recipes are traditionally prepared in most Anglo-Indian homes at the onset of the Christmas season:

Dark Fruit Cake

Makes 2 cakes

450 gm raisins
450 gm candied cherries (red and green), chopped fine
450 gm candied pineapple, chopped fine

250 gm crystallized ginger, chopped fine
450 gm mixed peel, chopped fine
1 cup of ginger preserves or orange marmalade
A bottle of dark rum
6 eggs, separated
½ tsp cream of tartar
450 gm butter
1 cup sugar, or to taste
1 tsp each vanilla, almond and lemon extract
1 cup cake flour
450 gm coarsely ground almonds
2 cups fine semolina
1 tsp baking powder
1 tsp ground cinnamon
½ tsp ground cloves
½ tsp ground nutmeg

Place first six ingredients in a large basin, pour over one cup dark rum. Cover and allow to soak for between twenty-four to forty-eight hours, stirring frequently. Separate eggs, beat egg whites stiff with cream of tartar. Set aside. In a large basin cream butter, sugar, egg yolks and essences. Sprinkle half a cup of flour over the fruit mixture and mix in with your hands until fruit is coated with flour. Mix together dry ingredients (ground almonds, semolina, baking powder and spices). Stir fruit into butter/sugar mixture, then mix dry ingredients into fruited batter. Pour a little rum into the batter as required, to facilitate the blending. Lastly, fold in stiffly beaten egg whites. Line two nine-inch cake pans with a double thickness of greased brown paper, and divide the batter equally among the pans.

Bake in preheated slow oven (150° C) for three hours, or until a cake tester, inserted, comes out clean. Remove cakes from pans, peel away brown paper, and allow cakes to cool. Pour a liberal amount of rum over each cake. Wrap in cheesecloth or plastic wrap and store in a cool dark place. The cakes should be moistened with rum occasionally Fruit cake should be allowed to ripen for at least three weeks before serving

Light Fruit Cake

Makes 4 cakes

450 gm coarsely ground almonds
450 gm red and green glace cherries, chopped fine
300 gm raisins
250 gm citron peel, chopped
250 gm candied pineapple, chopped
150 gm crystallized ginger, chopped
6 eggs, separated
1 tsp cream or tartar
2 cups fine semolina
2 cups cake flour
½ tsp salt
1 tsp baking powder
2 cups butter
2 cups sugar
1 tsp almond extract
1 tsp vanilla extract
1 tsp orange extract
1 cup milk
1 cup rum

Grease cake pans and line with brown paper. Set aside. Combine first six ingredients. Sprinkle two tablespoons flour over the almond/fruit mixture, and blend until the fruit is lightly coated with the flour. Separate eggs, combine cream of tartar with egg whites and beat until stiff. Mix together semolina, flour, salt and baking powder, and set aside. In a large bowl place egg yolks, butter, sugar and essences. Cream the mixture until all ingredients are well blended. Stir in almond/fruit mixture. Mix in dry ingredients, adding a little milk each time to facilitate the blending. Lastly stir in stiffly beaten egg whites. Divide the batter equally between cake pans and place in preheated slow oven (150° C). Bake fruitcakes until tester comes out clean. (Approximately two hours.)

Remove cakes from oven, and when cool, peel away the brown paper. Pour a liberal amount of rum over each cake. Wrap in cheesecloth or plastic wrap and store in a cool dry place. Moisten with rum every three or four days. Allow cakes to ripen for at least ten days before serving.

Marzipan

Makes approx. 2 cups

1 cup blanched almonds
2 tsp almond extract
2 cups sifted confectioner's sugar
2 egg whites, slightly beaten

Grind almonds extremely fine in an electric blender. Combine with almond extract and confectioner's sugar. Working with the tips of the fingers, knead the mixture, adding a little egg white at a time until you have a smooth dough.

Use the marzipan to cover fruitcake, or to make marzipan shapes.

Plum Pudding

Makes 1 pudding

450 gm candied peel, chopped fine
250 gm citron peel, chopped fine
250 gm candied pineapple, chopped fine
1½ cups golden raisins
1 cup currants
250 gm beef suet, chopped fine
½ cup chopped pecans
1 tbsp powdered cinnamon
¼ tsp powdered nutmeg
½ tsp powdered allspice
½ tsp powdered cloves
½ tsp fresh ground ginger
¼ tsp salt
1 cup sugar
½ cup strawberry preserves
1½ cup dry breadcrumbs
4 eggs
¼ cup milk
1 cup brandy

In a large bowl place chopped pineapple, peel, suet and pecans. Add in raisins, currants, spices, salt, sugar, preserves and bread crumbs. Beat eggs until thick and lemon-colored. Pour in milk and brandy, mix well. Add egg mixture to fruit mixture, and mix batter until well blended. Turn batter into a buttered one to one-and-a-half quart pudding steamer or glass mould. Cover top of mould with aluminum foil. Secure with several thicknesses of cheesecloth, and tie with string. Place mould on a trivet in a large deep pan of water. (Water should come halfway up the side of the mould). Steam the plum pudding for about four hours, replenishing water as required. Remove from pan and allow to cool. Refrigerate pudding for about four to six weeks still, in mould wrapped in cheesecloth. Alternatively, plum pudding can be stored in a cool, dry place.

To serve plum pudding: Steam for an hour or until heated through, in a large pan with water coming halfway to the top of the mould. Remove cheesecloth; loosen edge of pudding from mould with spatula; turn out on a serving platter.

To flame plum pudding: Pour several tablespoons brandy over hot pudding. Heat half cup brandy gently in a small saucepan until vapour rises. Ignite, and pour flaming over pudding. Carry it to the table. Serve with either custard or brandy hard sauce.

Note: Double ingredients given in recipe for custard sauce when serving with plum pudding.

Brandy Hard Sauce

Makes 12 servings

2 cups butter, softened
2 tsp vanilla extract
3 cups confectioner's sugar
½ cup brandy

Blend all the above ingredients together until smooth, and serve with plum pudding.

Condensed Milk Toffee

Makes approx. 900 gm

2 cans sweetened condensed milk
2 cups sugar
¼ tsp salt
½ cup water
250 gm butter
1 tsp vanilla extract

In a deep, heavy-based saucepan over medium heat, place the first four ingredients. Stirring continuously, bring the mixture to a boil. Lower heat and continue stirring until a candy thermometer inserted into the mixture registers 120° C or, (soft ball). Remove from heat. Add in butter and vanilla extract. Beat with electric beater. When the fudge becomes smooth, creamy and loses its gloss, turn onto a lightly buttered pan, spreading quickly with a spatula. Allow the fudge to cool before cutting into squares.

Note: When making fudge, toffees or other sweets, having a sugar thermometer on hand guarantees perfection every time.

Chocolate Fudge

Makes approx. 1 kg

250 gm unsweetened cooking chocolate
¼ cup water
3 cans condensed milk
2½ cups sugar
¼ tsp salt
120 gm butter
2 tsp vanilla extract

In a heavy-based saucepan, melt chocolate in water over very low heat. Remove from heat. Add condensed milk, sugar and salt to the saucepan. Place over moderate heat and stir continuously until the mixture comes to a boil. Continue stirring until a candy thermometer registers 120° C, or, (soft ball). Remove from heat, add butter and pour in vanilla extract. With electric beater, beat the fudge until smooth and creamy. When it loses its gloss, turn fudge onto a lightly buttered pan, spread evenly with a spatula.

Allow the fudge to cool before cutting into squares.

Coconut Toffee

Makes approx. 1 kg

450 gm freshly grated or unsweetened desiccated coconut
2 cups sugar
¾ cup water
1½ cups heavy cream

250 gm ground almonds
2 tsp vanilla extract
A few drops red food colouring

In a deep, heavy-based saucepan over high heat, make a syrup of the sugar and water. Lower heat, add in fresh or desiccated coconut, heavy cream and ground almonds. Cook, stirring continuously, until a candy thermometer inserted into the mixture registers 120° C, or (soft ball). Stir in vanilla extract and food colouring. Remove from heat and turn the mixture onto a lightly buttered pan, spreading quickly with a spatula. When cooled, cut into squares or diamonds. The coconut fudge will dry out further. Store in an airtight container.

Quick Fudge O'Brien

Makes 9" x 13" pan

My friend Gladys O'Brien was given this recipe by her mother, who prepared it for the family every Christmas. She generously agreed to share it with me, and I pondered long and hard on the unusual ingredients before finally deciding to give it a try. Viola, it worked! Yielding a sweet, delicious confection.

3 cups sugar
1 cup full cream or evaporated milk
250 gm butter
½ tsp salt

¼ cup cocoa powder
1 tsp vanilla
1 cup flour

Place first five ingredients in a heavy-based saucepan and stir over moderate heat until the mixture comes to a boil. Allow to boil for ten minutes. Remove from heat. Stir in one teaspoon vanilla essence. With an electric beater, beat in flour a tablespoonful at a time until well blended. Pour into a 9" x 13" buttered pan and allow to cool before cutting into squares.

Kul Kuls

Makes approx. 1½ kg

450 gm sifted cake flour
250 gm fine semolina
1 tsp baking powder
½ tsp salt
125 gm butter
6 eggs, separated
125 gm sugar
1 cup of thick coconut milk
2 tsp vanilla extract
Vegetable oil for frying
FOR SUGARING
250 gm sugar
1½ cup water

Sift together first four ingredients. Rub in butter and gently work into the flour/semolina mixture. Separate eggs. Whip egg whites frothy. In a large bowl place egg yolks and sugar, beat until thick and lemon coloured. Pour in coconut milk and stiffly beaten egg whites. Combine flour/semolina dough with egg/sugar/coconut mixture and knead until you have a soft, pliable dough. Form into a ball, smear a little butter over the top, cover with a tea towel and set aside for an hour.

To make kul kuls: Grease the tines of a fork and pinch off a piece of dough the size of a marble, pressing it onto the tines. Roll into a scroll. Set formed kul kuls on a lightly floured pan.

To fry kul kuls: Place a deep fryer or wok over moderate heat and pour in vegetable oil. When the oil is hot lower kul kuls into the wok, and fry to a light, golden colour. Drain on a paper towel. When cool, the fried kul kuls may be sugared if liked.

To sugar kul kuls: Melt sugar and water in a deep saucepan and cook over moderate heat until you have one-third-height syrup. Drop kul kuls into the syrup. Coat evenly, remove from saucepan with a slotted spoon and transfer to a platter.

Allow kul kuls to cool before storing in an airtight container.

Turkish Delight

Makes approx. 1 lb

2 tbsp gelatin
½ cup cold water
2 cups sugar
½ cup boiling water

½ cup orange juice
¼ cup lime juice
Icing sugar

Soak gelatin in cold water. Combine sugar and boiling water, heat until sugar is dissolved. Add gelatin, bring to a boil and simmer for twenty minutes. Remove from heat, add orange and lime juice. Colouring may be added if desired. Pour into pan to a depth of about three-quarters of an inch. When set, cut into squares with a hot knife and roll in icing sugar.

Rosa Cookies

Makes approx. 500 gm

4 eggs
¾ cup sugar
½ tsp salt
2 tsp vanilla essence
2 cups thick coconut milk–(fresh or canned)
1½ cups sifted cake flour
2 tbsp vegetable oil
Vegetable oil for frying

In a large bowl beat the first four ingredients until thick and lemon coloured. Mix in coconut milk. Stir in flour a little at a time, beating continuously until you have a smooth batter (batter should not be thick). Blend in two tablespoons vegetable oil.

Half fill a wok over moderate heat with vegetable oil. Place the rosa cookie mould in the wok and allow it to get hot. Shake off excess oil and dip mould into the batter, ensuring the batter only comes three-quarters up the side of the mould. Immerse once more into hot oil and gently shake the mould, and the cookie will slide away into the hot oil. Repeat this procedure until you have four or five cookies floating in the hot oil. Fry to a light golden color. Remove from oil and drain on a paper towel. Should the batter become too thick, thin with a little milk. When all the batter has been utilized, allow the rosa cookies to cool. They are very fragile and should be loosely stored in a large container.

Cashew Nut Toffee

Makes about 1 kg toffee

This delicious recipe was given to me by a friend Tess da'Cunha, who shares her cashew nut toffee with my family every year at Christmas.

450 gm ground cashew nuts
450 gm sugar
½ cup butter
1 cup full cream or evaporated milk
1 tsp vanilla extract
1 tsp almond extract

In a heavy-based saucepan over moderate heat, place first four ingredients and stir until the sugar dissolves. Continue stirring until the mixture thickens and begins to leave the sides of the pan. Remove pan from heat and rapidly stir in vanilla and almond extract. Mix well and pour into a greased tray. Cut into squares and allow to cool. Store cashew nut toffee in an airtight container.

Shortbread Biscuits

Makes about 2 dozen biscuits

1 cup butter at room temperature
2/3 cup icing sugar
1¾ cups cake flour
½ cup rice flour

Place butter and icing sugar in a bowl and beat together with an electric beater until light and fluffy. Blend together cake and rice flour, and add to the butter/icing sugar mixture a tablespoon at a time until all the flour has been utilized. Remove dough from bowl and lightly knead until smooth. Roll out dough onto a lightly floured surface, and cut into strips or shapes. Place on ungreased cookie sheet about half an inch apart. Prick shortbread all over with fork. Bake in preheated oven (150° C) until golden brown around the edges. Remove from oven, cool, and store in an airtight container.

Strawberry Coconut Bars

Makes approx. 60-70 bars

1¼ cups sifted cake flour
½ tsp salt
1 tsp sugar
1 tsp baking powder
½ cup butter

1 egg yolk
2 tbsp milk
1 cup thick strawberry jam
2 eggs
1 cup sugar
2 tsp vanilla extract
6 tbsp melted butter
2½ cups sweetened desiccated coconut

Sift flour, salt, one teaspoon sugar and baking powder together. Blend in butter, egg yolk and milk. Press the mixture into a greased rectangular pan (11" x 7" x 2"). Spread strawberry jam over, leaving an edge of about a quarter inch all around the pan. In a separate bowl beat eggs and sugar until thick and lemon coloured. Pour in vanilla extract and melted butter. Blend in desiccated coconut. Spread mixture evenly over jam.

Bake in preheated (180° C) oven for about half an hour, or until the top is golden brown and set. Cool and cut into squares.

Coconut Cookies

Makes about 4 dozen cookies

¾ cup butter
1 cup firmly packed brown sugar
1 egg
1 tsp vanilla extract
2 cups sifted all-purpose flour
½ tsp baking powder
1 cup desiccated coconut, lightly toasted

Cream butter and sugar until smooth. Beat in egg and

vanilla extract. Sift flour and baking powder, and combine with toasted coconut. Mix flour/coconut mixture in with butter/ sugar mixture and knead into a soft dough. Shape into a ball and refrigerate for about twenty minutes. Roll cookie dough out onto a lightly-floured surface, and with cookie cutter, cut into shapes. Place on ungreased cookie sheet and bake in preheated (180° C) oven until golden brown around the edges. Loosen with a spatula and allow cookies to cool before storing.

Cheese Straws

Makes about 5 dozen cheese straws

2 cups sifted all-purpose flour
¾ tsp salt
½ tsp chilli powder
¾ cup chilled butter
227 gm grated sharp cheddar cheese
Cold water

Sift together flour, salt and chilli powder. Cut in half a cup of butter, and add grated cheese. Mix well. Blend in enough cold water to hold the ingredients together. Roll out dough into a rectangle and dot with two tablespoons butter. Fold corners into the centre of the dough. Roll out again and dot with two more tablespoons of butter; fold again. Wrap dough in foil and chill for half an hour. Roll into a rectangle about a quarter-inch thick, and cut into strips (about ½" x 4") with a pastry wheel. Place on ungreased cookie sheet and bake in a preheated oven (180° C) for about ten minutes, or until golden. Remove from oven and allow cheese straws to cool before transferring to an airtight container.

Pickles, Chutneys, Sauces and Salads

Pickles, Chutneys, Sauces and Salads

Woe to the cook whose sauce has no sting.

—Geoffrey Chaucer, 1345-1400

Pickling is one of the oldest methods of food preservation known to man. In European countries vegetables are pickled in vinegar, sugar and salt, with an assortment of spices added for flavouring. Dill is a favourite seasoning, as are coriander seeds and bay leaves. In India, limes and mangoes are soaked in a salt brine in glass or earthen containers which are placed on a sunny window sill, to catch the warming rays of the sun, which serves to speed up the pickling process. Vegetables are infused with a pungent combination of mustard seeds, chillies and turmeric, and are sometimes cooked in sesame seed oil (til) or mustard oil, before being stored away in burnees for a time, so that the spices can marry and penetrate the vegetable.

The Anglo-Indian community enjoys every type of pickle available in the market, but when preparing pickles in the home, the quantities of ingredients may differ a little, and there is a subtle shift in taste. To begin with, sugar is almost always added, and no matter how hot or sour the pickle proves to be, there is an underlying sweetness to it. Secondly, the ingredients for the pickle are almost always ground in vinegar and cooked in oil, as opposed to many Indian pickles in which whole or ground spices are often mixed in raw.

Chutneys are a particular favourite with the community, and in some cases, ground fresh on a daily basis, just before lunch. Chutneys are made from fresh mint, green coriander, green chillies, ginger, sugar or jaggery (gur), and, generally, a tablespoon or two of tamarind purée is included as well.

Sauces and salads are unique, since the Anglo-Indian diet is a blend of eastern and western cuisine. Albeit, the profusion of spices used may on occasion render the dish unrecognizable to the western palate. The pristine Béchamel sauce may contain just a tad too much of black pepper, and the gravy accompanying roast beef may have a distinct flavour of garlic. Which only serves to lend colour and spice to the cuisine.

Pickles

Mango Kasaundi

Makes 3 bottles

2 kg green mangoes (Pare the fruit, discard the seed and cube)
½ cup salt
1½ cup mustard oil
2 stalks curry leaves
1 tsp fenugreek seeds
2 large pods of fresh garlic, peeled and sliced fine
3" piece of fresh ginger, peeled and sliced fine
10 green chillies, slit
1 cup sugar, or to taste
Salt to taste
Malt vinegar

GRIND TO A PASTE

3 tbsp cumin seeds
2 tbsp mustard seeds
2" piece fresh ginger, peeled and chopped
3 whole pods fresh garlic, peeled and chopped
10 red chillies
2 tsp turmeric powder

Place mango pieces in a glass basin and sprinkle over with salt. Work the salt into the mango, cover and set aside. The next day, drain the accumulated salt water from the mango, and set mango pieces in the sun for a few hours. Place a large pot over moderate heat, pour in oil and throw in curry leaves. When the oil is hot, stir in the whole fenugreek seeds. Add sliced garlic and ginger. Lower heat and fry for a few minutes. Grind spices in vinegar, mix with turmeric powder and stir into the pot. Add green chillies. Fry on very low heat, stirring continuously until the spices are fragrant, and the oil rises to the surface. Mix in mango pieces, and continue stirring until the mango is well coated with the spices. Add salt and sugar. Pour in a further two cups vinegar. When the mixture comes to a boil, remove from heat. Cool the kasaundi and bottle.

Brinjal Pickle

Makes 2 bottles of pickle

3 large brinjals (wash and wipe dry. Cut brinjals lengthways into 2" slices)
2 tbsp salt
1 cup mustard oil
½ tsp fenugreek seeds
1 tsp mustard seeds
10 curry leaves
6 green chillies, slit
1 large pod garlic, peeled and sliced fine
1½ tbsp salt, or to taste
¾ cup sugar
Malt vinegar

GRIND TO A PASTE
10 red chillies
1 whole pod garlic, peeled
2" fresh ginger, peeled

Toss slices of brinjal in salt and set aside for an hour. Place a heavy-based pot over moderate heat. Throw curry leaves, fenugreek and mustard seeds into the hot oil. When the seeds start to sputter, lower heat, add green chillies and sliced garlic to the pot. Stir until the garlic becomes a light golden colour. Grind spices in a little vinegar and place in the pot. Fry spices until fragrant and the oil begins to separate. Strain away excess liquid from the brinjal, and mix the pieces in with the frying spices. Add salt and sugar to taste. Lower heat. Pour over one cup vinegar and allow the brinjals to simmer until firm and tender. Remove from heat. Adjust seasoning according to taste. Allow the pickle to cool before bottling.

Mixed Vegetable Pickle

Makes 1 large bottle

250 gm carrots (scrape and cut into matchsticks about 2" long)
250 gm French beans (top and tail, cut into 1" pieces)
120 gm green chillies, slit
2 large capsicums (remove seeds and cut into 1" pieces)
1 tbsp salt, or to taste
1 cup cooking oil
6 curry leaves with stalk
½ tsp fenugreek seeds
Malt vinegar

GRIND TO A PASTE

1 large pod garlic, peeled
3" piece of green ginger, peeled and chopped
1" piece turmeric
5 red chillies

Salt
¼ cup sugar, or to taste

Toss vegetables in a teaspoon of salt and set aside for one hour. Grind spices to a paste in vinegar. Place a heavy-based pot over moderate heat. Pour in oil. Throw curry leaves and fenugreek seeds into the pot. When the seeds begin to brown, lower heat and add masala paste. Fry until the oil separates from the spices. Stir vegetables into the pot, mixing well to ensure they are coated with the spice mixture. Add sugar and salt to taste. Pour in a cup of vinegar and allow the pickle to simmer until the vegetables are cooked but firm. Remove from heat. Bottle the pickle when it is cool.

Apple Pickle

Makes 2 bottles

2 lb sour green apples (core and cut into 1" cubes)
1 cup mustard oil
1 stalk curry leaves
½ tsp fenugreek seeds
1 tsp mustard seeds
1 large pod garlic, peeled and sliced
6 green chillies, slit
2 cups malt vinegar
1 tsp turmeric powder
1 tbsp Kashmiri chilli powder
2 tsp salt, or to taste
½ cup brown sugar

GRIND TO A PASTE

5 red chillies
1 large pod fresh garlic, peeled
2" piece fresh ginger, peeled

Sprinkle a teaspoon of salt over diced apples and set aside. Grind red chillies, ginger and garlic in a little vinegar, and mix with turmeric and Kashmiri chilli powder. Pour oil into a heavy-based pot over moderate heat. Throw in curry leaves, fenugreek and mustard seeds. When the mustard seeds start to sputter, lower heat and stir in sliced garlic and fresh green chillies. Blend in masala paste and stir continuously until the spices release their fragrant aroma. Add apple pieces and continue frying until they are well coated with the spices. Mix in salt, sugar and remaining vinegar. Allow the pickle to simmer on the top of the stove until the apples are cooked but firm. Adjust seasoning and remove from stove. Allow the pickle to cool before bottling.

Salt Fish Pickle

Makes 2 bottles

500 gm salt fish (wash fish in a little vinegar, wipe dry, cube and set aside)
1 cup mustard oil
6 curry leaves with stalk
½ tsp fenugreek seeds
1 tsp mustard seeds
½ tsp turmeric powder
5 green chillies, slit

1 tsp salt, or to taste
¼ cup sugar
3 tbsp tamarind purée
½ bottle malt vinegar

GRIND TO A PASTE

6 dried red chillies
1 tbsp cumin seeds
1 large pod fresh garlic, peeled
2" piece fresh ginger, peeled

Pour oil into a heavy-based pot over moderate heat. When oil gets hot, fry the pieces of salt fish. Remove with a slotted spoon and set aside. Add curry leaves, fenugreek and mustard seeds to the pot. Grind chillies, cumin, garlic and ginger to a paste with vinegar, and mix with turmeric powder. When the mustard seeds begin to sputter, stir in the masala paste and fry until fragrant. Place pieces of fish in the pot, and continue frying until they are well coated with the spices. Place green chillies, tamarind purée and sugar in the pot. Pour over one cup vinegar. Allow the salt fish pickle to simmer a further fifteen minutes. Add salt if required. Adjust seasoning and remove from heat. Allow the salt fish pickle to cool before bottling.

Prawn Balchow

Makes 1 large, or 2 small bottles

1 cup dried prawns
8 curry leaves with stalk
1 cup mustard oil
1 tsp mustard seeds

½ tsp fenugreek seeds
1 large pod garlic, peeled and minced
3" piece fresh ginger, peeled and minced
4 large onions, peeled and minced
6 green chillies, slit
Malt vinegar
1 tsp chilli powder
1 tbsp Kashmiri chilli powder
½ tsp turmeric powder
5 or 6 whole peppercorns
3 tbsp sugar
1½ tsp salt, or to taste

Place a heavy-based pan over moderate heat and pour in oil. Add curry leaves, mustard and fenugreek seeds to the pan. When the seeds begin to sputter, lower heat. Stir in minced garlic, ginger, onion and green chillies. Fry until fragrant. With a little vinegar make a paste of the next three ingredients and lower into the pan. Stir in whole peppercorns. Fry the masala paste until the oil separates from the spices. In a blender, grind the shrimp coarsely with a little vinegar. Add to the spice/onion mixture, stirring continuously. Add sugar and salt to taste. Pour in one cup vinegar. Simmer the balchow over low heat until the spices are well blended, and the raw smell disappears. Remove from heat. Allow to cool before bottling.

Lime Pickle (1)

Makes 2 large bottles

24 limes (cut limes in quarters and remove pips)
1 cup table salt

2 cups sugar
2 whole pods fresh garlic, peeled and sliced
3" piece fresh ginger, peeled and sliced
250 gm green chillies, slit lengthways
Malt vinegar

Mix the ingredients together and place in a glass jar on a sunny window sill. Shake the jar at least once every few days. When the limes become soft and light brown in colour, they are ready to be served.

Lime Pickle (2)

Preserved limes as in previous recipe
1 cup mustard oil
½ tsp fenugreek seeds
1 tsp mustard seeds
Malt vinegar
1 large pod fresh garlic, peeled
2" piece fresh ginger, peeled
1 tbsp Kashmiri chilli powder
1 tsp turmeric powder
Salt and sugar to taste

Pour oil into a heavy-based pot and place over moderate flame. Throw in mustard and fenugreek seeds. Grind ginger and garlic to a paste in a little vinegar, mix with chilli and turmeric powder. When the seeds begin to sputter, place masala paste in the pot and fry until the raw smell disappears. Stir in preserved lime mixture. Lower heat and allow the pickle to simmer for about twenty minutes, or until the spices are well blended. Adjust seasoning and remove from stove. Bottle when cooled.

Chilli Pickle

Makes 1 bottle

250 gm green chillies (wash, wipe dry and slit lengthways)
1 cup cooking oil
A few curry leaves (optional)
1 tsp mustard seeds
½ tsp fenugreek seeds
1 cup vinegar

GRIND TO A PASTE

1 tbsp cumin seeds
1 large pod garlic, peeled
2" piece fresh ginger, peeled

MIX INTO A PASTE WITH

½ tsp turmeric powder
1 tbsp Kashmiri chilli powder
1 tsp salt, or to taste
2 tbsp sugar

Place a heavy pot over moderate heat, and pour in oil. Throw in curry leaves together with mustard and fenugreek seeds. When the mustard seeds begin to sputter, lower heat. Grind cumin, garlic and ginger to a paste in a little vinegar, and mix with turmeric and chilli powder. Stir masala paste into the pot and fry until the raw smell disappears. Mix in green chillies. Add salt and sugar to taste. Pour over remaining vinegar. Allow the pickle to simmer for about half an hour. Remove from stove and cool before bottling.

Chutneys

Sweet Mango Chutney

Makes 2 bottles of chutney

1 kg mangoes (pare, discard seeds and slice)
450 gm sugar
2 cups vinegar
1 large pod garlic, peeled and sliced fine
3" piece of fresh ginger, peeled and sliced fine
6 whole red chillies
150 gm raisins
2 tsp salt, or to taste

Place a heavy-based saucepan over moderate heat. Add in sugar and vinegar. When the sugar dissolves, stir in the next four ingredients together with mango slices. Add salt to taste. Simmer the chutney over low heat until it has thickened to the consistency of a soft jam. Remove from heat. Bottle mango chutney when cool.

Tomato Chutney

Makes 1 large bottle

½ cup cooking oil
1 tsp mustard seeds
500 gm firm, ripe tomatoes (plunge tomatoes in hot water and remove skin. Chop)

3 large onions, chopped fine
1 tsp chilli powder
½ cup sugar
½ cup vinegar
2 tsp salt, or to taste

Pour oil into a saucepan over moderate heat. Add mustard seeds to the pan, and when they begin to sputter, lower heat and stir in the next six ingredients. Allow the tomato mixture to simmer until it thickens to the consistency of a soft jam. Adjust seasoning. Remove from fire and allow to cool before bottling.

Green Coriander Chutney

Serves 4-6 persons

½ fresh coconut, or 150 gm desiccated coconut
1 large bunch of green coriander, washed and chopped fine
1" piece of fresh ginger, peeled and chopped
3 green chillies
2 tbsp tamarind purée
2 tbsp sugar
1 tsp salt, or to taste

If using desiccated coconut, soak in half cup hot water for an hour. Place coconut with water in a blender, together with next six ingredients. Grind to a paste. Remove from blender and adjust seasoning. Some prefer green coriander chutney a little sweeter than others.

Serve as an accompaniment at lunch. Green coriander chutney keeps well in the refrigerator for a week or two.

This chutney makes excellent sandwiches. Thinly butter two slices of bread and top with a liberal layer of chutney. Enjoy!

Devil Chutney

Serves 4-6 persons

1 cup raisin
1" piece fresh ginger, peeled and chopped
2 tbsp tamarind purée
Malt vinegar
2 green chillies, chopped
½ tsp red chilli powder
1 tbsp sugar, or to taste
Salt to taste

Place all the ingredients in a blender with enough vinegar added to make a smooth paste. Remove from blender and adjust seasoning to taste. Devil chutney should be hot, with a sweet and tangy after-taste. This chutney keeps for two or three weeks in the refrigerator. Store in a bottle with tight-fitting lid.

Devil chutney is particularly delicious served as an accompaniment with junglee pulao, kitcheree, or with a savoury side dish.

Mint Chutney

Serves 4-6 persons

½ fresh coconut, or 150 gm desiccated coconut
1 large bunch of fresh mint, wash, remove stalks and chop
1" piece of fresh ginger, peeled and chopped
3 green chillies
2 tbsp tamarind purée
1 tbsp sugar
Salt to taste

If using desiccated coconut, soak in half cup hot water for an hour. Place with water in a blender together with next six ingredients. Grind to a paste. Remove from blender and adjust seasoning to suit. Serve as an accompaniment at lunch or dinner.

Sauces

After mastering the technique of preparing a good white and brown sauce, one can create all kinds of interesting variations. White sauce or Sauce Béchamel is the basis of many other sauces such as cheese sauce, egg sauce and Sauce Mornay. Brown sauce or Sauce Espagnole is the basis of many game and poultry sauces, and is made from scraps of meat and poultry that combine to produce a rich, flavoursome creation.

White Sauce

Makes 3 cups

3 tbsp butter
3 tbsp cake flour
2 cups full cream milk
½ cup whipping cream
1 tsp salt, or to taste
½ tsp pepper

Place a heavy-based saucepan over low heat and melt butter. Stir in flour to make a roux, ensuring the flour does not burn. Pour in milk, stirring continually; the sauce will start to thicken. Add cream, salt and pepper. Remove from flame. Use Béchamel or white sauce as a base for creating cheese sauce, or any of the other sauces mentioned above.

Brown Sauce or Sauce Espagnole

½ cup diced carrots
1 large onion, peeled and chopped
2 sticks celery, chopped
120 gm cooked ham, chopped
6 tbsp butter
6 cups beef stock
3 garlic flakes, chopped fine
2 tbsp parsley, chopped
1 bay leaf
½ tsp dried thyme
1 cup tomato purée

1/3 cup flour
½ cup white wine
½ tsp black pepper, powdered
1 tsp salt

In a large heavy-based pot over moderate heat, place three tablespoons butter, ham, carrots, onion and celery. Cook until the carrots are tender. Pour in stock and next four ingredients tied in a bit of cheesecloth. Simmer the stock-based mixture for two hours, skimming the surface every little while. Remove from flame and strain through a sieve, pressing down in order to extract all the essence. Pour in white wine and tomato purée, mix well and place the mixture in a pot over low heat. Add three tablespoons butter to a saucepan over moderate heat, and as the butter melts, stir in flour. Continue stirring until you have a roux. Mix roux into the stock mixture and stir until the sauce thickens and coats the back of a spoon. Blend in pepper and a teaspoon salt. Remove from heat. When the sauce is cooled, bottle and freeze until required. Additional salt may be added when using Sauce Espagnole as a base for gravies, etc.

Mint Sauce

Makes 1 cup

1 cup malt vinegar
2 tbsp sugar
1 medium-sized bunch fresh mint leaves, chopped fine
Salt to taste

In a small saucepan place vinegar and sugar. When the sugar melts, stir in mint leaves and continue cooking over moderate heat until the mixture comes to a boil. Add salt to taste. Remove from heat and allow to cool. Serve with mutton chops or roast leg of mutton.

Tamarind Sauce

Makes 1 cup

1 cup tamarind pulp
1 tsp fresh ground ginger
1 tsp salt
2 tbsp sugar
½ tsp chilli powder

Place ingredients in a small saucepan over low heat. Stir until the ingredients are well blended, and the mixture comes to a boil. Remove from heat and adjust seasoning to taste. Serve tamarind sauce with roast pork.

Delicious Tomato Sauce

Serves 6 persons

1 can condensed tomato soup
½ can of vinegar
1 tsp chilli powder
1 tsp garlic powder
2 tbsp brown sugar
1 tsp salt, or to taste

Place the ingredients in a heavy-based saucepan over low heat, and stir until well blended. Adjust seasoning to suit. Remove from stove and pour into a sauce boat. Serve with potato or meat cutlets. Delicious!

Bread Sauce

Makes 2 cups

2 tbsp butter
1 onion, chopped fine
½ cup fine breadcrumbs
½ tsp salt
½ tsp freshly ground black pepper
1 cup full cream milk

Place a heavy-based saucepan over low heat. Add butter and minced onion to the pan, and cook until the onions are transparent. Mix in breadcrumbs, salt and pepper. Pour milk over the mixture, stirring continually. Cook for ten minutes until thickened. Add a little more milk if required. Remove from heat and serve with roast chicken or game birds.

Salads

Onion and Cucumber Salad

Serves 4-6 persons

1 large onion, peeled and sliced into thin rings
1 whole cucumber, peeled and sliced into rounds
3 green chillies, slit lengthways
Juice of 1 lime
½ tsp salt
1 tsp sugar

Toss ingredients in a salad bowl. Cover and refrigerate at least three hours. Just before serving, toss the mixture once more.

Cucumber salad makes an excellent accompaniment when served with pork chops, glace or any other savoury side dish.

Beetroot Salad

Serves 4-6 persons

3 medium-sized beetroots, cooked, peeled and cut into rounds
1 large onion, peeled and sliced into rings
1 tsp sugar
½ tsp salt
2 tbsp malt vinegar

Toss ingredients in a glass bowl, cover and refrigerate for about two hours. Toss the salad once more just before serving.

Green Mango Salad

Serves 4 persons

2 medium green mangoes (peeled and cut into slivers lengthways)
1 large onion (peeled and sliced fine)
2 green chillies (sliced lengthways)
2 tbsp sugar
½ tsp salt, or to taste
2 tbsp fresh lime juice

Place first three ingredients into a glass dish and sprinkle over with sugar and salt. Toss lightly. Pour over fresh lime juice and mix until well blended. Cover the dish and store in refrigerator for at least an hour before serving. This allows the flavours to marry. Serve with curry, rice and vegetables.

Kachumbur

Serves 4 persons

1 large onion, minced
2 green chillies, chopped fine
1 medium tomato, diced fine
2 tbsp malt vinegar

½ tsp salt
1 tsp sugar

Mix ingredients in a glass dish, cover and refrigerate for about one hour prior to serving. Kachumbur makes an excellent salad accompaniment when served with curry, rice, dal and vegetables.

Raita

Serves 4-6 persons

2 cups curd
½ cup milk
2 tbsp sugar
1 tsp salt, or to taste
1 large onion, minced
2 green chillies, minced
1 medium tomato, minced
1 small bunch green coriander, washed, stalks removed and chopped fine
A pinch of chilli powder

In a glass bowl beat together first four ingredients, and adjust seasoning to taste. Stir in next four ingredients. Sprinkle chilli powder over top, cover and place in refrigerator. Serve chilled.

Raita makes a refreshing salad accompaniment when served with Junglee pulao, chicken pulao, or coconut rice and kofta curry.

Green Salad

Serves 6 persons

1 head lettuce, washed, outer leaves removed and torn into pieces
3 green onions, washed and chopped fine
1 medium cucumber, peeled and sliced into rounds
1 medium onion, peeled and sliced into rings
1 small bunch red radish, washed, stalks removed and cut into quarters
2 medium tomatoes, washed and sliced into rounds
6 hard-boiled eggs, peeled and cut in half, lengthways
Salad dressing

In a large salad bowl combine first five ingredients. Arrange tomato slices around and garnish with halved hard-boiled eggs. Serve with bottled dressing on the side. Thousand Island, or a simple oil and vinegar dressing are excellent choices.

Chicken Salad

Serves 6 persons

Leftover cold roast chicken (700-800 gm) (Remove skin and bones—cube meat)
1 medium cooked potato, peeled and cubed
½ head lettuce, shredded
1 medium onion, minced
1 small cucumber, peeled and cut into rounds

4 hard-boiled eggs, halved
1 large tomato, cut into wedges
Mayonnaise
1 tsp prepared English mustard
½ tsp freshly ground pepper

Place first six ingredients in a large salad bowl. Toss with mayonnaise, mustard and pepper. Arrange tomato wedges and hard-boiled eggs around the bowl, and serve chilled.

Chicken salad makes an excellent light supper on a hot summer night.

Fruit Salad

Serves 6 persons

1 large apple, peeled, cored and diced
2 large pears, peeled, cored and diced
1 can pineapple chunks, drained
2 large, firm, ripe mangoes, peeled—flesh cut away and seeds discarded (cut flesh into 1" pieces)
10 firm, ripe strawberries, washed and sliced lengthways
2 large oranges, peeled, segments opened and pips removed
1 small bunch seedless green grapes
2 firm, ripe bananas, peeled and sliced
½ cup sugar
1 tbsp fresh lime juice
Custard sauce

Place first seven fruits in a large salad bowl. Sprinkle sugar and lime juice over the fruit and toss. Just prior to serving, add banana slices to the bowl. Serve fruit salad chilled, accompanied with custard sauce.

Note: Papaya, peeled and cubed, melons, peeled and cubed, or any other fruit in season may also be added to the fruit salad. The greater the variety of fruit, the more delicious the end result will be.

Snacks and Appetizers

Snacks and Appetizers

Where snacks and appetizers are concerned, Anglo-Indian tastes lean more towards spiced creations such as pakoras and samosas. That is not to say that stuffed mushrooms, cheese aigrettes and petits fours do not feature at cocktail parties, teas and other functions where snacks are served; they certainly have their place. However, when in the company of intimate friends or family, their tastebuds tend to stray in the direction of such earthy stuff as onion bugeas, alu bondas and chutney sandwiches.

On formal occasions there is a need to serve an assortment of snacks in order to cater to the .varied tastes of the guests. Today one can fairly well dispense with snobbery and serve up beluga caviar alongside devilled eggs—anything goes. In fact, any or all appetizers and snacks, when cooked to perfection, garnished with care and properly presented, can satisfy even the most fastidious tastes. Everything rests in the presentation—properly garnished, one may even serve chutney sandwiches to the Queen!

Before embarking on the preparation of snacks and appetizers, it is essential for the creative cook to know the rudiments of making a perfect puff pastry and simple Genoise sponge; and, of course, one must not forget to have on hand a reliable recipe for potato sabzi, in the event one would like to include alu bondas or samosas on the menu. A bottle each of freshly made green coriander, mint and devil chutney are essential as they make excellent accompaniments. Towards this end I have set down below a few tried and tested recipes that have served me well on many occasions.

Perfect Puff Pastry

500 gm unsalted butter
500 gm cake flour
1 tsp salt
1 tbsp fresh lime juice
1½ cups cold water

Roll the butter in three tablespoons flour, coating all over. Cover with plastic wrap or aluminium foil and place in the refrigerator until perfectly chilled. Place the remaining flour in a basin and stir in salt. Sprinkle over lime juice and a little cold water. With your hands work the mixture into a dough, adding water as required, until you have a firm dough. Continue working the dough until it is smooth and elastic. Place on a well-floured surface and roll out the dough to form a large square. The dough should be thinner at the edges. Place the chilled butter in the centre, and fold the four corners of the dough over the butter, sealing the edges. The butter should be completely encased in the dough. Cover in foil or plastic wrap and chill in the refrigerator once more for about half an hour. Remove from refrigerator, and on a well floured surface, roll out the dough in a rectangular shape. It should be of even thickness all over. Fold dough into thirds lengthways, and re-place in the refrigerator to chill for about twenty minutes. Remove from refrigerator, and with the folded side towards you, roll dough out again and fold into thirds. This process should be repeated at least four more times before the pastry is ready for use. The dough should be chilled for at least twenty minutes between each folding. The dough is then ready for use.

Note: Puff pastry can be stored in the refrigerator, and is good for two weeks.

Choux Pastry

1 cup water
125 gm butter
¼ tsp salt
1 cup cake flour
4 large eggs, beaten

Place a heavy-based saucepan over moderate heat and pour in one cup water, butter and salt. When the mixture comes to a full boil, lower heat and stir in flour, mixing vigorously until the dough begins to leave the sides of the pan and forms a ball. Remove from heat and with an electric mixer, blend in eggs, one at a time. Drop the dough in mounds, a tablespoon at a time, onto a greased baking sheet. Bake in preheated hot oven (180° C) for about half an hour. Remove from oven and cool on a rack.

Choux pastry puffs can be frozen without filling for a week. When required, they need only be placed for a few minutes in the oven, cooled, split open, filled with cream (whip with a little sugar and a teaspoon of vanilla extract), and served.

Pastry for Savoury Tarts

Makes 24 small tart shells

2 cups cake flour
1 tsp salt
¾ cup shortening
¼ cup cold water

Mix together flour and salt. Cube chilled shortening and mix into the flour with fingers until the mixture resembles coarse meal. Sprinkle water over the mixture a tablespoon at a time, until the ingredients are moist enough to hold together. Gather together the dough and shape into a ball. Cover in plastic wrap and chill until ready for use.

Sweet Pastry for Tarts

Makes 24 small tarts

2 cups cake flour
¼ cup sugar
½ tsp baking powder
½ tsp salt
¾ cup shortening
1 egg, beaten
A little milk

Mix together flour, sugar, baking powder and salt. Cut in shortening, and add egg. Working with your fingers, form the mixture into a dough by adding a little milk at a time until the dough holds together. Form into a ball, wrap in plastic or foil, and store in the refrigerator until ready for use.

To make tart shells: Divide pastry into twenty-four equal portions, and roll each portion into a round that will fit into a tart mould. Fit each round of pastry into the mould. Prick with a fork and bake in preheated hot oven (180° C) for about eight minutes, or until golden. Fill as desired.

Note: A dozen tarts made with the recipe given above and filled with lemon curd (Recipe in cakes, cookies and custard) and topped with whipped cream, is a delicious tea-time treat.

Genoise for Petits Fours

Makes 1 cake

½ cup pure ghee
6 large eggs
1 cup sugar
1 cup sifted flour
¼ tsp salt
1 tsp vanilla extract

Lightly grease a shallow cake pan (17" x 11"), and line with wax paper. Place eggs and sugar in a bowl over a basin of hot water. Whip until the mixture turns warm. Remove from heat and beat with an electric beater at high speed until the mixture triples in volume and becomes very light and fluffy. Add salt to flour and vanilla extract to the ghee. Pour flour over the egg/sugar mixture, beating continuously. Stir in ghee and vanilla, ensuring the mixture does not loose volume. Pour into prepared pan and bake in preheated oven (180° C) until done. Peel off wax paper and allow the Genoise to cool overnight before cutting into shapes or rectangles to make petits fours. Decorate with buttercream or fondant frosting.

Curry Puffs

Makes 24 curry puffs

Puff pastry
Green masala mince

Prepare a dry green masala mince (recipe in 'Curries and Fries'). Omit potato from the recipe. On a lightly floured surface, roll out puff pastry into three-inch squares. Place a spoon of mince in the centre of the square. Moisten the edges and seal together. Pastry may be folded in half, or into triangles. Transfer to a lightly greased baking sheet and bake in preheated (180° C) oven for about twenty minutes, or until the pastry is golden brown and flaky. Remove from heat and serve immediately.

Freeze remaining puff pastry for use at a later date.

Prawn Puffs

Makes. 24 prawn puffs

Puff pastry
500 gm tiny prawns, cleaned and deveined
2 tbsp cooking oil

3 fresh curry leaves, chopped
3 large onions, minced
1 tbsp fresh ginger/garlic paste
½ tsp chilli powder
½ tsp turmeric powder
1 small bunch green coriander, wash, remove stalks and chop fine
2 green chillies, minced
1 tsp tamarind purée
1 tsp sugar
Salt to taste

Place a heavy-based saucepan over moderate heat. Pour in oil, curry leaves and minced onion. Fry until the onion is transparent. Make a paste of the next three ingredients and add to the pan. Fry spices until they release their fragrant aroma. Add prawns to the pan and continue frying. Stir in green coriander and green chillies. Add tamarind purée, sugar and salt to taste. Continue rapidly stirring; remove prawns from heat when most of the liquid has been absorbed. Adjust seasoning. Allow the prawn mixture to cool.

On a lightly floured surface roll out puff pastry and cut into circles or three-inch squares. Place a spoon of prawn mixture in the centre, moisten the edges and fold over. Crimp. Transfer prawn puffs to a lightly greased baking tray and bake in preheated oven (180° C) until light and flaky. Serve immediately.

Freeze remaining pastry.

Eclairs

Makes 12 eclairs

Choux pastry

CREAM FILLING

3 cups full cream milk
1 cup sugar
6 tbsp cornstarch
¼ tsp salt
2 tbsp butter
2 large eggs, lightly beaten
2 tsp vanilla extract

CHOCOLATE GLAZE

100 gm semi-sweet cooking chocolate
100 gm butter
2 tbsp hot water
1½ cups icing sugar
Pinch of salt
1 tsp vanilla extract

Spoon choux pastry into a pastry tube, and pipe into fingers on a lightly-greased baking tray. The pastry should be about four inches in length and one and a half inches broad. Bake in preheated hot oven (200° C) for half an hour, or until pale and golden. Remove from oven and allow to cool. Split the pastry and fill with cream filling.

To make cream filling: Place a heavy-based saucepan over low heat and scald milk. Lower heat and add sugar and cornstarch to the pan, stirring continually until thick. Mix in salt and butter. Stir in beaten eggs and vanilla. Remove from heat. Transfer the cream filling to a glass bowl. Sprinkle a little sugar over top to prevent a skin from forming. Chill in the refrigerator. Split cooled choux pastry shells in half and fill with cream.

Cover with chocolate glaze and serve.

To make chocolate glaze: Place a heavy-based saucepan over moderate heat and place the first three ingredients in the pan. Stir until the chocolate has melted. Remove from heat. When cool, beat in icing sugar, salt and vanilla. The mixture should be smooth and slightly runny. Drizzle over eclairs, allowing the glaze to run down the sides of the pastry. Serve.

Beef Tarts

Makes 12 tarts

12 baked tart shells made from savoury tart pastry
1 cup roast beef, finely diced
1 medium onion, finely minced
1 tbsp cooking oil
½ tsp garam masala
1 tsp Worcestershire sauce
1 tsp fresh ginger/garlic paste
1 tsp chopped fresh green coriander
1 green chilli, chopped fine

Place a saucepan over moderate heat, pour in oil and fry minced onion until transparent. Stir in diced beef, garam masala and next four ingredients. Add salt to taste. Fry the beef until it is nicely browned. Remove from heat. Fill tart shells, garnish with a bit of chopped green coriander. Serve hot.

Ham-Stuffed Eggs

Serves 6 persons

6 hard-boiled eggs
½ cup minced cooked ham
1 tsp dry mustard
½ tsp salt
¼ tsp ground black pepper
4 tbsp mayonnaise
A few sprigs parsley

Cut boiled eggs in half, lengthways. Remove yolk and place in a bowl together with the next five ingredients. Mix well. If required, add a little more mayonnaise. Fill egg whites with the mixture. Garnish with a sprig of parsley and serve.

Devilled Eggs

For devilled eggs, the recipe is the same as above. However, omit the ham and parsley. Fill hard-boiled egg whites with the yolk/mayonnaise mixture and sprinkle a dash of paprika over each halved egg. Chill and serve.

Cheese Aigrettes

Serves 6 persons

125 gm butter
125 gm cake flour

¾ cup cold water
80 gm aged cheddar cheese
1 tsp lime juice
¼ tsp dry mustard
½ tsp salt, or to taste
½ tsp chilli powder
2 eggs, separated
2 tbsp grated Parmesan cheese
Cooking oil for frying

Place a heavy-based saucepan over low heat and melt the butter. Stir in flour and cook for a few minutes. Add water, and stirring continuously, bring the mixture to a boil. Add next five ingredients to the pan and continue stirring. Remove from heat. Beat egg whites until stiff. Stir yolks into the cheese mixture, fold in egg whites.

Place a heavy skillet over moderate heat and pour in half a cup of oil. When the oil is moderately hot, drop the egg/cheese mixture into the skillet a tablespoon at a time, and fry until golden brown. Drain on a paper towel. Serve immediately, garnished with grated Parmesan cheese.

Alu Bonda

For 6 persons

FOR THE POTATO

6 large potatoes, peeled and cooked in salt water
¼ cup cooking oil
A few fresh curry leaves, minced
½ tsp whole mustard seeds
1 large onion, minced

2 tbsp fresh ginger/garlic paste
1 level tsp turmeric powder
1 medium-sized bunch of green coriander, washed and chopped fine
3 green chillies, chopped fine
1 tsp fresh lime juice
Salt to taste

GRAM FLOUR MIXTURE (BESAN)

1½ cups gram flour
1 tsp salt
½ tsp turmeric powder
½ tsp chilli powder
½ tsp baking powder
Water
Oil for frying

Cube cooked potatoes. Place a saucepan over moderate heat and pour in oil. Add curry leaves and mustard seeds to the pan. When the seeds begin to sputter, lower heat and stir in onion. Fry until transparent. Make a paste of the next two ingredients with a little lime juice and mix in with pan ingredients. Fry the spices until they release their fragrant aroma. Add chopped green coriander and chillies, together with cooked potatoes. Fry the potato mixture. Add salt to taste and remaining lime juice. The potatoes will become very soft; mash them while frying until well blended with spices. Remove from heat and set aside.

Sift gram flour together with next four ingredients. Pour in enough cold water to make a smooth paste. With your hands form potato mixture into balls, each the size of a large walnut. Place a heavy skillet over moderate heat and pour in one cup of oil. When the oil is hot, dip potato balls into gram flour mixture and coat evenly. Place in hot oil. Fry bondas golden on all sides. Remove from heat and drain on absorbent paper. Serve alu bondas with green coriander chutney.

Pakoras

Serves 6 persons

500 gm gram dal
2 cups water
6 green chillies, chopped fine
2 large onions, minced
A few curry leaves, chopped fine
1 tbsp fresh ginger/garlic paste
½ tsp turmeric powder
½ tsp methi seeds (roast fenugreek and pound)
1 tsp baking soda
1 tbsp vegetable shortening
2 tsp salt, or to taste
Water
Cooking oil

Soak gram dal for about three hours in two cups water. Grind to a paste. Place the next nine ingredients in a glass bowl. Stir in ground gram dal. Mix well. Adjust salt and add enough water to make a stiff batter. Place a heavy skillet over a moderate flame and pour in a cup of cooking oil. When the oil is hot, drop tablespoons of batter into the skillet and fry until golden and cooked through. Drain on absorbent paper. When all the pakoras have been fried, serve with chutney.

Moorku (Chukli)

500 gm rice flour
750 gm gram flour, sifted
1 tsp baking soda
1 tbsp chilli powder
½ tsp black pepper powder
1 tbsp sesame seeds
1 tbsp whole cumin
2 tsp salt, or to taste
1 tbsp butter
Water
Cooking oil

Place a heavy skillet over moderate heat and roast the sesame seeds; set aside. Add whole cumin to the skillet and roast until fragrant. Set aside. In a large bowl mix together first five ingredients. Add roasted seeds to the mixture, and rub in butter. Add salt to taste. Sprinkle a little water at a time over the mixture, and with a wooden spoon work into a stiff batter. Cover and set aside for half an hour. Place a wok or karai over moderate heat and pour in cooking oil. Fill moorku press with dough, and when the oil is hot, press batter into oil, working in a circular motion. Allow moorkus to fry until golden brown. Lift out of hot oil with slotted spoon and drain on absorbent paper. Repeat the process until all the batter has been utilized. Cool moorkus and store in a large air-tight tin.

Onion and Potato Bugeas

Serves 6 persons

2 cups gram flour
1 tsp baking powder
1 tsp salt, or to taste
½ tsp turmeric powder
½ tsp chilli powder
Water
2 onions, sliced fine
3 green chillies, sliced fine
A few curry leaves (optional)
1 medium-sized bunch of green coriander leaves, washed, stalks removed and chopped fine
2 medium potatoes, peeled and cooked in salted water
Oil for frying

Sift together first five ingredients and place in a large bowl. Add enough water to the mixture to make a stiff batter. Add next four ingredients to the bowl and mix well. Slice potatoes into thick rounds and mix in with the batter, taking care not to break them up. Place a heavy skillet on moderate heat and pour in a cup of oil. When the oil gets hot, drop tablespoons of onion/potato batter into the skillet and fry until crisp and golden brown in colour. Remove from skillet and drain on absorbent paper. Serve immediately with chutney.

Koftas

Serves 6 persons

1 kg lean ground beef or mutton
2 large onions, minced
4 green chillies, minced
2 tbsp freshly ground ginger/garlic paste
1 medium bunch fresh green coriander, washed and chopped fine
1 tsp garam masala
½ cup breadcrumbs
1 large egg, lightly beaten
1½ tsp salt, or to taste
Oil for frying

Place the ground meat in a large bowl together with the next eight ingredients. Blend well. Cover and set aside until ready to serve. Place a heavy skillet over moderate flame and pour in a cup of oil. Form the mince into koftas the size of medium walnuts. Lower into hot oil and fry a rich brown colour. When the koftas are cooked through, remove from skillet. Pierce each kofta with a fancy pick and serve immediately, accompanied by a bowl of mint chutney.

Tea, Coffee and Refreshments

A Note on Tea

'Tea is not only the antidote to drowsiness,' said the poet,
'but one of the ways whereby man may return to his source.'

Tea has always enjoyed immense popularity in India, and the ever hospitable Anglo-Indian will entreat guests who may want to depart in a hurry to linger just long enough to share a last cup of tea. When visiting an Indian home, one is always asked to 'take tea,' no matter what time of the day or night it may happen to be. An old friend of the family once described his miserly cousin as one who would invite you to a restaurant, and then proceed to order 'one cup of tea and two saucers'. The word 'chai' is synonymous with comfort and camaraderie. Indians, I feel, are more comfortable drinking tea than any other beverage. 'Chai' insidiously works its way into everyday life and becomes the focal point of social interaction. Friends confide in one another over a cup of tea; and even when describing trips and picnics, some are apt to mention the fact of how they stopped at a wayside 'dhaba' to refresh themselves with tumblers of 'thousand-mile chai', the type enjoyed by lorry drivers. This potent brew simmers endlessly in large kettles over a low fire, and is constantly replenished with hot water and a further handful of tea leaves. It is sweet, strong and milky, and undoubtedly keeps the drivers awake as they hurtle across the plains of India towards their destinations.

Darjeeling tea, that grows on the tea estates of Assam in the shadow of the mighty Kinchinjunga, is famous the world over for its flavour and aroma, which is delicate and fragrant. Because of its elevation, Darjeeling was also a much-favoured holiday spot during the time of the 'British Raj'. In this rarefied atmosphere, between cups of tea and games of bridge at the club, the wives and families of English army officers and civil servants escaped the scorching heat of the plains during the summer months.

The English, who today are known as a nation of tea drinkers, refined the art of serving and drinking the brew. In spite of a tax being imposed, and much adverse publicity at first, 'tea caught on,' and by the 18th century, became a 'must' at elegant gatherings. At high teas, the upper crust of English society sat around drinking tea from cups of fine china; while thumb and fore-finger delicately circled the handle of the cup, the little finger or 'pinkie' stood poised snobbishly in the air. Tea cakes, delicate watercress and cucumber sandwiches, and shortbread biscuits were served as the guests sat around and made polite conversation.

Fashionable 'memsahibs' brought all the rituals surrounding the service of tea along with them to the colonies, and some of these have stayed with us and can still be seen in the pretentious establishments of the nouveau riche. Not for nothing has the Anglicized Indian been called at times, 'More British than the British.' Anglo-Indians, while borrowing heavily from these rituals, have nevertheless managed to side-step the ceremony surrounding them. Characteristically, they enjoy the best of both worlds, quite comfortable serving seed cake, treacle buns and sandwiches along with samosas, pakoras and sev ghatia.

My father was an army officer in the Second Punjab Regiment. The rigors of army life dictated we move every two years; consequently, our family travelled the length and breadth of India on posting. This entailed endless train journeys which, we, as children, looked forward to with a great deal of excitement. Peering out of the compartment windows, our hair and faces streaked with coal dust, we looked out expectantly as the train pulled into remote stations along the way. Suddenly, the otherwise desolate platform would become a hive of activity as vendors rushed up and down, loudly hawking their wares. What lingers in my memory is the cry of the chaiwallah, calling out at the top of his voice, 'Chai garam chai,' as he strode up and down the platform. Anxious travellers could be seen poking their heads out of carriage doors and windows, waving their hands, or shouting themselves hoarse in an effort to attract his attention. Rapidly moving from one compartment to another, he would serve them, pouring the milky sweet tea in a stream into the thick glass tumblers. Tea, and an order of onion bhajias, that were sold wrapped in newspaper, was truly an enviable treat.

The essence of tea leaves, when brewed with care, can be soul-satisfying, and a true lover of the 'leaf' would never deign to use a tea bag. The following is a recipe for making leaf tea:

Heat a kettle of cold water until it comes to a full rolling boil. Rinse your teapot in some of the boiling water. Add to the pot one teaspoon of leaves for each person, and one for the pot. Cover the leaves with the required amount of water (one cup of water for each person). Place the lid on the pot and cover with a tea cosy. Allow the tea to steep for a full five minutes, after which, remove the cosy and the lid of the pot. Give the brew a vigorous stir with a teaspoon. Replace the lid and pour into cups through a strainer. Serve immediately with milk and sugar.

Iced tea is a great thirst quencher, and is made by filling tall glasses with cracked ice and pouring sweetened hot tea over. Garnish with a sprig of mint and a slice of lemon. Serve cold.

To make delicious spiced tea for six persons, one needs only to place six teaspoons of Darjeeling tea together with five whole cloves, a stick of cinnamon and the rind of half an orange in a warmed teapot. Pour over seven cups of boiling water and steep for five minutes. Strain and serve together with a pot of honey.

Coffee

> Where coffee is served, there is grace
> and splendour and friendship and happiness.
>
> —Sheikh Ansari Djerzeri Hanball Abd-al-Kadir, 1587

A fitting conclusion to any meal is a fresh brewed cup of coffee. In India, most of the coffee is grown in the Nilgiris or 'Blue Mountains' of Karnataka state, so called because their grassy slopes are covered with strobilanthes, whose masses of blue flowers are said to have given these ranges their name.

Unfortunately, none of these precious coffee beans ever reach the North American market, and anyone spoilt by their delicate taste and aroma is hard pressed to get used to the Colombian brands.

In order to brew good coffee, one must choose beans that have been roasted a light brown colour. Once purchased, empty the bag of beans into a shallow pan and carefully look them over, making sure to discard any beans of a darker hue. One burnt bean can spoil the whole brew. In a coffee grinder, grind the beans coarsely. Rinse the glass container of your percolator before filling it with the required amount of cold water, and measure one tablespoonful for each person, pack down firmly, and percolate to optimum strength.

Fill coffee cups three-quarters full with the rich brew. For café au lait, fill to the brim with hot full cream milk and cover with a generous dollop of whipping cream; for café noir, fill to the brim with boiling water. Serve immediately with sugar.

Cold coffee is particularly delicious served after dinner on a hot summer night. Cold coffee is best made in a blender.

For six medium-sized glasses: place six teaspoons coffee, quarter cup hot water and twelve teaspoons of sugar in the blender. Blend at high speed. Add two cups of ice cubes and pour over six cups of full cream milk. Pour into serving glasses, top each glass with two tablespoonfuls of vanilla ice cream. Serve immediately.

Refreshments

During the summer months, hot, heavy meals do not whet the appetite. Instead, one constantly dreams of sipping all kinds of cooling drinks in an effort to combat the unrelenting heat. Recipes for cordials, syrups and concentrates abound, all of them offering to cleanse the body and cool the limbs. I have always felt refreshed after downing a frosty glass of sweet lassi. From among the countless recipes that exist, I list below but a few:

Sweet Lassi

Serves 4 persons

Made in a blender, sweet lassi is a frothy, delicious concoction.

1 cup ice cubes
1 cup curds
2 cups full cream milk
1 drop rose essence concentrate
Sugar to taste

Place ingredients in a blender and blend at high speed. Divide between two glasses and serve. Delicious!

Summer Thirst Quencher

Serves 6-8 persons

1 cup orange juice
1 cup pineapple juice
1 cup lime juice
4 cups soda water
1 cup ice cubes
Sugar to taste

Place ingredients in a blender and blend at high speed. Divide between six glasses and serve. Slice one orange into rounds and garnish glasses.

Sparkling Apple Quencher

Serves 4-6 persons

2 cups apple juice
2 cups ginger ale
1 cup ice cubes

Sugar to taste
A few sprigs of mint

Place ingredients with the exception of the mint in a blender and blend at high speed. Pour into glasses, garnish with mint and serve.

Falooda

Serves 6 persons

4 cups full cream milk
2 cups whipping cream
1 tbsp cornflour
2 tbsp isabgul seeds
2 cups rose syrup
Sugar to taste

Mix together milk and cream, refrigerate for four or five hours. Cook cornflour with two cups of water until thick and transparent. Strain the cooked mixture through a sieve into a bowl of icy water and set aside. Place the isabgul in a pan of cold water until the seeds swell. Drain and set aside. Combine milk/cream mixture with rose syrup and sugar to taste. Stir in isabgul. Strain the set droplets of cornflour through a sieve once more. And mix in with the milk/cream mixture. Divide between glasses, and serve the falooda cold.

O.T.—The Temperance Drink

Makes 1 bottle

500 gm sugar
4 cups water
2" piece of fresh ginger, peeled and sliced
8 cloves
10 cardamoms
2 1" cinnamon sticks
½ nutmeg, roughly chopped
Juice of 6 limes

Place sugar and water in a heavy-based pot over moderate heat and cook until the mixture is the consistency of a heavy syrup. Lower heat and add next five ingredients to the pot. Simmer for a further twenty minutes. Add lime juice. Remove from heat and allow the O.T. to cool. Strain through a double thickness of muslin, and bottle. The liquid should be clear and amber-coloured.

To serve, place in a wine glass with crushed ice; a little cold water may be added if preferred.

Mango Fool

Serves 6-8 persons

2 large green mangoes
4 cups water
½ tsp salt
3 cups sugar, or to taste
4 cups full cream milk, chilled

Pare the fruit and slice away the flesh from the mango seed. Pour two pints water into a pot, add mango flesh and half-a-teaspoon salt. Cook until the flesh is pulp. Remove from heat and strain through a fine sieve, stirring continually to ensure that all the pulp passes through. Stir in sugar and refrigerate until cold.

To serve: mix together mango pulp and cold milk. Pour into tall glasses.

Milk Punch

The following is an English verse which gives the ingredients required to prepare milk punch. It is believed to have been written by Alexander Pope.

From far Barbadoes on the Western Main
Fetch sugar, ounces four, fetch sac from Spain,
One pint, and from the East Indian coast,
Nutmeg; the glory of the Northern Toast,
On flaming coals let them together heat,
Till the all-conquering sac dissolve the sweet,
On such another fire put eggs, just ten,
(New-born, from tread of cock and rump of hen),
Stir them with steady hand, and conscience pricking
To see the end of ten fine chicken,
From shining shelf, take down the brazen skillet,
A quart of milk from gentle cow and fill it
When boiled and cold, put milk to sac and eggs,
Unite them firmly, like the triple league,
And on the fire let them together dwell.

A less complicated recipe follows:

2 cups sugar
8 cups boiling water
1½ cups fresh lime juice
1 bottle brandy
1 bottle rum
4 cups hot milk

Wash and dry a large glass jar with a fitting cap. Place sugar in a deep pot and pour boiling water over it. Set aside until it cools. Add lime juice to the sugar water and stir. Allow to sit overnight. The next day add rum and brandy to the pot and stir well. Boil the milk and pour into the pot. Do not stir the mixture. Cover and allow the mixture to sit for five hours. Strain through muslin, do not press, or milk solids may escape into the liquid. For improved flavour, a cup of Benedictine may be added to the punch. Strain once more into glass jar. Store in a cool dark place. Keeps indefinitely.

Rum Punch

1½ cups sugar
5 cups water
4 cups fresh lime juice
6 cups rum
1 cup peach brandy

In a large punch bowl, dissolve sugar and water. Stir in remaining ingredients, and allow to marry for about two hours. Place two trays of ice cubes in the bowl. When the punch has perfectly chilled, serve in punch glasses.

Glossary

A mixture of spices	*Garam masala*
Allspice	*Kabab chini*
Almonds	*Badam*
Aniseed	*Anisoo*
Apples	*Sev*
Apricot	*Khurbani*
Apricot (dried)	*Jardaloo*
Asafoetida	*Hing*
Aubergine	Brinjal, *baingan*
Banana	*Kela*
Barbecue	*Bhoojan*
Bay leaf	*Tej patta*
Beef	*Gai ka gosht*
Beetroot	*Chukundar*
Black pepper	*Kali mirch*
Bombay duck	*Boomli*
Bone	*Huddi*
Brain	*Bheja*
Bread	*Roti*
Butter	*Makhan*
Buttermilk	*Lassi*
Cabbage	*Bandh gobi*
Capsicum	*Simla mirch*
Cardamom	*Elaichi*
Carrot	*Gajar*
Cashewnut	*Kaju*
Cauliflower	*Phool gobi*
Cayenne	*Lal mirch*
Charcoal	*Koela*
Chick pea	*Channa*
Chick-pea flour	*Besan*
Chicken	*Murgi*
Chilli (green)	*Hari mirch*
Chilli (red)	*Lal mirch*
Cinnamon	*Dalchini*

Clarified butter	*Ghee*
Clotted cream	*Malai*
Clove	*Lavang*
Coconut	*Naryal*
Coconut (dried)	*Copra*
Coconut oil	*Naryal ka tel*
Coriander seeds	*Dhania*
Corn	*Makkai*
Crab	*Kekra*
Cream cheese	*Paneer*
Cucumber	*Kheera*
Cumin seeds	*Jeera*
Curd (Yogurt)	*Dahi*
Curry leaves	*Curry patta*
Custard apple	*Sitaphul*
Dates	*Khajoor*
Dill	*Sua Saag*
Dripping	*Churbee*
Duck	*Batak*
Eggs	*Anda*
Fenugreek seeds	*Methi*
Fish	*Machchi*
Flour (Whole wheat)	*Atta*
French Beans	*Phalli*
Fruit	*Phul*
Game	*Shikar*
Garlic	*Lusson*
Ginger	*Adrak*
Gourd (bottle)	*Dodhi*
Gourd (snake)	*Chichinda*
Grapes	*Angoor*
Green Peas	*Mattar*
Guava	*Amrud*
Hare	*Khargosh*
Heart	*Dil*
Ice	*Burf*
Jaggery	*Gur*
Juice	*Rus*
Kewra	*Kewrah ruh*
Kidney	*Goordah*
Knife	*Chhuri*
Ladies finger	*Okra*
Lamb	*Bher*
Lemon	*Nimboo*
Lentil (split)	*Masoor dal*
Lime	*Limboo*
Lime juice	*Limboo ka rus*

Liquor	*Daroo*	Pineapple	*Anaras*
Liver	*Kaleji*	Pistachio nut	*Pista*
Mace	*Jaffantry*	Pomfret	*Chamna*
Mango	*Aam*	Poppy seeds	*Khus Khus*
Marrow	*Gooda*	Pork	*Suar ka gosht*
Meat	*Gosht*	Potato	*Alu*
Melon	*Kharbuja*	Prawns	*Jingha*
Minced meat	*Keema*	Preserve	*Murubba*
Milk	*Doodh*	Pumpkin (red)	*Kaddu*
Mint	*Podina*	Pumpkin (white)	*Petha*
Molasses	*Gur*	Radish	*Moolee*
Mushroom	*Guchian (dhingri)*	Raisins	*Kishmish*
Mustard	*Rai*	Refined flour	*Maida*
Mutton	*Bakri ka gosht*	Rice	*Chawal*
Nutmeg	*Jaiphul*	Rice Flour	*Chawal ka atta*
Olive oil	*Jaithun ka tel*	Rind	*Chilka*
Oyster	*Kaloo*	Rose essence	*Ruh Gulab*
Papaya	*Papita*	Saffron	*Kesar*
Peanut	*Moongphulli*	Salmon (Indian)	*Rawas*
Pear	*Jamphul*	Salt	*Namak*
Peas	*Mattar*	Semolina	*Sooji*
Pepper (black)	*Kali mirch*	Sesame	*Til*
Pickle	*Achar*	Spinach	*Palak*
		Spogel seeds	*Isabgul*

Stock	*Yakhni*
Sugar	*Chini*
Sweetmeat	*Mithai*
Tamarind	*Imli*
Tea	*Chai*
Tongue	*Jeeb*
Turmeric	*Haldi*
Turnip	*Shalgam*
Vegetables	*Tarkari*
Venison	*Hiran ka gosht*
Vermicelli	*Seviya*
Vinegar	*Sirka*
Walnut	*Akhrot*
Water	*Pani*
Wheat	*Gehun*
Wine	*Sharab*
Wood apple	*Nashpati*

Index

A Simple Meat and Potato Curry 211
Alu Bonda 386
Amti 291
Apple Pickle 352
Apricot Jam Tart 314

Baked Ham in Pineapple Sauce 157
Baked Rice Pudding 315
Banana Fritters 325
Battered Brinjals 278
Beef Cutlets 134
Beef Macaroni Soup 108
Beef or Chicken Curry 86
Beef or Mutton Buffath 221
Beef Stock 102
Beef Tarts 384
Beetroot Salad 366
Boiled Raisin Spice Cake 306
Brandy Hard Sauce 334
Bread Sauce 365
Breaded Shrimp 269
Brown Fried Rice 196
Brown Sauce or Sauce Espagnole 362
Buttered Eggs 298

Cabbage Foogath 280
Café au lait 399
Café noir 399
Caramel Custard 312
Carrot Halwa 326
Cashew Nut Toffee 341
Cauliflower Foogath 280
Cauliflower in Cheese 275
Ceylon Curry 224
Cheese Aigrettes 385
Cheese Straws 344
Chicken and Corn Soup 113
Chicken Biryani 188
Chicken Country Captain 120
Chicken Fricassee 122
Chicken in Orange Sauce 130
Chicken Jal Frezi 235
Chicken Korma 238
Chicken on Rice 129
Chicken Pie 127
Chicken Pulao 186
Chicken Roast 124
Chicken Salad 369
Chicken Shakuti 231
Chicken Stew 121
Chicken Stock 101

Chilli Fry—Green Masala 149
Chilli Pickle 357
Chinese Fried Rice 199
Chocolate Cake 309
Chocolate Fudge 336
Choux Pastry 378
Clam Fry 268
Clear Tomato Soup 103
Coconut Cake 305
Coconut Cookies 343
Coconut Custard Pie 311
Coconut Rice 180
Coconut Toffee 336
Cold Coffee 400
Cold Cucumber Soup 106
Cold Roast Beef Hash 146
Coorgi Pork Pickle 250
Coq au Vin 126
Cream of Cauliflower Soup 105
Cream of Celery Soup 108
Curried Ladies Fingers (Okra) 285
Curry Paste 85
Curry Puffs 381
Custard Sauce 319

Dal Soup 107
Dark Fruit Cake 329
Delicious Tomato Sauce 364
Devil Chutney 360
Devilled Eggs 385
Dodol 322
Dry Fry 210
Duck Vindaloo 236

Eclairs 383
Egg Curry with Gram Dal 293
Egg Moley 295

Falooda 402
Fish Balchow 257
Fish in Sweet and Sour Sauce 263
Fish Moley 256
Fish Rissoles 264
Fish Stock 99
Foogath of French Beans 282
Foogath of Red Pumpkin 281
Fried Chicken 123
Fried Vermicelli 323
Frithath Curry 218
Fruit Salad 370

Garam Masala 85
Genoise for Petits Fours 380
Ginger/Garlic Paste 90
Glace 133
Goa Fish Curry 255
Gram Dal and Meat Curry 213
Green Coriander Chutney 359
Green Mango Salad 367
Green Masala Mince 214
Green Masala Pulao 185
Green Salad 369
Gulab Jamuns 320

Ham-Stuffed Eggs 385
Hyderabadi Chicken Curry 233

Iced Tea 398

Jalebi Pudding 325

Junglee Pulao 191

Kachumbur 367
Kitcheree 182
Kofta or 'Ball' Curry 215
Koftas 391
Kul Kuls 338

Lemon Curd 315
Lemon Sponge Pudding 316
Light Fruit Cake 331
Lime Pickle (1) 355
Lime Pickle (2 356
Liver and Onions 142
Luscious Chocolate Rum Cake 310

Maharashtrian Curry (Roasted Masala) 219
Mango Fool 403
Mango Kasaundi 349
Marmalade Pudding 317
Marrow Bone Soup 112
Marzipan 332
Masala Brinjal 283
Masala Fried Bombay Duck 261
Masala Fried Fish 259
Masala Fry 148
Masala Pork Chops 248
Masala Prawns 265
Masoor Dal 287
Meat Loaf 150
Methi Bhajee with Prawns 286
Milk Punch 404
Mint Chutney 361
Mint Sauce 363
Mixed Grill 140
Mixed Vegetable Pickle 351
Moorku (Chukli) 389
Mushrooms and Capsicum Fry 279
Mutton Biryani 189
Mutton Korma 225
Mutton Mulligatawny 110

O.T.—The Temperance Drink 403
Omelette 296
Onion and Cucumber Salad 366
Onion and Potato Bugeas 390
Onion Soup 103
Orange Pound Cake 308
Oxtail Soup 109
Oyster Soup 104

Pakoras 388
Pancakes 327
Pastry for Savoury Tarts 379
Peas and Potato Sabzi 284
Peas Pulao 179
Pepper Steak 137
Pepper Water 209
Pepper Water and Dry Fry 207
Perfect Puff Pastry 377
Phirni 324
Pickled Pork Vindaloo 242
Plum Pudding 333
Pomfrets in Tomato Curry 261
Pork Assado 154
Pork Bhoonie 153

Pork Chops Arthur 151
Pork Curry 251
Pork Fry 152
Pork Indad 247
Pork Sorpotel 246
Pot Roast 143
Potato Croquettes 277
Potato Cutlets 135
Prawn Balchow 354
Prawn Puffs 381
Prawn Pulao 197
Prawn Vindaloo 267
Puran Polis 292

Quick Fudge O'Brien 337

Raita 368
Rasam 290
Roast Duck in Orange Sauce 131
Roast Haunch of Venison 158
Roast Suckling Pig 170
Roasted Carrots and Potatoes 276
Roasted Pork Tenderloin with Egg Noodles 155
Rolled Beef 138
Roly Poly Pudding 318
Rosa Cookies 340
Rum Punch 405

Salt Fish Curry with Tomatoes 260
Salt Fish Pickle 353
Salted Beef Tongue 144
Scrambled Eggs 297
Seed Cake 305
Shortbread Biscuits 342
Simnel Cake 307
Snake Gourd Curry with Mince Meat 222
Sparkling Apple Quencher 401
Spiced tea 398
Steamed Carrot Pudding 313
Stella's Chicken Korma 239
Strawberry Coconut Bars 342
Stuffed Tomatoes 276
Stuffing for Roast Duck 132
Stuffing for Roast Suckling Pig 171
Summer Thirst Quencher 401
Sweet and Sour Meatballs 145
Sweet Lassi 400
Sweet Mango Chutney 358
Sweet Pastry for Tarts 379

Tamarind Sauce 364
Tandoori Chicken 88
Tandoori Mix 87
The Curry 230
Tina's Lime Rice 198
Tomato Chicken 234
Tomato Chutney 358
Tomato Pulao 181
Trifle 319
Turkish Delight 339

Vegetable Sambar 289
Vegetable Stock 100
Vindaloo Paste 89

White Sauce 362

Yakhni Pulao 194